Please remember that this is a library book, and that it belongs only temporarily to each person who uses it. Be considerate. Do not write in this, or any, library book.

WITHDRAWN

WITHDRAWN

Human Sexual Behavior and Sex Education

With Historical, Moral, Legal, Linguistic, and Cultural Perspectives

Health Education,
Physical Education, and
Recreation Series

RUTH ABERNATHY, Ph.D., EDITORIAL ADVISER

Director, School of Physical and Health Education,
University of Washington, Seattle, Washington 98105

Human Sexual Behavior and Sex Education

With Historical, Moral, Legal, Linguistic, and Cultural Perspectives

WARREN R. JOHNSON, Ed.D.

Professor of Health Education and Director,
Children's Health and Developmental Clinic
University of Maryland, College Park, Maryland

EDWIN G. BELZER, JR., Ph.D.

Associate Professor of Health Education
Dalhousie University, Halifax, Nova Scotia

Third Edition

Lea & Febiger · *Philadelphia* · *1973*

Library of Congress Cataloging in Publication Data

Johnson, Warren Russell, 1921—
  Human sexual behavior and sex education.

  (Health education, physical education, and recreation series)
  First published in 1963 under title: Human sex and sex
education.
  1. Sex customs. 2. Sex instruction. I. Belzer, Edwin G., joint
author. II. Title. [DNLM: 1. Sex behavior. 2. Sex education.
HQ21 J71h 1973]
HQ21.J6 1973   612.6'007   73-8941
ISBN 0-8121-0420-X

ISBN 0-8121-0420-X

Copyright © 1973 by Lea & Febiger. Copyright under the International Copyright Union. All rights reserved. This book is protected by copyright. No part of it may be reproduced in any manner or by any means without written permission from the publisher.

Published in Great Britain by Henry Kimpton Publishers,
London

Library of Congress Catalog Card Number: 73-8941

PRINTED IN THE UNITED STATES OF AMERICA

392.6
J71h
1973

To Our Children:

Traci and Doug
Andrealisa, Anton and Terry

31596

Tempora mutantur nos et mutamur in illis.
("Times change and we change with them")

Preface

The first edition of this book was written because the paucity of useful literature for teaching the subject virtually required it. The second edition was undertaken because of the need for updating so as to keep pace with rather sudden scientific, medical, and educational developments. The third is presented now because even though many fine, up-to-date books on human sexuality now exist, none has the scope or educational perspective that we consider so needed in the present crucial era of change and, hopefully, of more rational social and educational reconstruction along the sexual way.

One of the highest compliments paid the earlier editions of this book was that they were fun to read. We hope that this edition is, too—and that it is not only mind-stretching but challenging as well.

May we particularly note two new features of the book. We are quite happy with both.

1. The book is now addressed specifically to Canadian readers as well as to those of the United States.

2. In its presentation, it unabashedly and explicitly recognizes the female members of humanity by not merely *implying* their involvement. That is, rather than use such words as "he" or "him" to refer to a person of undetermined sex, we have made explicit the heretofore implied "or she" or "or her." Similarly, we have used such terms as "people," "humans," and "humanity" instead of such terms as "man" or "mankind." We are well

aware that such adjustments of the text are not demanded by the traditions of accepted English usage. ("Anyone can judge from the context whether or not females are included in the nondeterminant use of masculine pronouns or nouns.") However, such traditions have been passed on to us from bygone ages when it was *assumed* that the important tasks, such as the solving of social problems and the making of significant cultural contributions, were the prerogatives of masculinity. And so our language bears the burden of history. The fact that even "enlightened," highly educated people can have their thinking distorted by such verbal pitfalls is attested to by the report (*Sexism Skews Theories of Human Nature.* 1973) that psychological research involving only male subjects tends to have its results interpreted as applying to both sexes, whereas the results of psychological investigations in which only females serve as subjects tend to have their findings viewed as applicable only to females.

Acknowledging that our plan to make female involvement explicit was something of an affectation which took some contrivance on our part, we sought the opinions of a number of women. Typically, their reaction was something like: "It's such a little thing. It could be awkward. 'He' or 'man' implies 'she' and 'woman,' so why bother?" Then, presently, they would come around to the thinking of the young woman who said: "It's a very little thing. But the problem of femininity is not one or a few big things, but hundreds of little things like this—like girls' roles in children's books and the relative passivity expected of girls—which add up to the big problems. I think it's a great idea." Thus, this little verbal gesture is in harmony with the spirit of the entire book in which we wish to affirm the *primacy of the individual,* and in this connection echo the conviction of John Stuart Mill:

. . . the principle which regulates the existing relations between the sexes . . . is wrong in itself and (is) now the chief hindrance to human improvement . . . it ought to be replaced by a principle of perfect equality, admitting no power or privilege on the one side, nor disability on the other (1869).

College Park, Maryland   WARREN R. JOHNSON
Halifax, Nova Scotia   EDWIN G. BELZER, JR.

REFERENCE

Mill, J. S.: The Subjection of Women. 1869.
Sexism skews theories of human nature. Psychology Today, 6:14, January, 1973.

Acknowledgments

We are particularly indebted to Doris Sands and Daniel Leviton, both of the University of Maryland, for their critical reading of the manuscript. Brent Rushall helped to update the material on Australia. Walter Chizinsky of Briarcliff College made a number of helpful suggestions. Barbara West and Terri Pottie helped greatly in the preparation of the manuscript.

W. R. J.
E. G. B.

Contents

Introduction

A Decade in Review and a Glance Ahead

The First Edition of this book appeared just ten years ago. Favorable critical reactions to it from people like A. S. Neill, Albert Ellis, Lester Kirkendall, Emma Layman, and E. James Leiberman encouraged the author to believe that the drastically different approach of the book was not without merit. Quite frankly, however, it was rather remarkable that the book was published at all at that time, considering the unique coverage, ranging as it did from intercultural comparisons of "moralities" and historical review of our strange sexual tradition, to critical analysis of our sex laws, the attitudinal traps our sexual language sets for us—and considering the book's studied efforts to avoid trying to appear to provide *the* answers for parents and educators.

Five years later, when the Second Edition appeared, circumstances of sex education were quite different. More and more prominent people had begun looking to education as the reasonable means whereby an obviously conflict-ridden, confused, self-defeating society might find its way to a saner, healthier, and happier way of perceiving and otherwise behaving sexually. The Sex Information and Education Council of the United States and of Canada (SIECUS and SIECCAN) had now been formed and were becoming highly influential; The American Association of Sex Educators and Counselors (AASEC) had just been formed and showed good promise for growth and influence; Masters' and Johnson's *Human Sexual Response* was still shaking the

1

nation nearly as vigorously as Kinsey's first report had some twenty years previously; the newly produced magazine, *Medical Aspects of Human Sexuality,* reflected the growing awareness among physicians of their need for competency in this field; large segments of the "respectable" public were finding it increasingly easy to read without furtiveness, and to talk openly about, such publications as *Sexology Magazine, Playboy, Eros,* and the numerous writings of Albert Ellis; clergymen were beginning to attend sex-related courses and seminars in their efforts to find ways of re-establishing viable contact with their congregations; and, finally, with all of its good and not so good reasons for a "nervous Nellie" stance on this subject, the field of education was being prodded—by itself and others—into some experimental programs of sex education. In brief, the upper classes of society were beginning, reluctantly perhaps, to admit to an interest in a major preoccupation of the common people.

Also, the inevitable had begun. On a well-organized and well-financed scale, fundamentalist religious groups had begun to sense the implications of these new developments for much of their theological morality. Far-right political groups began to appreciate the windfall that spreading sex education offered to them. What a chance to draw large numbers of uncommitted voters into their ranks, with the motive of defending morality against its most dangerous enemies: the corruptors of the young and innocent. The backlash of easy progress of sex education was on with a vengeance. Popular, often highly respected, even famous sex educators were harassed most viciously, threatened, declared communist, and denounced in that safest repository of libel, the Congressional Record.

Now, after another five years, the Third Edition goes to press. These years need to be talked about a little because they have tended to further some cultural changes which have had drastic social-educational implications. During these last years, sex science, medicine, and education have made considerable progress, the same forces that have granted acceptance of increasing amounts of body exposure and sex in popular entertainment having, doubtless, facilitated respectability of openness about sex in some professional groups. Of course, entertainment and "serious" sex have reinforced each other, at the very least with regard to greater ease in talking about and viewing the forbidden subject.

Education, more than the fields of science and entertainment, has been vulnerable to protesting groups and by-laws of boards of education, and has therefore not kept apace except in such isolated situations as some independent (private) schools, universities, and medical schools. On the one hand, then, openness and objectivity in dealing with sex education and counseling are a professional obligation (Sheppe, 1972, p. 17). For example:

> The physician is entitled to his own individual feelings, values, and standards about sexuality, but he is obligated to keep abreast of current information and remain objective when dealing with his patients and their sexual lives (Mathis, 1967, p. 51).

In other words, doctor, you can be as irrational as you wish on your own time, but when you're treating patients, you're obligated to be informed and objective. Thus the physician who by training abhors oral-genital sexual play may well feel the need to show paraplegic patients films about such play as a form of realistic rehabilitation. The gynecologist who devoutly believes that erotic expression belongs within the context of love and preferably marriage may feel obligated to treat a single person by teaching him/her to masturbate or function successfully with a paid, surrogate lover—as *treatment* for sexual inadequacy. The public school teacher might be well aware of the prevalence of sexual dysfunction and other sex problems due largely to sexual dys-education. Still, personally enforced loyalty to traditional morality tends to make impossible discussion of, let alone illustrated explanations of, common sexual maladjustments or preventive education concerning them. Thus, the physician may thrive on treating some of the very conditions the educator would be crucified for preventing.

It seems reasonable to predict that the maturing of sex education will be like a good business *trend*—generally upward over a period of years, but with occasional setbacks of varying degrees and kinds. Indeed, sex education has been swept along to some extent with the trend away from dogmatism and anti-sensualism; but it is *not yet at all sure what it is being swept toward.*

It is the nature of an upward trend or of progress to be uneven. Moreover, progress may be very uneven on different fronts of the same undertaking. For example, in a single city where sex education is officially encouraged, one junior high school may be moving boldly and happily forward, whereas its neighboring junior high—for reasons of leadership, teaching staff, or community attitude—may have nothing to do with the subject.

Often a curious discrepancy exists between formal sex education as provided and the community context within which it occurs. For example, in New York State, some "conservative" Catholic schools provide rather progressive sex education programs, but the presumably more liberal Protestant-dominated schools avoid it completely. California prides itself on being progressive, and surely it enjoys a reputation for unusual sexual freedom and experimentation (its phenomenal divorce and VD rates would seem tangible support for this reputation), but it may well be one of the most repressive of all states when it comes to public school sex education. There, "sex" is a dirty word in school. Teachers who forget themselves are faced with penalties. This poses a serious problem in some subject matter areas, such as VD and preparation for marriage. The state legislators recently made a major concession: it may now be acknowledged in classes on VD that these diseases are transmitted mainly via sexual contact. No such luck with regard to senior-year preparation for marriage, contraception education being an especially punishable offense.

Research that is generally viewed as respectable (even California legislators have been known to avail themselves of Masters and Johnson type treatment for sexual dysfunction) and audio-visual technology have combined to pose a new threat to "respectable" sex education. It is now possible to purchase or rent quality slides and movies depicting virtually any desired sexual activity. Many if not most sex educators would cringe at the thought of using such materials in educational settings even if not forbidden to do so. But lo and behold! A large, influential organization is doing just that: showing sexually explicit pictorial materials to children, ages twelve to fourteen years. Among other things, films of actual masturbation, sexual intercourse, and homosexual love-making, male and female. And God help us, it is a religious group, the Unitarian-Universalist Association, that is responsible for this heretical letting of children into the secrets of (vicarious) sex—in the name of education, of all things!

Of course, this kind of thing has been one of the most interesting, if confusing and disconcerting, developments in this field. We used to think we knew where religion stood. Oh, of course there were the Mormons and the strange nineteenth century colony at Oneida, N.Y. Still, by and large, sex did not exist for the religious except in monogamous marriage, and that for reproductory purposes. Thus, who would expect the Quakers and now, to a greater degree, the Unitarians not only to accept but to act upon logic like that of Cody Wilson, former director of the U.S. Presidential Commission on Obscenity and Pornography ". . . people have to be taught about sex . . . it is better to be explicit and organized in our socialization process than implicit and haphazard."* One does not expect people to go so far as to put this generally acceptable philosophy into practice—especially religious groups! For a major function of education has always been to inculcate the young with accepted traditional values and ways of thinking and doing. The unenviable task of today's educator is to carry out this function when there is no generally "accepted" tradition to teach.

A reverse-English variant on the chicken-egg controversy has it that the task of the egg is to produce another chicken which will lay another egg. . . . Thus through all the controversy and bold and timid posturings over sex education, the young and not so young the world over have gone about their evolutionarily appointed task of being fruitful. Evolutionary tyranny may have meant the destruction of the individual—for whom evolution cares not one jot—but with its overriding concern for numbers, it has kept the species going. Among some peoples, as among the early Jews and the modern Marquesan Islanders, as we shall note in a later chapter, the seeking of sexual pleasure has coincided with population growth needs. In much of

* For details of the Unitarian-Universalist sex education program and its rationale, see *SIECUS Report* of April and September, 1972.

the world today, however, human survival needs and overwhelming sexual drive are increasingly at odds, the consequences of the drive—ova creating more people to create more ova—meaning suffocating numbers of people.

Thus, evolutionary forces that have tended to spell survival of the species may now have become self-defeating for the species. However, a technology has emerged which can, on a wide scale, lead to an alteration in consequences of evolutionarily based sexual cravings. That is, the technology concerned with population regulation which makes possible the having of children deliberately rather than whimsically, fortuitously, or recklessly: If the technology is put to use on a grand scale.

Increasingly, the idea seems to be spreading that nonreproductory sexual activity between consenting adults is not a matter of social or, therefore, legal concern. At the same time, reproductory sex is becoming a matter of enormous social concern. Each newborn makes demands upon our precarious living conditions, our energy resources, food supply, transportation facilities, and education, health, and recreation systems. A new baby is not a drop in the bucket, for new babies continue to arrive by the millions as older people live longer; and millions of drops eventually overflow any bucket. And the wealthier the baby's family, the more of everything baby will consume. A wealthy baby is many drops in the bucket.

In other words, if "immoral" behavior were to be defined generally as behavior that detracts from or damages ongoing social welfare, any nonreproductive sexual activity between or among consenting adults could hardly be designated immoral. On the other hand, in spite of the obvious fact that reproduction is a condition of survival of any species, human reproduction, except under very special conditions, now tends to be suspect on moral grounds, as defined above.

So what is the function of sex education today? To teach "morality"? To teach how to control fertility? To teach toward joyful sexual expression? To teach about human reproduction? To educate about sex roles, traditional and emerging?

We think that these are some of its functions. But why stop with this short list? The coverage of this book suggests a good deal of what we believe modern sex education needs to concern itself with. *Human Sexual Behavior and Sex Education* provides an introduction to specific subject matters which need to be included in any basic education concerning human sexual behavior. But far more important, we feel, are the implications to be drawn from the subject matter. Consider the following examples.

Why are the Latin words of sexual structures and functions translated into English? (Ch. 2) To make the point that they do have meaning in English. But we hide the language of sex away in a long dead language, thereby, perhaps, clearly illustrating the traditional rejectionist attitude toward the subject.

Why consider the conflicted dynamics of growing up in our society as a sexual creature? (Ch. 3) Because we can thereby see some of the problems that are posed for any child expected to grow up ignoring and usually rejecting his/her sexuality and that of others while at the same time managing some kind of adjustment to society's adore-sex-hate-sex dilemma.

Why review and contrast sexual behaviors of primitive and modern societies? (Ch. 9 and 10) To gain perspective as to the fantastic range of possible patterns of behavior considered normal and abnormal by different peoples. Clearly, human flexibility is impressive. We are not *necessarily* locked into any particular posture;

and with some knowledge of our possibilities and with the benefit of rational assessment of our needs and problems, we may learn to live happily with our sexuality in modern circumstances rather than being in perpetual conflict with it.

Why discuss the "language barrier"? (Ch. 5) Because most sex education does not deal directly with sex as affective or feeling experience but as verbal, cognitive communication about it. Moreover, the language of sex tends to interfere with communicating about it, and is therefore one of the major obstacles to progress in this field. 'Tis an ambitious undertaking: to try to intellectualize a "feeling" experience and communicate about it with emotionally charged, deceptive, often unusable language.

Why review the historical tradition lying behind our sexual attitudes, morality, and laws? Isn't this so much muckraking? (Ch. 4) Not really. It does no good to fix blame for foolish, even wicked behavior. But it does help to know that sex has always been a major human interest, that it has been and continues to be reflected in art and religion, and that we are a product of a long tradition, most of whose rules were formulated by struggling middle-Eastern tribal people well over 2000 years ago to meet their needs, not ours. Historical accidents rather than divine plan or human nature must account for our strangeness, sexually speaking.

Why survey our sex laws and their origins? (Ch. 6) Because a sexually informed and rational people would recognize their inappropriateness to the present day and would not tolerate many of them.

Why take into account intersocietal comparisons, primitive and modern? (Ch. 9 and 10) To gain a fuller appreciation of the possible range of patterns of sexual behavior and of the various experiments in sex education that are being tried. There is no escaping the conclusion that prospects for the future are many, encouraging—and frightening.

What is the point of enumerating "theories" of sex education? (Ch. 11) Well, these seem to suggest the possible approaches from which we have to choose. A theory is a kind of tentative compass heading. It keeps you pointed in the "right" direction, once you've decided where you want to go.

Yes, it seems to us that the implications of the factual material are what really concern us, for as educators, we perceive education's role as not only conveying knowledge, but also as helping people perceive problems clearly and prepare for action in solving them. We do not feel qualified to tell readers which of the seven theories of sex education to favor as guidelines into the future. But we do feel qualified to help isolate the possibilities for inspection by persons who have troubled to identify the problem and explore its various facets.

This little book does not pretend to provide the answers to today's or tomorrow's sex education questions. However, it is our hope that it will help to improve the quality of questions that urgently need asking and the perceptiveness of proposed answers. For as John Steinbeck said on the occasion of receiving the Nobel Prize for literature: "The roads of the past have come to an end and we have not yet found new pathways to the future." We have new pathways to build.

REFERENCES

Mathis, J. L.: Iatrogenic sexual disturbances. Medical Aspects of Human Sexuality, 1:49-51, 1967.

Sheppe, W. M., Jr.: The family physician and human sexuality. Medical Aspects of Human Sexuality, 6:10ff, July, 1972.

1

The Sexual Revolution and the Challenge to Education

Human Sexual Behavior and Sex Education: With Historical, Moral, Legal, Linguistic and Cultural Perspectives is intended to deal broadly with various aspects of the subject matter of sex. However, as the title suggests, the concern is with the interaction of the subject matter with its educational context. The purpose of this chapter is to explore this interaction, as sex is becoming viewed increasingly as educational subject matter.

There is today great agitation throughout the land to do something about sex education in schools and colleges. In colleges, generally, sex courses of one kind or another are being offered by numerous departments, departments which only a few years ago would have nothing to do with the subject. At the school level, however, there is unevenness of enthusiasm, the earlier widespread spirit of get-the-show-on-the-road now being countered by a powerful get-the-show-off-the-road movement. Of course, the usual foci of concern are unwanted pregnancy among the young, teenage marriage, and venereal disease; but we also hear much about teaching "responsibility," "morality," and "male and female sex roles." It would be difficult to take a position against teaching such things, and school board

11

members, school administrators, presidents of institutions of higher learning, as well as large numbers of parents and clergymen, are on record as being very much in favor of initiating sex education programs. Still, the fact remains that few schools have sex education programs that go much beyond basic reproduction education and information pertaining to venereal disease and most of those do not appear to stand up very well to scrutiny (Breasted, 1970). Perhaps in response to a focusing of attention during the late sixties and early seventies (Malfetti and Rubin, 1967; Cohn and Belzer, 1970) on the need to increase teacher training for sex education responsibilities, many American institutions of higher learning have hastened into the breach. The February, 1972 issue of *SIECUS* (Sex Information and Education Council of the United States) *Report* listed 31 sex education workshops being offered at various colleges and universities and such groups as The American Association of Sex Educators and Counselors, the American Institute of Family Relations, and the Institute for Sex Research (better known as the "Kinsey Institute"). This was only a partial listing of the special workshops and summer courses being offered throughout the United States that summer. Boards of education continue to order their schools to provide sex education at all levels. Canadian universities and schools are also showing increased interest in the subject, but not without strongly mixed feelings.

Clearly there is in the dynamics of this situation something strange and formidable which has to do with the subject matter, but not just with the subject matter. It has to do with the other aspects of the teaching-learning process as well, the learner and the teacher, all operating or trying to operate within the context of the history-making sexual revolution of modern times.

To begin with, in speaking of the "sexual revolution,"

we are not referring so much to the increased ability of young people to drive through the red lights and stop signs of traditional sexual morality. After all, sexual permissiveness has fluctuated continually between extremes through the centuries. More importantly, this revolution has to do with the increased ability of people, especially professional people, to raise questions about, talk about, study about, and teach about sex as a major factor in the total dynamics of human life—from infancy to old age and among all people. In brief, sex education is no longer to be left entirely to chance, the entertainers, the advertisers, and other exploiters of our sexual ignorance, conflicts, and tensions. What implications has this revolutionary development for education?

Let us examine sex education as it relates to the basic anatomy of the teaching-learning process: the characteristics of the learner; the characteristics of the subject matter; and the characteristics of the teacher.

Characteristics of the learner. This is obviously a good starting point, but not exactly a simple or neat starting point, for would-be learners in North American schools report to their classrooms from an incredible range of culturally different neighborhoods (Johnson, 1973). And the mixing of subcultures within schools and classrooms! A single classroom may accommodate not only students from the dominant middle class, with its Puritan sexual ideals and conflicts, but also ghetto blacks or whites, whose one- or two-room homes have allowed them exposure to sexual activity—along with nudity, dancing, playing, fighting, eliminating, and eating—from their earliest years. Still other groups that may be represented are country children, children from the industrial community, and children who have grown up in foreign lands. What an unbelievable diversity of background, of notions of sexual "morality," and of readiness for learning. And yet, an interest in sex and in learning about it tends to be one of the things they have in common.

As a matter of fact, numerous studies have been done to assess the health education interests of school-age children and youth. Invariably, pupils rank sex education at or very near the top in interest. A teacher commented recently that she gave a stiff examination on basic sex education to her lowest track class, her "E" group—isn't it nice that we teachers are not so classified?—and every child earned an "A" grade. In brief, it seems reasonable to characterize the school-age population as potentially "eager learners" when it comes to sex education. *Playboy* magazine has been used successfully as an aid to developing junior high school nonreaders into eager readers (Herndon, 1965). Such learning aids slyly encourage intellectual functioning by appropriate arousing of feeling.

Now who are our school and college age young people? They are a very special population. Among other things they are perpetually forming and gradually elevating in sophistication our "educated" citizenry. The college graduates and especially those who go on to graduate study may be regarded as our intellectual leadership of the future, including the professional people to whom society must turn for guidance and help. Whether or not they finish high school or college they will become a huge proportion of their nation's husbands, wives and—if they have waited so long—parents, as well as the bulk of our "educated" public opinion and voters.

We believe that only when viewed in this light of broad social significance does the most impressive importance of an adequate sex education in our schools become apparent. Needless to say, in the course of his/her life, each person has been deeply interested in sex and has felt a need for greater knowledge of his/her own sexual self. But the Judeo-Christian-Puritan tradition—our tradition—has required us to be self-deprecating for having such an interest and need, and in due course to persecute our own children for evidencing similar interest and curiosity. To this day, in this area, ignorance is still widely considered a virtue, although less commonly so than even a decade ago. (The word "ignorism" has been invented to label the rather perverse value which holds certain kinds of ignorance to be superior to corresponding understanding.)

The young are in the strange, or perhaps we should say impossible, position of being pulled in opposite directions—in one direction by their biological drive as it is goaded by the sex-saturated environment, and in the opposite direction by the traditional sexual morality which disavows the existence of moral sex out of marriage. The young must attempt to function somehow in a sex-centric society which is profoundly anti-sexual—the young who as children are *supposed* to be totally "innocent" of sex, and as "youth" *supposed* to express their sexuality not at all before marriage.

Do we stop to consider that our young people are in a most ambiguous position with regard to their thoughts concerning, and actual expressions of, their sexuality? That is, regardless of their actual sexual behavior, in the past, people *knew* what "right" behavior was and when they deviated from it. "Right" and "wrong" were as easy to distinguish as black and white. This is no longer the case. Of course, spokesmen of the traditional view continue to insist on the traditional values, "right" obviously being right and incapable of misinterpretation or change. But increasingly, medical scientists, psychologists, psychiatrists—even educators and clergymen—are not only questioning the validity of traditional attitudes, but are also accusing these very attitudes of causing all manner of personal and social problems. Traditional views are being questioned at every turn. For example, highly regarded professional people now not only state that masturbation is harmless, but that it is very probably beneficial. Church leaders have called for greater understanding and tolerance of homosexuality, and one leading English clergyman recently recommended the encouragement of homosexuality as a means of world population control. In these times, ministers are even heard to assert in sermons to the young that sexual relations can be beautiful *and* responsible before marriage. Recently, the majority of a group of dedicated clergymen agreed that, in a particular case involving adultery, the adultery had to be considered "good" because it led to the higher good of saving a deteriorating family. The minority view was that this judgment was so wrong as to be unthinkable. Rev. Hunter Leggitt coauthored an article (Myers and Leggitt, 1972) in which many case studies are presented as examples of how adultery may be beneficial rather than harmful to one or more persons involved. Rabbi Roland Gittelson (1972) promptly challenged the assertion that in certain circumstances adultery can improve the quality of marriage. Authority pulling from opposite directions—and each person, young or older, must decide for himself/herself and choose his/her own way of life.

Is the young person capable of making wise choices in such sensitive areas as sexual behavior? If not, who will make the choices? We must confess that we personally are biased in that we have high regard for young people and their potential for self-direction and dedicated work. Harold Taylor, former president of Sarah Lawrence College, tends to look to young people for our salvation:

. . . they are willing to take risks, to test themselves and their
moral sense against the world . . . Yet this generation of students
has come of age when the educational system has fallen behind
them; they are ready for more than the schools, the colleges or
the society are ready to give.

What is the educator's role in this strange situation?
Should one be an aloof observer? A proponent of the traditional? For the anti-traditional? Should one be an objective analyst thinking together with the young? Let us
leave this question for the time being and turn to the
second major aspect of the teaching-learning process.

The characteristics of the subject matter. The first
question that must be faced is: Is sex properly a subject matter at all? Is it of sufficient importance to human
beings, and to their health and welfare, to justify its
inclusion in the school or college curriculum? Among
other things, this question raises the further question
of definition. A superintendent of schools of California
was once quoted in the press as being strongly opposed
to sex education in schools on the grounds that the
young get too much sexual stimulation already without
the schools adding to it. It would seem that he defines
"sex education" as sexual intercourse education or training in sexual stimulation of some such. Few educators
advocate sex education of these kinds, but admittedly
they are possibilities.

In a study (Johnson and Schutt, 1966) to determine
whether the people, school pupils, school and college
administrators, and school board members considered
human sexuality a legitimate subject for study in schools
and at the college level, the majority of each group
sampled reported believing that there should be sex
education in the schools. Most of the school administrators and the sampling of college presidents indicated
that such education is not only "needed" but "urgently
needed." Still, as the School Health Study Project

2

(N.E.A.) report showed, there are exceedingly few planned health education, let alone sex education, programs in the United States. The proportion of Canadian schools with such programs is still smaller. Most school officials explain this discrepancy between need for sex education and sex education actually provided by indicating two major problems: (1) fear of community, especially parental, reaction and (2) lack of qualified teachers.

Here, then, is one of the major characteristics of this particular subject matter. It is different. Who ever heard of having to sample the public, school officials, school board members, etc., over the question of whether an area within the disciplines of history, mathematics, literature, or chemistry should be studied in schools? Why this strong emotion, this fear and anxiety, this unique assumption of irreversible incompetence on the part of teachers to be able to teach this one subject? Why this dread of being caught by the community teaching children about sex?

Yes, why this dread of being caught—this dread which usually requires that if sex education is provided at all by schools, it is in response to epidemic levels of venereal disease and pregnancy among youngsters? This dread of being caught teaching the young about sex goes much deeper than our reticence about venereal disease and illegitimate pregnancy. In fact, these are not by any means the fundamental considerations which must be faced if we are really to come to grips with a sex education that is appropriate to our times. Let us consider these more fundamental matters and ask ourselves *whether we are bold* enough to examine them closely. For they are among our most inscrutable and ineffable taboos. And they are in the tribal sense sacred to us!

This means that we must do such things as ask:

whence came our sexual morality, sex attitudes and practices, which make a healthy sexual adjustment virtually impossible in childhood and adulthood? And whence came our unbelievable, impossible, sex laws? What will we say when we learn that this "morality" and these laws within which we aspire to live and to which we pledge our allegiance are largely the rules laid down by an ancient tribal people of the Middle East, the Old Testament Jews who, for all of their practical wisdom, could not possibly have anticipated modern circumstances?

How will we respond when we learn that our incredibly mixed feelings about sex are the result of a conflict between our biological drive—which has kept our interest as well as the species alive to this date—and an attitude instilled by the horrendous denunciations of sex and womanhood, not by Jesus, but by the early Christian church fathers? To anticipate a little of the more detailed and carefully documented discussion of this whole subject in our chapter on modern sexual customs in historical perspective, St. Paul's attitude toward sex as a troublesome distraction of other men is well known. Tertullian wrote: "Woman, you are the devil's doorway . . . It is your fault that the Son of God had to die." St. Chrysostom wrote: "Among all savage beasts none is so harmful as woman." But it was St. Augustine, that major architect of Christian theology, who in the Fifth Century concluded that sexual intercourse is the specific means whereby sin is automatically transmitted from generation to generation. It was he who permanently fixed the association of sex, sin and guilt in Judeo-Christian mentality. Only Jesus and (for about a century now) his mother have been born free of sexual contamination and therefore by definition—immaculate, clean, sinless. Former Catholic priest James Kavanaugh has protested this whole tradition saying: sex has been "the chief and single sin, man's fleshly battle with the world" (1967, p. 10).

As we shall see in later chapters, the Puritan movement, which began in the Sixteenth Century, has contributed some special things to our subject matter dilemma. These Puritan contributions are concerned mainly, perhaps, with the language of sex and our ideas about obscenity, including nudity. In the Puritan spirit, Shakespeare was "cleaned up" by Bowdler, serious efforts have been made to clean up the Bible, and many's the small boy's mouth which, dirtied in some strange way by words, has been cleaned up by soap. Mainly because of the Puritan attitude toward words, the parent or teacher who would teach about sex soon finds himself/herself in the position of trying to talk about a taboo subject with words which he/she was taught and has been teaching children are not "nice," but are "gutter talk." How do you teach about something which, for a great many people, has little if any acceptable language associated with it? Sex language is not only incommunicado, it is anticommunicative.

In brief, what other subject matter must, for historical-linguistic reasons, be looked at through such turbulent emotions, through such conflicting feelings of attraction and rejection? What other subject matter cannot be talked about freely because of an unacceptable, emotion-laden language and inner inhibitions, as well as fear of punishment or criticism?

For reasons suggested by the foregoing historical-linguistic considerations, much of what needs to be taught about sex at the present time should be *remedial* in nature: "remedial sex education." That is, there are all manner of widely held misconceptions about, as well as ignorance associated with, sex: and since some of these are harmful in their effects, they require immediate attention.

They have to do with clearing up still widespread and erroneous notions about such things as menstruation, masturbation, contraception, homosexuality, the sex play of children, the effects of pornographic literature and pictures, and so on. Some of this remedial sex education is differential as to male or female sex, even though both sexes need to be aware of it. For example, a significant portion of a girl's self-concept should probably not depend on such things as whether she is "beautiful" or has breasts of a size and shape that happen to be stylish right now in Hollywood, Montreal, or on television. She should not fear that her masturbating will cause a disease or incapacitate her as a future sexual partner. She should not be capable of being trapped in the double bind of, "If you give in you're a tramp or a slut; if you don't you're hung up." She should not be slave to the tradition that she is only a romantic and reproducing creature, and not a rational or sexual one—for today, because of education and contraception, those women *who so choose* need not be virtually exclusively sexual objects to be drooled over and possessed, or species replicating mechanisms. And this is a major dimension of the sexual revolution.

With further remedial intent, the male needs to realize that his worth as a person and his effectiveness as a male and male sex partner are not really dependent upon his physical size, his having a mesomorphic, muscular body build, his "handsomeness," or the size of his genitals. Also in need of remediation at the attitudinal level is the still rather prevalent notion of many males that females who *will* deal with them sexually are contemptible for doing so. In our opinion this is reflective of an evil view of both women and sex that is now archaic. However, urgent as the need may be to meet individual, personal and family needs, sight must never be lost of the social significance of tomorrow's "educated" citizens. They must be prepared to evaluate many sex-related matters which concern the entire society. The educated citizenry, the voters of tomorrow, need to be informed about and capable of taking remedial action concerning various things of great social significance such as our absurd sex laws and overwhelming population problems.

Let us consider a few things about our sex laws. Again we are anticipating a later chapter in order to make the point that even a moderately sex-educated citizenry would probably refuse to live under the existing ones. These laws are archaic, inconsistent, unrealistic and, as New York attorney Pilpel (1965) has demonstrated, fundamentally hypocritical. An educated citizenry is needed which will insist that they be changed. How many people realize that they can be jailed for extended periods in some states for "necking"? That husband and/or wife can be jailed for years, up to thirty years or more, for committing "sodomy" together—but that the legal definition of sodomy is so varied that there is no telling what is meant by the word when you hear that someone has committed it? Did you know that laws concerning homosexuality have given rise to untold police corruption, unpunished robbery, and murder, as well as the creation of innumerable, confirmed homosexuals? These are but a few examples of our incredible sex laws, which need the attention of a sex-educated citizenry.

And our censorship laws. It is time that we admit some things to our future educated citizens on this score. Whence came our postal obscenity laws? These laws, which set a kind of standard of what is considered obscene and have made possible very questionable jailings and a secret harassment of the public by postal authorities, came from rather dubious sources. For example, the American laws are primarily attributable to

Anthony Comstock, a veteran of the American Civil War, who believed as most people did at that time that masturbation causes various diseases, insanity, death, and damnation. That which appeals to the "prurient" interest—that is, the sexual interest—was therefore a deadly threat. No sex educated person today believes that masturbation has any such dire effects—but we live under laws which *presume* such effects. Imagine being in the intriguing position of the judges who try people in obscenity cases. In effect, they have to decide whether the long-dead Anthony Comstock would consider the literature or picture likely to arouse sexual feelings in young men which might tempt them to masturbate. Believe it or not, this is the judge's problem even though we no longer regard masturbation as a sickening evil, and even though no one has shown sexy books or pictures to be harmful to the viewer or to society (The Report of the Commission on Obscenity and Pornography, 1970)! Isn't it time for education to confront the educated citizens and intellectual leaders of the future with the issues in matters of such concern?

Let us turn now to the third major aspect of the teaching-learning process.

The characteristics of the qualified teacher of sex education. The person whom school officials still tend to claim, with considerable justification, does not exist. (Before going on, let us emphasize parenthetically that we are talking about something *very* special when discussing childhood sexuality and sex education from the perspective of the adult, especially perhaps, that of parents, teachers and society's officials.)

Thus, for example, the typical adult attitude toward childhood sexuality may be exemplified by the incident in which a small child had set fire to the grass and weeds of an isolated vacant lot. In minutes, there was a swarm of neighbors on the lot stamping away at the

flames, beating at them with brooms and wet gunny sacks. Several were asked the reason for desperation.
Obviously the fire had nowhere to spread and it was, in fact, destroying some pollen-producing weeds in a bad season for hay fever. The questioner received only wild-eyed stares in response. When he left, the neighbors were still shouting each other on and stamping and beating at the busy little flames, which finally became smoldering embers and ultimately died out completely. Is our analogy with adult attitudes and the tenacious flames of childhood and youthful sexuality overdrawn? We don't think so. And the frequent dying out of the flame in adulthood is attested to by the overwhelming numbers of people seeking help for sexual inadequacy. At any rate, the would-be sex educator has to make a crucial decision as to whether he is really an educator or a stamper-outer of the flames. But back to the "qualified" teacher of sex education.

We have no studies to back up our views with regard to the qualities needed by a teacher of sex education; but the foregoing discussion would seem to imply certain things which may serve as a starting point in setting criteria for such teachers.* Clearly, impossible standards must not be set. It should go without saying that the teacher needs to be one with whom the learner is willing to talk openly.

1. First of all, we think, the teacher must have come to terms with his or her own sexuality, and to have admitted not only to its existence but to its full status in the dynamics of his or her total personality functioning. That is, he/she must be able to deal directly with his/her pupils and the subject matter without having at every

* The American Association for Sex Educators and Counselors (AASEC) has taken the first steps in formulating standards for the accreditation of sex educators. Its special committee's initial reports will appear in 1973.

step to struggle with personal conflicts, anxieties, and tensions. For this reason, the individual who is either extremely eager or extremely reluctant to teach this subject may well not be the best choice to teach it. A teacher once gave an accurate talk on human reproduction to a group of girls—and left them severely upset because of the way in which she did it. This incident recalls the case of the superintendent of schools of a medium sized city who actively blocked sex education—not, as he insisted to his board and himself, for moral reasons—but because, as he suddenly realized and confided, he resented his own impotency so profoundly. The teacher of sex education cannot be caught up in such personal conflicts if he/she is to be effective.

2. It should go without saying that the teacher needs to know the appropriate factual material associated with the subject that he or she is to teach. Most emphatically, the traditional misconceptions concerned with sexual adequacy, masturbation, the sex play of children, and homosexuality must not be passed on by anyone who teaches this subject. Moreover, he or she should know far more about the broad subject of human sexuality than merely the principles of reproduction education. This point is of special importance in sex education because questioning by students is bound to give rise to "instant escalation" into unexpected, oftentimes sensitive, threatening territory.

3. The teacher of sex education needs to be able to use the language of sex easily and naturally, especially in the presence of the young. This is impossible for many people; however, most can probably learn to do so.

A rule of thumb which we have found useful in counseling potential teachers of sex education has been: "If you feel uneasy about the prospects of speaking directly to youngsters about sexual matters, but believe that this uneasiness is rather silly and wish you could be rid of it, you should be encouraged. Usually in such cases the uneasiness is due to lack of experience. On the other hand, if you feel uneasy about the prospects of discussing sexual matters with youngsters, and you feel that direct, frank communication about such matters is basically wrong, very probably you will not get over these feelings simply by becoming active in sex education programs."

4. He or she needs to be familiar with the sequence of psychosexual developmental events throughout life; and to have a sympathetic understanding of common problems associated with them.

5. The teacher needs an acute awareness of the enormous social changes that are in progress and of their implications for changes in our patterns of sexual attitudes, practices, laws and institutions. Acknowledging that even though the old and traditional is not necessarily useless because it is old and traditional, neither is it necessarily valid or useful because it is old and traditional, he or she must be prepared to reckon with the fact that marriage and propagation have lost much of their historical functions. Men and women no longer need each other as they used to for economic reasons. Nor do men and women need to produce children who will serve as sickness and old age insurance, free labor, and a family fighting force. The teacher in this field must help the society to adjust to such facts, to help the society evolve through a most difficult transitional period, and to help evolve new patterns, new ways, new institutions. In short, at present, we are caught between the murderous pressures of the fading era and the strange new era that is being born; and the sex educator must not try to pretend that all of this is not happening and that we can return to the simple past with its clear-cut, arbitrary solutions. By "arbitrary

solutions" we mean solutions that are "right" because someone or some group has simply defined them as "right" with no feeling of obligation to provide supporting evidence. (We recognize that *ultimately* all value judgments are based upon unprovable assumptions. However, as members of a culture that has a strong rational tradition, we are inclined to be skeptical of axiological prescriptions for which the prescriber fails to give at least a "reasonably reasonable" case.)

Refusal to accept the arbitrary authority of any so-called traditional morality will be difficult for many educators—until they pause to realize that a professional ethic is at stake. The would-be sex educator needs to realize that he or she can no more base his or her teaching upon the arbitrary authority of some group than he or she could justify making the study of the subject of nutrition conform to the ritualistic dietary practices of the Hindus, the Zulus, the Sioux, or the Hopi Indians. Thus we know of no modern textbook on nutrition that finds it necessary to devote space to, and certainly not advocate, the ritual of communion or the Jewish or Blackfoot Indian sacred food taboos. The sex educator, like other educators, would seem wise to stick to the subject matter. He or she is neither theologian nor professional moralist.

It is possible that some readers will find a summary of main points of this chapter on the teaching-learning process and the challenge of sex education useful. The highlights are therefore as follows.

The most significant feature of the sexual revolution may well be that science and professional education are at last crowding their way upon the sex education scene, and an atmosphere conducive to rational thought and communication on the subject of sex seems finally to be emerging. The educator needs to view this development as it relates to three crucial factors in the teaching-learning process: the learner, the subject matter, and the teacher. With regard to sex education, salient characteristics of learners are that they are eager to learn and that their personal needs and future roles as parents and "educated," voting citizens, and perhaps intellectual leaders make it urgent that they be sex-educated.

The characteristics of the subject matter are that it fascinates and repels the minds of Judeo-Christian-Puritan people and is uniquely inaccessible to rational scrutiny or easy communication. The language of sex tends to be unacceptable and is commonly a barrier to education. Partly because of it, some people still doubt that sex is properly a school subject matter at all. However, the urgencies of modern circumstances have given rise to a demand—perhaps a near tidal wave demand—for a straightforward, rational approach to sex education in schools. Widespread misinformation requires that much sex education be remedial in nature. Although no information should be withheld from either sex, some has special significance for one or the other.

One can only speculate about what should be the characteristics of the individual qualified to teach sex education. We think that he or she must have come to terms with his/her own sexuality, know the subject matter and something of its extraordinary social significance, be able to talk about it easily, know what is appropriate to the different developmental levels, and be acutely aware of his or her role as educator, which forbids serving as advocate for any arbitrary authority, traditional or otherwise.

The word "challenge" appears in the title of this chapter, and indeed the material covered would seem to abound with implied challenges. However, before moving on to an analytical overview of perspectives and problems in this field, we will conclude this particular discussion with the key challenge which we hope the reader will keep in mind throughout the book: As we shall see in later chapters, anthropological and sociological data make it clear that people are capable of creating fantastically varied patterns of sexual behavior. Perhaps the basic question on this subject that educators will need to raise and help to answer is this: Since our present patterns of sexual behavior are demonstrably not in our individual or collective best interest, what patterns *might be* in our best interests—and how might we fashion them? Some future historian is likely to say that education has rarely if ever been confronted with such a challenge.

We can think of no words more fitting to the present situation than those of Lincoln, when he said:

The dogmas of the quiet past are inadequate for the stormy present. We must think anew, we must act anew, we must disenthrall ourselves.

REFERENCES

Breasted, M.: Oh! Sex Education. New York, Praeger, 1970.

Cohn, F., and Belzer, E. G., Jr.: Who is to teach the sex educator? Journal of Medical Education, 45:588-93, August, 1970.

Gittelson, R. B.: Selling love short. Sexual Behavior, 2:2-3, April, 1972.

Herndon, J.: The Way It Spozed To Be. New York, Simon and Schuster, 1965.

Iseman, M. F.: Sex education. McCalls, January, 1968.

Johnson, W. R.: Sexual awakening in girls. Sexual Behavior, 3:2-6, March, 1973.

Johnson, W. R., and Schutt, M.: Sex education attitudes of school administrators and school board members. Journal of School Health, 36:64+, February, 1966.

Kavanaugh, J.: A modern priest looks at his outdated church. Saturday Evening Post, 240:10+, December 16, 1967.

Malfetti, J., and Rubin, A.: Sex education: Who's teaching the teachers? The Record—Teachers College, Columbia University, 69:213-222, December, 1967.

Myers, L., and Leggitt, H.: A new view of adultery. Sexual Behavior, 2:52-62, February, 1972.

Pilpel, H. F.: Sex versus the law: a study in hypocrisy. Harper's, 230:35-40, January, 1965.

Report of the Commission on Obscenity and Pornography. New York, Bantam Books, 1970.

Taylor, H.: Portrait of a new generation. Saturday Review, 45:10-12, December 8, 1962.

2

Biology, Etymology, and Some Misconceptions

The discussion in this chapter will not be entirely repetitious of what appears in other books concerned with the basic biology of human sex. For one thing, we have included a translation, from the ancient sources, of some of the not-so-easy-to-use terminology of the sex structures and functions. For another, we have endeavored to begin weaving into the hopefully objective, "scholarly" element which rests on historical or clinical authority and/or scientific data, the intensely personal human element which is so often swept under the rug in such discussions—swept away even as it protests that all these things have meaning only in terms of this subjective referent.

In brief, as aspiring human beings, educators, and even scientists, we have attempted to write about human sexual behavior and sex education, not as exclusively academic or scientific matters, but as fundamentally human and personal matters of the utmost importance to every human being. Furthermore, although there are possibly ugly and darkly mysterious and subterranean as well as fascinating and even beautiful aspects of sexuality, there is also always the *fun* side of sex which is as much a part of it as "love." We have made no effort whatever to divest the subject of this fun aspect which has always ben a major source of amusement in human life.

When people speak of sex, they do not ordinarily think of anatomy and physiology. But when they speak of sex education, they do tend to think in anatomical and physiological terms, almost exclusively in fact. Motion and emotion tend to figure in people's conceptions of sex. Both are excluded in so far as possible from sex education. Making a cognitive (intellectual) experience of something that is basically an affective (feeling) experience is no simple trick.

The title of this chapter includes the word "etymology." This word refers, of course, to determining the origin or derivation of words. We are not entirely sure that it is correctly used in the title, but it is intended to be a notice that we will be peeking into a more or less esoteric field in order to see what meanings lie behind some of the terms of sex which are, to most people, nothing but unpleasant, though perhaps at times somewhat exciting words. No effort is made to trace all sex terms, but only those which seem somehow, to us at least, of special interest.

This attention to the words of sex is certainly not intended to be an extra added attraction thrown in as a collection of hopefully interesting curios, but rather as an important dimension of our subject. After all, our sex and sex-related words were once alive and functional in human communication and were in close contact with and perhaps descriptive of human experience. Of course, some of these words are functional today but not at the usual familial or educational levels. It may be profoundly reflective of our attitude toward sex that its terminology is not of English derivation, but instead, for the most part, is retained from a long-dead language that is incomprehensible to most of us and adds to and reenforces the mystery, remoteness, and ineffability of the whole subject. At any rate, many a person has felt somehow quite differently about the words "penis" and "vagina" upon learning that they derive from Latin words, the former meaning a little pencil or artist's brush and the latter meaning sheath or scabbard. "Pudendum," which has reference especially to the external genital parts of the female, derives from the Latin meaning "to be ashamed." The "shamefuls" as it were. The slang word "pud" referring to penis is a shortened form of pudendum. The Oxford English Dictionary tells us that "phallus," on the other hand, is the image of the male generative organ, symbolizing the generative power of nature, venerated in various religious systems, specifically that carried in solemn procession in the Dionysiac festivals in ancient Greece. In later times the phallus was commonly worn as an amulet for protection against the evil eye. In Eastern India the direct representation of the penis (the lingam) is today a revered symbol of life and fertility, and is of major importance in religious observances (see, for example, Kaplan, 1957, pp. 24 and 26). Isn't it interesting that drawing a phallus is a commendable act in some societies and an obscenity in others—such as ours?

Let us now turn our attention to the male reproductory structures and their functions.

Anatomically, the male system includes the penis, the sensitive head of which is known as the glans. (As does "gland," the word "glans" derives from the Latin for "acorn," there being quite a resemblance, especially if the foreskin is not removed by circumcision: *circum*, around + *cision*, cut. Once, when the two-year-old son of one of us was riding in an elevator in a large bank building his gaze focused upon the rococo ornamentation at the top of the car's walls. He pointed upward and said "penis." There among the ornate wood carvings were many acorns which evidently looked like penises to him. In a way, this youngster's perception was as keen as that of the obscure anatomist who officially dubbed the head of the penis "glans." The most sensitive part of the penis, the frenulum, is located on the under surface, just behind the glans. The male system also includes: the urethra, a tube which extends from bladder to glans and serves as an outlet for both urine and semen (from L., to sow), the opaque, slippery fluid which carries the sperm; the seminal vesicles (reservoirs where semen is stored); the vas deferens, or spermatic duct, the excretory duct of a testicle; the epididymis (epi, upon + didymos, testicle), a mass of convoluted tubing, where sperms are stored and mature after they leave the testicle proper; and the testicle, a gland of internal and external secretion, which produces sperm (L., denoting seed) and male sex hormone (from Greek, "to excite"). The two testicles are housed in the scrotum (L., bag).

The etymology of the word "testicle" or "testis" deserves further explanation. According to *An Etymological Dictionary of Modern English,* testis means "witness" in Latin; that is, the testis is a witness or testimony to male virility. "Testament" (as in New and Old) is related to "testis," meaning witness, last will, and in the Biblical sense, covenant. According to Shipley's Dictionary of Word Origins, the Latin diminutive of testis is a testiculus—from the early practice of placing the hand "on the seat of manliness" when swearing rather than upon the heart as we do today. Hindu and Arab men "swear oaths by putting their hands to the generative parts of their body" (Raphaelian, 1957, p. 78), as did some American Indians. This practice was also followed by the ancient Hebrews, as evidenced by Biblical references to oath taking while placing the hand "under the thigh" (*e.g.,* Genesis, 24:2; Genesis, 47:29).

The penis is capable of greatly increasing its size and

becoming erect when the spongy tissue of which it is composed becomes filled with blood. We suppose that the foregoing statement is a properly dry way of describing one of the arch peculiarities of being a male. Unlike the other appendages of the body, the penis has a kind of will of its own and cannot always be depended upon to behave in a way that is entirely acceptable to the cerebral cortex. Not only is it inclined to become erect as a result of sexual stimulation, such as love making, dancing, pornographic pictures, and a lively imagination, but also it might become restive in response to a full bladder, irritation from clothing, riding a bicycle or horse, or no particular thing that its possessor is aware of. In fact, an erection may occur under most disconcerting conditions—just as under various conditions it may fail disconcertingly to occur.

An older woman in one of our sex education classes—in the middle of her indignation at the way the course was going—startled herself and the class by exclaiming an insight that had hit her. She said, "Sex is to human life as salt is to the sea." This is a very important idea and if appreciated would help people to absorb unexpected events like having the penis begin to harden when one is fondling his own infant son or daughter, or when one is dancing with an attractive woman who happens to be the boss's wife; or in the woman's case, would help her to feel without self-incrimination her labia become warm, full and moist at times that are not entirely in keeping with her notions of propriety—when nursing one's infant, for example. (See the reference by Niles Newton.)

But to go on with the business at hand. Rhythmic movements of the penis within the vagina or comparable close-fitting structure eventually give rise simultaneously to orgasm (L., "violent excitement of feeling") and ejaculation (L., out + throw, as of semen from the body in the adult male). Ejaculation does not occur in males until their sexual structures have sufficiently matured at around the time of puberty. On the other hand, orgasm can occur in both males and females very early in life. Perhaps indicative of the profound involvement of sex in human behavior is the fact that male infants oftentimes get erections on the first day after birth. Although we have no idea who goes around conducting research of this kind, it is reported that before the age of one year, male infants respond to manipulation of the genitals by making thrusting movements which culminate in a general spasm that at least appears to be like the adult climax or orgasm (Ford and Beach, 1951, p. 179). Many boys as well as girls masturbate to climax long before puberty. After sexual maturity has been attained, orgasm accompanied by ejaculation may occur as a result of self-stimulation or during sleep (nocturnal emission or "wet dream"). As we shall see in a later discussion, and as many males know from personal experience, both these types of solitary sexual experiences are likly to be the occasion of enormous distress, fear, and guilt as well as pleasure and relief. In regard to "self-stimulation," or "self-relief" as it has also been called, this is true of many females too, but is perhaps even more difficult to deal with. For whereas sex is accepted though perhaps regretted in the male, it does not exist in the really "nice" female, or so our traditional inculcating of the young would have it.

Sperm, the male sex cells, are formed in the testicles and are carried in the semen fluid during ejaculation. They are microscopic and are shaped like tadpoles. (To appreciate how small they are, it has been estimated that enough sperm to form an object smaller than an aspirin tablet would be sufficient to give the earth its present population.) Their thrashing tails propel them about and are the means whereby they move through the vagina and womb and into the oviduct of the female, where conception usually takes place. Well over 250,000,000 sperm cells may be present in a single ejaculation of semen.

The testicles or testes, also called gonads (Gr., that which generates), are carried outside the body in a bag, the scrotum. The testes produce sperm and male sex hormone, androgen (Gr., male + producing), also called testosterone (androgen produced chemically from testes). It is this hormone which, as a result of stimulation of the testes by the "master endocrine gland," the pituitary, gives rise to the appearance of the secondary sex characteristics at puberty. Just how androgen affects human male behavior before and after puberty is not known, for there are of course so many learning and other possible factors involved in "behaving like a man." However, this hormone is certainly a factor. It is, of course, rarely if ever entirely safe to draw comparisons between humans and animals further down the evolutionary scale, but anyone who has worked with animals is aware how much more docile and manageable jackasses, rams, stallions, and bulls tend to become after they are castrated.

Similarly teachers of children have to watch few little girls as they have to watch most of the little boys when it comes to keeping discipline from going to pieces as a result of aggressiveness, enthusiasm, or just plain "messing around." Might socialization of females versus males account for *all* such observed differences in behavior? Probably not all. But the absurdly artificial nature of traditional sex role socialization has succeeded in making it extremely difficult for people of either sex to simply be and enjoy being themselves, regardless of their genital sex. The famous and increasingly available "transsexual" operations may represent the ultimate reaction to sex *role* confusion: "I am so confused and uncomfortable being what I am, genitally, that my only recourse is to have myself changed surgically to the only available alternative, the other sex" (Benjamin, 1966; Green and Money, 1969; Money, 1970-71). Today, a great many people, not just Women's Lib, are protesting the imposing of male or female stereotypes on children in the name of genital sex.

The prepuce (L., foreskin) is a loose skin which surrounds the end of the penis in a hood-like manner and can cover or be drawn back from the glans. Although among some people the routine amputation of the prepuce, circumcision, is based on religious beliefs, this practice is no longer generally considered to be medically justified. Whereas only a few years ago the great majority of North American male neonates were circumcised, precisely the opposite is true in many regions of this continent today. (Consult the Quarterly Cumulative Index Medicus of recent years for a blow by blow account of this controversy.)

Before leaving the subject of the male prepuce (there is a female kind also), we should note that the inside of the foreskin normally adheres to the penile glans in infants. This adhesion usually disappears during the second and third years of life, thereby allowing the foreskin to be pulled back to expose completely the penile head. Parents who decide against automatic circumcision (i.e., in the absence of a specific indication, such as phimosis—a too-tight foreskin) should realize that the early nonretractable foreskin is "normal," usually not requiring circumcision or forceable retraction of the prepuce so as to break adhesions. Male infants, who are free to do so, do a great deal of manipulating and tugging on their genitals. They thereby encourage freeing of prepuce from glans themselves.

Now a few words about genital pain following extended, nonorgastic love-making. It is well known that males as well as females sometimes experience more or less severe pain in the genital region following prolonged sexual arousal unrelieved by orgasm. This is usually explained on the basis of the large accumulations of blood in the pelvic region and associated swelling of the sex organs. For example, Masters has observed the uteri of prostitutes to be several times normal size after hours of seeing customers without experiencing orgasm themselves. Upon masturbating to orgasm, these women have had immediate relief from lower back and pelvic pain and their uteri have returned quickly to normal. However, the situation seems different with males. About 200 college level males were questioned as to (1) whether they had ever experienced such pain (variously termed "lover's nuts," "blue balls," and—a new one to us, "stone gullion,' apparently an Ohio localism), (2) whether they were wearing clothing at the time, and (3) whether the pain was relieved by orgasm. To our surprise, only about half had experienced such pain. In almost all cases those who had experienced it were wearing clothing or the erection was otherwise subjected to prolonged downward pressure at the time, and orgasm sometimes brought relief, especially if the pain were of short duration, and sometimes it did not. Since an ancient sexual technique involves maintaining peak erection for extended periods without orgasm, and no pain or other ill effect is ever reported, it seems reasonable to conclude that male groin pain is caused not by congestion of blood but by muscular soreness due usually to the downward pressure of clothing against the erection.

So much for the male sex structures and their functions. Now for the female.

The external sexual structures of the female are the "lips" or labia, the labia majora and within them the smaller lips, the labia minora (also called collectively the vulva and, as we have pointed out, the pudenda, "the shamefuls"). Some peoples attach great importance to the labia as being sexually attractive, as many of us do breasts, and they therefore stretch and irritate them to exaggerate their size (Ford and Beach, 1951, p. 176).

Within the labia are located, from front to rear: the clitoris, the urinary opening, and the vaginal opening, inside which lies the vaginal tract leading to the uterus or womb. Incidentally, it is of some interest that the surgical operation involving removal of the womb is called "hysterectomy," from the Greek word *hystera* meaning womb. Now, *hystera* is also the root word for hysterical, pertaining to wildly emotional behavior, for it was believed that what we call "hysterical behavior" is a female trait having its cause in the womb or hystera and having as perhaps its treatment of choice, ℞: *Penis normalis dosim repetatur* (The best medicine would be an ordinary penis, repeatedly) (Kaplan, 1957).

The clitoris (Gr., "to close," and allied to such words as closet and closure) is the counterpart of the penis in the male, although it is much smaller and is not capable of ejaculation. It is about one-eighth to one-half inch in length, like the penis has a shaft, glans, and foreskin and, again like the penis, is capable of tumescence when stimulated intentionally or unintentionally. During sexual excitement, the engorged clitoris draws back to a fairly inaccessible position beneath the hood formed where the labia minora join. Marriage manuals of yesteryear were wont to stress the necessity of each couple's discovering which coital position resulted in maximal contact of the particular penis with the individual clitoris. In light of today's knowledge, it seems considerably preferable to acknowledge that couples

may have to try various positions if they are to discover which afford(s) them optimal mutual satisfaction. The clitoris, while not directly stimulated by the
penis, usually is stimulated pleasurably by the movement of the labia produced by coital thrusting. Sometimes a woman will not find this stimulation to be what
she requires to experience orgasm, but stimulation by
a tongue, a well lubricated finger, or an electric vibrator
will usually prove entirely adequate.

In the early 1950s, a neurologist presented a scientific paper on the subject of his minute study of the
cellular structure of the clitoris. He was surprised that
apparently he was the first to examine this structure
in such close detail, and he permitted himself unscien-
tific astonishment at the number of nerve cells crammed
into such close quarters. He concluded, with some
apparent reluctance, that on a strictly neurological
basis there seems to be no reason to suppose that the
female sexual experience is less intense than that of
the male. It was nice to have a scientific explanation
of what more than a few in the course of history have
been forced to suspect on their own.

But there are surely more interesting things to be
noted about the clitoris than all this business of anatomy, histology, and fundamentally pointless specula-
tion about the relative sexual sensations of male and
female. In *Cannery Row* (1945) John Steinbeck commented that two generations of Americans knew more
about the Model T Ford coil than about the clitoris. As
a matter of fact, it is probably safe to say that numerous
generations of men have not even known of the existence of this little structure. It has been the subject of
immense *intra*personal communication among women
but it has traditionally been blacklisted as a subject of
of *inter*personal communication: like "the little man

who wasn't there." In her outlawed personal history, *The Housewife's Handbook on Selective Promiscuity* (1961), Rey Anthony does describe lubricating and playing with her "little bump" but this is a rare admission. Linguists have long noted that things which are important to people tend to acquire many names. Thus the Eskimos have numerous names for snow, the Arabs numerous names for the camel, and we have numerous names for automobiles and the penis. In contrast, we have had many male college students who first encountered the word clitoris in our classes, and some apparently suspected that both word and structure were inventions of ours.

Intensive philological research reveals that there have been and are alternative terms for the clitoris, some of which are quite expressive of attitudes toward it, *e.g.*, Bad Fellow, Badge of Shame, Gaiety, Gem, Madness, Instigator, Narrow Strip, Place of Secrecy, Bride. In a mild way these terms are suggestive of the extremes of attitude toward the female genitalia which we have heard many times described variously by men as the most beautiful and the most ugly things in the world. At any rate, there must be some significance to be attached to the fact that the Germans have the word Kitzler or "tickler" for clitoris. This is not popular slang at all but straight-faced medical terminology.

Psychoanalytical interpretations of this vocabulary deficiency are in terms of the exaggerated evaluation of the phallus of the male and a corresponding depreciation of its absence in the female, all of which is the result of the strongly patriarchal, male-dominated tradition. The cultural attitude toward female sexuality certainly seems reflected in the extraordinary lack of terminology, or as Blau (1962, p. 69) suggested, it "seems to highlight the extreme cultural suppression of female sexuality. . . ."* The coming chapter on historical considerations may shed light, if somewhat obliquely, on this entire matter. At any rate, it is depressing to be able to report that so negative still is the attitude toward female sexuality that one of us personally has been instrumental in preventing more than one clitoris removal, which had been medically prescribed to stop little girls' "masturbating," and a book published in the 1960's describes a woman psychiatrist's accomplishing incredible mutilation of a woman's external genitals so as to prevent her masturbating when her on-again-off-again husband left her frustrated and frantic (Bonaparte, 1962, p. 192).

Regarding the urinary opening, two points should probably be made. The first is that most women would prefer that their lovers know of its existence and not in their eager feeling about confuse it with the vagina. The second is that the urethra, the tube which connects the opening with the bladder, is very short. Germs can relatively easily pass from the urinary opening area to the bladder and set up infections such as painful cystitis (inflammation of the bladder). However, not all urinary tract infections cause burning upon urination or other symptoms which could prompt their victims to seek medical aid. About one in every 100 school girls has an unrecognized urinary tract infection (Holland, Jurich, and Clemons, 1969). It is thought that many of these "silent infections" can and do lead to irreversible kidney damage, complications of pregnancy, and other troubles. Cleanliness of the labia area and

---

* Consult the references by Blau (1962) and Kanner (1962), if you can, for rare discussions of the clitoris. *Eros,* the magazine in which they were published, appeared for one year and was the basis for the five-year jail sentence and $42,000 fine in 1967 of its publisher, Ralph Ginzburg. *Eros* is now a collector's item.

anything that comes into contact with it is of practical importance.

The entryway to the vagina is usually partially blocked by a bit of skin called the hymen, maidenhead, or in slang, "cherry," which if torn during the first coitus may bleed. This bleeding has traditionally been taken to symbolize the end of virginity. However, those interested in this kind of testing should realize that bleeding is no real test of virginity because many females have such small and flexible hymens that they never tear, and others stretch or rupture the hymen by means other than coitus, *e.g.*, by the fingers and objects early in life, by inserting vaginal tampons during menstruation. A medical examination and counseling before a first coition can virtually assure freedom from tearing or other pain.

The vagina itself (L., sheath) is a stretchable flattened tube, somewhat like a deflated, small ball bladder, which can stretch and adjust its size to that of the particular erect penis during coitus and can stretch even more when serving as the birth canal during childbearing. It lubricates itself during sexual stimulation by means of a process wherein the lubricating fluid is evidently squeezed through the vaginal wall by the greatly increased blood accumulation in the genital area. More mysteriously, when an artificial vagina is constructed for a woman from skin from another part of her body, this skin presently "learns" to function as a natural vagina if coitus is engaged in within a few weeks.

Incidentally, during erotic response the outer third of the vaginal barrel tightens, with the result that male orgasm is encouraged. On the other hand, with heightened sexual arousal the walls of the inner end of the vagina actually are drawn apart, as though a collapsed tent had been erected by pulling taut its guy wires. This favors pooling of the semen close to the cervix.

Thus the female copulatory organ has evolved in a way that encourages conception. Unfortunately, reflex and forceful gripping of the penis by the outer portion of the vagina may encourage early ejaculation by the male. Skilled female lovers oftentimes emulate but improve on the vaginal response by firmly gripping the base of the erect penis with one hand and at the same time stimulating the glans, etc., and especially the frenulum (under portion of penis just back of the glans corona) lightly with tongue or lubricated fingers. In this way, sensitive adjustment may be made to the male's wish to prolong enjoyment. Conversely, the female may find erotic response more gratifying if tongue or well-lubricated fingers are used gently to stimulate labia minora and clitoris (unscented cold cream is excellent lubrication). Indeed, some couples find such forms of direct stimulation so controllable and enjoyable that these are not considered foreplay, penis-in-vagina coitus rarely if ever being practiced.

The vagina connects the outer with the inner female sex structures, joining as it does with the cervix (L., neck) of the uterus. The nonpregnant uterus (Teutonic and Old English meaning belly, abdomen, or hollow place) is a hollow, muscular organ, roughly the size of a small pear, which angles upward from the vagina. This angling away from the plane of the vagina needs to be taken into account in placing diaphragms, and IUDs, and in examinations of the cervix and uterus. In pregnancy, shortly before delivery the uterus has grown and stretched to hold some 20 inches and 7 pounds of fetus, but it is still able to exert tremendous pressure against the fetus in the process of expelling it. The uterus is also the source of the menstrual flow in that its lining, the endometrium, builds up a layer of blood and tissue each month and discharges it if pregnancy does not occur.

The fallopian tubes (ova or egg ducts) arch upward, one to the right and one to the left, like horns from the uterus, and terminate like extending fingers (fimbria) near the respective ovaries. The lack of direct connection between tube and ovary has raised the question of how the ovum gets into the tube on better than a pure chance basis. Photographic studies of animals have shown that the fingers literally reach out and grab eggs and suck them into the tube by a chemotaxic effect —a chemical drawing-in effect. Amazingly, specialists in obstetrics and gynecology testify to cases where a woman has had the ovary on one side and the fallopian tube on the other side surgically removed—and still became pregnant! Once the ovum is inside the tube, it is propelled toward the uterus by means of cilia, like those in the respiratory tract which push fluids and objects from the direction of the lungs and toward the mouth. This is all very well for the ovum, but it also means that the sperms have to fight their way up against the current, so to speak.

The ovaries are homologous to the male's testicles. That is, they develop from the same embryonic tissue and perform some similar functions. If the cortex of the embryonic gonad develops, an ovary is produced. If the medulla, the inner core, develops, a testicle results. Of course, the ovaries produce the ova, or egg cells.

The ovaries also produce estrogen, a hormone which promotes bone growth. The prepubertal growth spurt of young females is largely in response to their increased production of estrogen. You may have noticed how the girl who enters puberty earlier than her peers is often one of the tallest in her class. Such girls also often stop growing before their peers, whose slower growth patterns may well result in a taller height at maturity. This apparent mystery may seem less amazing in light of the fact that estrogen, in addition to bone growth, stimulates the maturation and cessation of activity of the epiphyses, the growth regions at the end of the long bones. The female preponderance of estrogen over androgen is also responsible for the broader pelvises of females and their narrower shoulders. Breast and nipple development are provoked by estrogen, as is the appearance of a wedge-shaped patch of pubic hair on the mons veneris (mound of Venus, goddess of love).

In light of the aforementioned roles of estrogen, we think it would have seemed more appropriate had this particular hormone been given a name with a derivation comparable to that of "androgen." Whereas "androgen" (Gr., man + beginning) means substance that induces masculine characteristics, "estrogen" is derived from a root that refers to being in sexual heat, the word translating out to such things as gadfly, sting, and frenzy. While it may be true that a great many females from time to time act sexually frenzied, we can hardly attribute much of this to the hormone we call estrogen. Actually, it seems to be androgen *in both sexes* which is the hormone primarily responsible for our erotic zip. Part of the evidence that leads to this realization has been obtained from women who have had their adrenal glands removed for medical reasons. The adrenal glands produce not only such hormones as cortisone, epinephrine, and norepinephrine, but they are a major source of androgen in the human female. It was found that adrenalectomized women who were receiving adequate corticosteroid therapy to maintain life, but no androgen supplementation, quickly reported a loss of interest in erotic activity and a marked reduction in sexual responsiveness (Drellich and Waxenberg, 1966). Interestingly enough, these women did not lose their desire for affectionate contact and tender interpersonal relationships. These desires continued in the absence of any urge for coitus or drive toward orgasm. When androgen supplementation was provided, the erotic drive returned. Greenblatt (1971, p. 25) has reported an experiment in which women who had lost their orgasmic capacity were treated with a variety of hormones. Whereas only about 30% of those receiving estrogen experienced improved sex drive, over 75% of those who received androgen had an increase in libido. Some women who have received androgen during medical treatment for various disease problems have experienced orgasm for the first time. Others have complained of "almost intolerable" increases in sexual desire.

The ovaries produce a second important hormone, progesterone. This hormone interacts with estrogen in bringing about the events of the menstrual cycle and is chiefly concerned with the uterus, the fertilized egg, and the adjusting of the body during pregnancy. For example, due to its action, ovulation and menstruation stop when conception occurs, and presently the breasts begin to enlarge to prepare to produce milk. Incidentally, an increasing number of mothers are deciding that their own milk is probably the best natural food for their infants, and is wonderfully convenient and preheated, and they are therefore electing to breast-feed. Moreover, the uterus of the woman who breast-feeds returns to normal size sooner. Breast feeding is also associated with earlier return of sexual interest. Sexual feelings stimulated by suckling the breasts are natural, to be expected, and they certainly should not give rise to guilt feelings or the abandoning of breast feeding. It has been pointed out that survival of the human species has probably depended upon the large pleasure payoff to two sexual functions—coitus and suckling infants. Whereas we are repeatedly reminded that the first payoff potential is naturally programmed into us, most of us have been in the dark relative to the second.

Several years ago, a "health fair" in a large Eastern city included a live demonstration of a mother breast feeding her infant. This exhibit created a great commotion because a large number of people considered the sight of a mother feeding her child in this way obscene and damaging to public morality. Others insisted that this is perhaps the least obscene of sights, and the battle was joined.

Increased circulating levels of progesterone (for + gestation) during pregnancy are important in stimulating the body adjustment necessary for successful gestation (L., to bear). As a matter of fact, when John Rock and his associates first developed their progesterone pill, "the pill," it was not for the purpose of contraception, but to help women who tended to abort spontaneously early in pregnancy to maintain their pregnancies successfully. It was an afterthought that recognized the possibilities of artificially interrupting ovulation (Enovid, the trade name of the original "pill," means eggless or no egg).

The menstrual (L., monthly) cycle constitutes an obvious example of human behavior control via the endocrine glands. True, as humans evolved, the upper brain acquired more and more influence upon behavior —which is to say that in comparison with animals more of our behavior is determined by learning than by evolutionary programming of lower brain and endocrine mechanisms. In fact, we have progressed to the point where we are often absurdly arrogant about our upper brain control of what we do, and we are prone to feel a certain aloofness from our lower, biological functions. But menstruation is among those things that keep us reminded of our base in biological life. Indeed, the extent to which different phases of the menstrual cycle

3

influence any given woman's thought, feeling, and action processes is largely unknown, although most husbands and many doctors have no doubt that a causal relationship does exist. For example, extreme irritability associated with menstruation may be due to pressure of fluid accumulations in the brain. Edema of this kind is treatable medically. (We know still less about hormonally mediated sexual and other kinds of cycles in males. Among the things for which we have to thank "Women's Lib" is increased attention to this inequity between the sexes.) Graves (1954) has attempted to call attention to the great but often subtle role of the endocrine glands in daily living by pointing out that: "The secretions that pour forth from the testicles and ovaries have an essential part in the endocrine symphony and their contribution is far more complex than the sexual aspects of reproduction ever indicated. Recent discoveries relating to these chemical processes of the body are revolutionizing medical practice as did the investigations of Pasteur, and all of them emphasize the importance of the role of physiological sex for both the man and the woman."

Generally speaking, each month from puberty (around thirteen) to menopause (around fifty), the walls of the uterus gradually build up a layer of tissue and blood, and if pregnancy does not occur, this is discharged as the menstrual flow. About fourteen days *before* the beginning of the next menstrual period, the ovaries expel an ovum (ovulation) which soon enters the oviduct. If sperm are in the oviducts during the few days it takes for the ovum to be transported to the uterus, pregnancy is likely to occur. Some women with very regular cycles can predict when they will ovulate by counting backward about fourteen days from their *next expected beginning* of menstruation. Unfortunately, many if not the great majority of women cannot predict just when their next menstruation will begin; so of course they cannot predict the time of ovulation accurately. After the egg of the month (*usually* there is only one) has erupted, a women's basal temperature rises slightly but measurably, and remains at the higher level until that particular cycle ends with the onset of a new menstrual flow. The unfertilized ovum seems to be viable for only about 24 hours. Therefore, a woman who has established that she is four days past ovulation can be quite confident of ten days of infertility. Perhaps you are asking yourself "Why do they say 'four days past ovulation' when they just said the egg is viable for only 24 hours?" The four days are an added safety factor in consideration of the possibility of a second ovulation during the same menstrual cycle. Evidently, when a second ovulation does occur, it can be depended upon to do so no more than 24 hours after the first.

The matter of female receptiveness to intercourse is of interest in this connection, for this too seems to be related to the menstrual cycle, to have a rhythm, and like menstruation itself, it seems to be a nice example of how basic biology intrudes upon god-like humans, sometimes surreptitiously and disconcertingly—upon their feelings, thoughts, and overt behaviors. Periodically because of glandular activity, most female birds and animals provide some sensory cue such as a sight, smell, or kind of movement to which males respond sexually. And usually at only this time, the female is receptive to sexual overtures by the male which would ordinarily bore or annoy her. In animals such behavior is termed being "in heat" or estrus. In heat cows may mount other cows in a bull-like fashion, and in heat lionesses may attempt to crawl under Leo. On about the tenth day of being in heat, the female dog suddenly stops sitting down when the male attempts to mount her, stands still and attempts to facilitate penis entry.

However, all this is not to say that female animals can have interest in sexual gratification only when in heat. We have known female dogs which dearly loved to mount each other or other suitable objects which could contact their external genitals, and make pelvic thrusts just like males until they gave every appearance that orgasm was reached. But they never permitted male mounting or entry except on the tenth to twelfth day of being in heat.

Somewhat similarly, perhaps, human females tend to report special interest in sex during particular times in the menstrual cycle, often just before or just after menstruation when, interestingly, most cannot become pregnant. (They may masturbate or participate in coitus more or less frequently at other times during their cycles, but we are concerned here with periods of spontaneous, strong sexual desire.) Some investigators suspect that women are becoming increasingly uninhibited sexually as their repressions and fears are being eased, and they are therefore increasingly likely to permit themselves to experience intense sexual desire while they are ovulating—with all that this implies for hazards of unwanted pregnancy if contraceptives are not used habitually. Girls in homes for unwed mothers have reported incredible indifference to protecting themselves by avoidance, resistance, or contraception at the time when they were most likely to be ovulating, even though at other times they had been most concerned about avoiding pregnancy (Clark, 1968, and Rubin, 1964).

There is a widespread and growing tendency to provide menstrual education for girls in about the fifth or sixth grades in the hope of having knowledge of it precede its onset. However, individual differences are so great that onset may occur before the fifth grade for some girls and after college age for others. Ovulation may occur in some girls a few years before the menarche, which accounts for the rare cases of pregnancy in seven- or eight-year-old girls. On the other hand, it has fairly recently been learned that usually girls do not begin to ovulate until some months or even years after the menarche, which is to say that most girls cannot become pregnant until they have menstruated at least a number of times. Indeed, many do not ovulate until they are in their early twenties. But again, some ovulate and get pregnant before puberty. Unfortunately there is as yet no reliable way of knowing whether or not any given girl has begun to ovulate, but the basic point here is that the menarche is not a reliable indicator.*

There is common concern as to the extent to which the menstruating girl or woman should curtail her physical activities. A useful rule of thumb is that, generally speaking, she can continue to do while menstruating what she is *used* to doing the rest of the time. Thus, women athletes and dancers can usually continue their exertions while menstruating, even such events as long distance swimming in cold water. However, during menstruation would very likely be a poor time to begin engaging in such activities. As for sexual intercourse, in spite of a long-standing abhorrence of coitus during menstruation (some primitive peoples have considered menstrual blood poisonous to men, and in our own tradition, according to Leviticus, God himself instructed Moses that if a man should "lie with a woman having her sickness . . . both of them shall be cut off from among their people"), there is no medical reason for abstaining at this time.

To know oneself is a tall order indeed, but it begins

---

*For a discussion of the relationship of the onset of menstruation and the onset of ovulation in the adolescent girl, see Israel (1967, Ch. 7).

with knowing something about one's body, how to use it efficiently, and how it functions. For all of its often bizarre, embarrassing, and messy unpredictability, menstruation is a condition of womanhood. And no woman can hope to understand or accept herself if this basic tie-in with the biology of the race is hated or rejected. Mothers of daughters would seem especially obligated to convey a naturalistic acceptance of this function, for the mother's attitudes toward and statements about it have much to do with the daughter's and perhaps, in certain instances, with whether or not the daughter will have menstrual problems. Moreover, mothers and school personnel can reduce the emotional trauma of unexpected menstruating, dress spotting, and not having a coin for the napkin machine by making intelligent provision for these kinds of things and letting girls know that help is available.

For a short period of time after ovulation, conception can occur. Conception means that a male sperm cell has reached and penetrated an ovum and pregnancy has been started. The 23 chromosomes that carry the hereditary characteristics in the sperm join with the 23 carried by the ovum. That is, mother and father contribute equally to the hereditary background of the child, but it is the sperm that determines its sex. By meiosis, presumably half of the father's sperms carry a male factor, a so-called Y chromosome, and half a female factor, an X chromosome. Thus the sex of the child is determined at conception and depends on whether an X factor or a Y factor sperm reaches the ovum first ($X + X$ = a girl; $X + Y$ = a boy). Ova and sperm that do not bring about pregnancy are either digested by the female's "clean-up cells" or are passed from the body.

Conception usually occurs in an oviduct, and the fertilized egg continues moving toward the uterus; cell multiplication begins and after a few days the egg lodges in the wall of the uterus. (It can lodge and "take root" in the oviduct or on an intestine. Such pregnancies are called "ectopic," which refers to "out of place." But we are concerned here with the usual developments.) By this time it has divided into many cells and in an interactive process with the endometrium, the placenta or afterbirth is formed. In time it becomes the intermediary tissue between woman and fetus. At first the ovum is like a seed; with a few thin roots pushed into the ground, but in time it becomes like a plant with numerous roots locked into the ground. As the "root" system develops, abortion becomes increasingly difficult.

Nourishment passes from the woman to the fetus by way of the placenta, and waste products from the fetus are returned to the woman by this same means. The woman disposes of these waste products by way of her kidneys via her own urine, which is one reason her fluid intake should be maintained at a relatively high level. Nutrients and waste products are passed back and forth through the walls of the blood vessels in the placenta by osmotic pressure. Neither the circulatory nor the nervous systems of woman and fetus are directly connected. However, some specialists urge pregnant women to arrange as tranquil lives for themselves as possible because hormones such as adrenalin which are associated with emotional upsets can pass from woman to fetus causing upset and possibly harm to the fetus if frequent in occurrence.

There is a great deal of literature and other information available on pregnancy and birth, and so we will conclude this brief discussion now with a few points which seem to be of special interest.

Can a girl or woman become pregnant without having vaginal coitus? Yes. If she has ovulated or is about to and if male ejaculation has deposited semen where sperms can reach the moist labia, the incredible little fellows can actually wiggle and lash their way from as far away as the thigh if moisture is present, to and through the vagina and beyond to reach the ovum. This rarely happens, but it does happen.

How can a woman tell if she is pregnant? Traditionally, of course, failing to menstruate on schedule is the first sign, although this does not necessarily signify pregnancy. Emotional upset, such as that occasioned by fear of pregnancy, or beginning a new job, can interrupt the menstrual rhythm. Ten days after a missed period, the presence of a pregnancy can be detected with a number of highly reliable medical tests. Realizing that ten days after a missed menstrual period usually is equal to about 24 days after an ovulation, a pregnancy would already have been established approximately three weeks by that time. (When does a pregnancy exist? At the instant of fertilization? Or not until implantation of the embryo in the uterus, several days later? If the latter, would you consider the "morning after pill" to be an abortifacient?) It is of special interest that in many states a woman need not be married or, if a girl, have parental permission in order to get medical tests for pregnancy in local health departments. In some states physicians in private practice may, if they choose, diagnose and "treat" pregnancy as well as venereal disease without parental consent. Planned Parenthood and local health departments are especially good sources of information (confidential) on all such matters. In Canada, "do it yourself" pregnancy test kits can be purchased in drug stores without prescription.

What causes twins? There are two possibilities. Identical twins result when a single sperm and single ovum unite and then divide in such a way that two individuals are formed instead of one. Their hereditary backgrounds are then believed to be identical, they are always of the same sex (the sperm having either been an X or a Y), and they look very much alike. On the other hand, fraternal twins result when the female releases two ova instead of the usual one when she ovulates, and each is fertilized by a different sperm. They may be of the same or opposite sex and are no more alike in heredity than other brother and sisters.

Is "the pill" responsible for the cases of five and even more babies, usually premature and unable to survive, that are reported via news media so frequently these days? No. Multiple births are not increased by previous use of contraceptive pills. The cases referred to above involve the use of drugs taken to stimulate ovulation. Unfortunately, sometimes they stimulate the release of more than one egg. Notice that the news reports usually mention the number of boys and girls in the "litter." Such babies are the products of multiple ovulation, and as with fraternal twins, are no more closely related than are brothers and sisters born years apart. This is in contrast to such cases as represented by the famous Dionne quintuplets, who developed from a single original zygote or fertilized egg.

Is coitus harmful to the pregnant woman? Traditionally doctors have advised against coitus for as much as three months before and three months after birth—which is to say abstention for half a year. Not surprisingly, it has been during this period that many of those husbands who had extramarital affairs first began doing so. Investigators such as Masters and Johnson have established that this whole matter of coitus during pregnancy has to be put on an individual basis. Female libido is likely to be heightened during the second three months of pregnancy and coitus may be entirely safe until shortly before delivery—although orgasm may trigger labor as delivery time approaches. It is safe to say that the circumstances of advanced pregnancy tend to discourage coital interest in many women, and intense orgasm may be followed by discomfort as pregnancy progresses. However, this does not mean that women cannot provide very satisfying nonvaginal sexual release for their husbands during virtually the entire course of pregnancy.

Generally speaking, coitus may be resumed some weeks after delivery and, as indicated earlier, sexual interest tends to return most quickly to those women who nurse their babies. It is highly recommended that physicians who do see fit to limit or outlaw coitus for extended periods during and after pregnancy should explain their reasons fully to both husband and wife so that the man will not feel that his wife is rejecting him personally or needlessly. Again, we mention the fact that one need not be available as a coital partner to be a very satisfactory lover.

How can a woman get an abortion? Sometimes an unwanted pregnancy is terminated by the woman's body itself in what is called a spontaneous abortion. The fetus with developmental defect or disease is likely to be rejected in this way, although it may not be.

As for induced abortion, by a United States Supreme Court decision of 1973, the anti-abortion laws of 46 states were either invalidated (31 states) or required to be rewritten (15 states). During the first three months of pregnancy, the decision to have an abortion is now entirely up to the woman and her physician. During the next six months, states may regulate abortion only to protect a woman's health (Court decision: "the word person, as used in the 14th Amendment, does not include the unborn"). Even during the last 10 weeks, when life may be sustained outside the womb, abortion may be performed to protect the life and health, presumably including mental health, of the pregnant woman.

Although all ten provinces and the two territories of

Canada come under the same federal law regarding therapeutic abortion, there is great variation in practice from one community to another. In some places, over 90% of women seeking abortion receives them, usually on the basis of protecting their mental health (and most of those whose petitions are denied are women whose pregnancies have gone beyond the twelfth week, when the hazards of abortion rise markedly). In other locations, legal abortions are nonexistent.

Efforts at self-induced abortion by poking about in the easily punctured uterus, trying to jar the embryo loose, or by taking drugs are not only ineffectual, but exceedingly dangerous and sometimes fatal to women. Also, nonmedical abortionists who operate against the law are in the business for the money, do not tend to have optimal training or facilities and are therefore to be considered dangerous. On the other hand, there are cases such as that of a qualified, respected and well-to-do doctor in a large Eastern city of the United States who performed thousands of abortions at very low price over a period of some thirty years before he was finally "caught." He was proud of his modest contribution to the welfare and happiness of so many women, and his wonderfully disarming explanation of his villainy was that he did not know that it was against the law. The new court ruling should soon put illegal abortionists out of business in the United States.

Having talked a little about conception, let us consider something of the avoidance of it: contraception. (See Calderone, 1970 and other references on contraception and family planning.) In the course of history people have employed numerous and, in some cases, fantastic methods of population control. Infanticide and induced abortion have been very widespread. Contraceptive techniques have included stuffing various ma-

terials into the vagina to serve as a vaginal condom or
cervical plug, and tying off the uterus at the cervix
and washing out the vagina with various substances
after coition. Contraception in the male has been ac-
complished by covering the penis with some material
such as fish or sheep gut to catch the semen, or even
operating (with a stone knife) upon the penis in such
a way that the urethra is diverted at the base of the
penis, thus causing ejaculation to occur outside the female's body (Guttmacher, 1959, pp. 67ff). Withdrawal
or coitus interruptus has been a most common method,
for all its often frustratingly unsatisfactory characteristics.

Today people have available to them an array of
contraceptive methods, some of which are highly reliable—a fact that many teachers of sex education tend
to deny. The following methods are available by medical prescription only. "The pill" is probably 100% effective when used according to directions; the intrauterine
device (IUD) is very effective under certain conditions,
particularly as a means of population control for an entire population of an area or a country, and the diaphragm with spermicidal jelly or cream approaches
100% effectiveness when the fitting is correct and when
used without fail.

The pill is as easy to take as aspirin, and it stops ovulation in the same way that pregnancy does. It also
serves to regulate menstruation and render it entirely
predictable. That is, it is taken daily for 21 days, bleeding occurs two or three days later and the pills are
resumed on the fifth day of bleeding, whereupon bleeding stops. The pill is comparable in the contraception
field to the Wright brothers' airplane in the transportation field. The present and potential significance of the
work of John Rock and his associates, the developers

of the pill, is difficult if not impossible to appreciate (Rock, 1963).

Menstrual pain may be reduced or eliminated by taking the pill. This seems to be related to the observation that, generally speaking, anovulatory menstrual cycles do not produce dysmenorrhea, even in females who are normally laid low by their menstrual period. Many females who regularly suffer from menstrual pain can recall that when they first started menstruating they had no difficulty. Those relatively carefree days probably coincided with the post-menarche infertile period previously mentioned. These women would seem to be especially likely to be relieved of dysmenorrhea by having their ovulation suppressed by "the pill."

The intrauterine contraceptive device is an inexpensive plastic loop, coil, or ring which is fitted into the uterus by a physician or other carefully trained person. As long as it stays in place, pregnancy rarely occurs. Although they are more likely than are mothers to expel an IUD, or to need to have it removed owing to side effects, such as cramps or excessive menstrual flow, women who have never been pregnant *can* and *are* using the IUD. Just how it works is not known, but it usually works. Once it is inserted, it is likely to be effective for an indefinite period. It is being used extensively in India, and there is even a program there for inserting them into sacred cows as a means of reducing the number of these overpopulous, foodstuff-destroying creatures (killing them or castrating the bulls is profoundly sacrilegious).

On the other hand, the diaphragm is a thin rubber cap which is fitted across the cervix by the woman before each coitus. It prevents the sperms from entering the uterus. Creams and jellies which have been developed to kill sperms are placed around the diaphragm for additional protection.

Some effective methods of contraception do not require medical prescription. The rubber condom is inexpensive and highly effective, even without the spermicidal cream or jelly, which some women use as an additional precaution. Moreover, the condom provides considerable protection against gonorrhea if foreplay does not bring infectious material from the anus, for example, and if the condom is properly worn. However, even with these precautions, the condom is of considerably less value against syphilis because it does not cover areas other than the penis which are likely to come into contact with infectious female or male material (Fiumara, 1972).

Some aerosol foams kill sperms in the vagina quite effectively, but some brands do not. Thus, advice should be sought from a gynecologist or from a Planned Parenthood or Family Planning Association. Vaginal suppositories are suspect. The advertising of some gives the impression that they are reliable contraceptives, but they are merely scented deodorants.

Surgical contraception involves cutting and tying or cauterizing the vas (vasectomy) or sperm ducts of the male or the fallopian tubes of the female. It is generally not the contraceptive of choice for young, childless people. Vasectomy of the male is a very simple and effective operation, since the vas lies just under the skin of the scrotum; and it may be performed in the office of a physician. Follow-up studies of many vasectomized men have demonstrated that this procedure does not have ill effects, does not reduce sexual interest or ability (many such men report that this is improved after the operation, probably because of freedom from fear of starting pregnancy), and does not reduce masculine characteristics. It simply makes the male infertile (Reimann-Hunzikir and Reimann-Hunzikir, 1966).

On the other hand, research has shown that various

personality changes (e.g., increased "machismo," perhaps in unconscious efforts to compensate for a perceived assault upon masculinity) are liable to develop "in a significant proportion of men" (Ziegler, 1971, p. 73) following vasectomy. Emotional and personality problems seem most likely to occur in males who equate vasectomy with castration and/or who were in conflict with their mate over the wisdom of their having the operation. Adequate preoperative counseling would probably help to screen out such candidates for surgical contraception, or to eliminate the contraindication.

Vasectomy should not be confused with *castration,* which involves removing the testicles and thereby the source of both sperm and male sex hormone. Thus, generally speaking, boys who are castrated before puberty do not acquire the usual secondary sex characteristics, such as deepened voice, beard, more angular build, and so on. Interestingly, although castration has generally been thought to cause the end of sexual interest and activity, it sometimes does not; some castrated individuals report active and satisfactory sex lives. Apparently, such men produce sufficient androgen in their adrenals to keep the spark alive. At any rate, the simplicity and effectiveness of vasectomy make it a popular method of contraception in North America for men who have had all of the children they want, and it is widely practiced in such places as India as a population control measure. There is about a 50% chance that subsequent surgery can restore fertility.

Until recently, surgical sterilization of females required relatively major surgery. It could involve hysterectomy (removal of the uterus), or cutting and cauterizing the fallopian tubes. Access to the tubes was sometimes gained via vaginal incision, but usually through abdominal incision (laparotomy). Although these methods are still used, and in some cases required, a new, simpler operation is becoming more widely available. This method involves the use of laparoscope, an instrument that is inserted into the abdomen through a small incision, thereby enabling the surgeon to view the internal organs. During the laparoscopy, the tubes are located, cauterized, and sometimes severed. Skilled physicians can usually finish the operation in no more than 15 minutes (Keith et al., 1972). Recovery after sterilization through laparoscopy is usually much easier and faster than it is after the older methods.

In the past few years, the growing availability of reliable contraceptives has greatly changed the sex situation for young people, such as those of college age. Far less often is "going all the way" dependent upon building up to an overwhelming excitement which makes the possibility of pregnancy seem inconsequential. Many girls consider it only reasonable to make provision for their own safety with contraception in advance of a date which might include sexual intercourse. And both males and females seem increasingly interested in growthful, affectionate relationship within which coition is likely to occur.

In this general regard, many people who deal with college students have noticed that it is no longer true that the girl necessarily wants love, security and a permanent relationship, whereas the boy just wants to satisfy his "biological urges." It has been our observation and that of many other college level teachers that now, more and more, both young men and young women want a responsible and loving or at least affectionate relationship rather than an exploitative one. Large numbers of such relationships lead to marriage, but a great many do not. In the latter cases, as well as in the former, the experience tends to be prized—and this development is due in considerable part to the emergence of contraceptives which tend to take the desperation out of sexual relationships.

Perhaps the basic point is that effective contraception is now becoming available to virtually all North Americans who believe in responsible, intentional, planned parenthood. Federal, state, and provincial governments have, to various degrees, taken a stand in favor of contraception, free if necessary, for all willing to avoid unwanted pregnancy and regulate family size. Marriage is no longer a prerequisite for getting help. It seems that Guttmacher's famous question, "Babies By Choice Or By Chance?" is being seen, increasingly, as having only one rational answer.

We do not mean to paint an unrealistically rosy picture of family planning or population control. We are told that a group in California has set up a foundation to provide funds for selected graduate students so that they can afford to have children while still in school. This is a kind of desperate effort to get the intellectual into the reproduction business while still reasonably young. To cite another example, some black leaders view reproductory restraints as detrimental to their cause and they see in virtually unrestrained child-begetting the larger good of black population growth. Hark, the distant echo of an outnumbered people: "And be ye fruitful, and multiply; bring forth abundantly in the earth . . ." To them, Planned Parenthood and like agencies in the ghettoes are instruments of status-quo-seeking white people.

The larger picture of world population control and family planning is quite grim, except in a few places like the Soviet Union, where war so reduced population and technology so increased living space and the need for workers that overpopulation will likely not be a problem for some time. The modern advances in birth control techniques make it possible to dream of a day when food supply, general living conditions, health, and education levels can be brought into reasonable harmony with population size—*if there is but time.* If there is but time. To understand the nature of the present situation, it is necessary to face up to the fact that at present, and for the immediate future at least, the population problem is out of hand and totally unsolvable by known means other than massive warfare or other unthinkable catastrophe. There is no known way of making any contraceptive available to the vast majority of people in the world who need and/or want one. In the face of this fact, world population continues to grow at a rapid rate, especially in those places where it is already far beyond the rate of increase in foodstuffs and other necessities and educational opportunities. Poverty, ignorance, increased control of diseases of the young and old, and the persistence of traditional attitudes toward the importance of having many children are among the factors that greatly complicate the problem.

Birth rates *have* been falling in recent years. This should not be misinterpreted as saying that the population has been declining. Rather, the population continues to "explode," but at a slower rate. If the Zero Population Growth advocates had magical power to balance births with deaths very suddenly, say within five years, tremendous new problems would emerge. The population would "age," which is to say that the average age of persons living at a point in time would be greater. Just as baby booms give rise to problems by virtue of their producing a relatively large proportion of the population who are relatively "nonproductive," so do shifts to a relatively aged population. All in all the situation is complicatedly ominous beyond comprehension.

What about the schools and contraception education? Of course many school teachers bootleg information about contraception to their students because of their conviction that high school may be the last opportunity for many young people to acquire this vital information on a systematic basis. However, such teaching is contrary to stated policy in most schools as of this writing.

Private schools seem to have taken the lead in providing education about contraception, but not all public schools have shied away from this subject. As early as 1966, "family planning education" was taught in relation to a family relations course for seniors in the public high schools of Kansas City, Missouri. This part of the course included planned contraceptive education, although no contraceptive devices or aids, except a temperature chart and a booklet relative to the rhythm method were to be brought into the classroom. After thirty years of opposing contraception education in schools, in 1968, Howard S. Hoyman, an American pioneer in school health education, published an article entitled "Should We Teach About Birth Control in High School Sex Education?" Of course his answer was "yes." The evolution of his thinking seems to have typified that of other educational leaders who, while conservative, are capable of change in the face of overwhelming evidence of social need.

Reconsideration of this issue on a national and international basis, with careful reexamination of basic assumptions, pro and con arguments, new evidence and recent impressions, and ethical and religious implications, has finally brought me to a new position. I now believe that, whether we like it or not, we will have to face up to teaching *about* contraception in our junior and senior high schools (Hoyman, 1968, p. 549).

The Masters and Johnson research (1966, 1970) has illuminated many areas of human sexual behavior and, as we commented earlier, has established irreversibly that sex is a proper subject for scientific study in the laboratory and elsewhere. And people still carry on debates as to whether a sexual revolution is in progress!

Dr. Masters prepared for his work well in advance. While waiting for the years to pass which would give him the respectability of some greying and balding, he became not only a highly qualified obstetrician and gynecologist, but skilled research worker as well. When he felt that the time was ripe and he had learned what the literature and his colleagues had to tell him, he turned to the best source of sex information he could think of—prostitutes. Just as few people with adopted children think of their indebtedness to girls and women who conceive out of marriage, few have stopped to consider the knowledge that professional prostitutes have contributed concerning male as well as female sexual behavior and sexual happiness. Dr. Masters turned to them, and although in time he found it desirable to utilize more reliable subjects who were more likely to be free from pelvic diseases or the need to leave town suddenly, the fact remains that he learned much of value from them. They served as his first subjects in detailed studies of what happens physiologically in sexual excitement and orgasm by masturbation as well as by coitus. They taught him much about how the physician may help people overcome sexual dysfunction. And one of them, a high priced call girl who was also a university instructor with a Ph.D., taught him that neither he nor any man could hope to understand the female sexual experience, and she convinced him he needed a woman to help him with his research. This led to his seeking out and collaborating with Virginia Johnson.

We will not undertake to summarize the Masters-Johnson findings to date. This has been done in excellent fashion elsewhere (Belliveau and Richter, 1970). But we will comment briefly on a few points which have been of special interest to many people.

In the first place, Masters and Johnson have at last

shot down the masturbation bugaboo, once and for all. They have for years used masturbation as a routine laboratory procedure with many hundreds of people from all walks of life. It has been a major means of observing, filming, and measuring just what happens before, during and after orgasm of both men and women, and it is used as a basis for making comparisons among different methods of sexual stimulation. There is no longer a question of harmfulness but of usefulness. Indeed, due in part to the Masters-Johnson influence, many doctors now recommend to women who have not experienced orgasm and resist genital stimulation that they learn what it is and how to achieve it by means of gentle, clitoral, and other genital self stimulation. In time they learn to enjoy this and to achieve climax, and become able to accept such stimulation from their mates.

Masters and Johnson have demonstrated that orgasm is not anatomically localized, but rather involves the entire body. Indeed, the body undergoes a definite pattern of adjustments during the four phases of the erotic response cycle (excitation, plateau, orgasm, and resolution). Regardless of method of stimulation, these same four steps are experienced. For example, a few women can reach orgasm by stimulating their own breasts, fewer still by having their lower backs stroked, and a very few by having sexual fantasies. Still, the physiological events are the same in orgasms produced in these ways as in those produced by masturbation, coitus, or use of an artificial penis. (Incidentally, the artificial plastic penis used by Masters and Johnson is a remarkable device containing a motion picture camera which first made possible color photographs of just what happens within the female sex structures during sexual response. Among other things, it revealed the forming of the vaginal platform during sexual excitement, the process whereby the outer third of the vagina thickens and contracts, literally gripping the penis, while the inner two-thirds dilates; and it revealed the source of vaginal lubrication—the vaginal walls themselves.)

The fundamental social and perhaps socializing nature of the sexual experience has long been recognized simply on the basis that apparently almost everyone prefers sex with another person rather than solitary masturbation. However, Masters and Johnson went a step further in experiments comparing the subjective evaluation of the gratification of orgasm with physiological measurements of the intensity and duration of orgasm. For example, a woman masturbated in the laboratory while physiological measures were being taken. She rated the experience at the top of a four point scale with regard to its intensity. And the physiologist who had nothing but the recordings of the measures to go by also rated the orgasm at the top in intensity. A few days later, the woman participated in coition with her husband in the laboratory, but this time both the physiological measures and her subjective evaluation placed the experience much farther down on the scale than when she had masturbated, considerably less intense and shorter in duration. She was then asked which of the two experiences was more gratifying, more fulfilling, more enjoyable. Her response was without hesitation. Of course her experience with her husband was far the better in every way! When William Masters told this story to a small gathering, he paused and added slowly: "When will we men learn?"

We think that there is no more important finding in the Masters-Johnson research—and they are wont to stress this over and over—than that males and females are far more *alike* than they are different in their sexuality and sexual responses. Of course, this idea is not new. In the 16th Century, Montaigne commented:

Both male and female are cast in one mold; instruction and custom excepted, there is no great difference between them.

(See also the quotation by Mill in the Preface.) Modern research is confirming the prevalence of similarity over dissimilarity—and thus is further calling into question the traditional sex role stereotyping from infancy. As one scientist concluded at a recent American Association for the Advancement of Science meeting: there are four "absolute imperatives of sex differences: women menstruate, gestate and lactate, whereas men impregnate. Other differences are optional" (Money, 1972). The homologous nature of the male and female sex structures has been noted for years. But Masters and Johnson have gone far beyond this. The following are examples. The penis and clitoris are remarkably alike except in size and the lack of ejaculatory capacity of the clitoris. Male and female orgasms are the same physiologically, and they amount to contractions of the "muscles against the erectile chambers. The contractions expel blood in the woman's erectile chambers, and semen from the man's" (Salzman, 1967). With optimal stimulation (which frequently she has not received except perhaps when masturbating), the woman takes only slightly longer to reach orgasm than the male. In both it is a matter of total body involvement in approximately the same ways (e.g., many men's nipples also become erect). And so on.

In brief, we now have a physiological basis for improved male and female understanding and communication, for the mysteries of sex have been taken to be the basis of implacable strangeness, unfathomable distance. True, there are differences and Masters needed a Johnson on his team (Money and Ehrhardt, 1973).

But then, what man really understands any other man? As educators professionally concerned with the betterment of human relations, we find this showing of the essential closeness of maleness and femaleness most exciting and promising.

Let us conclude this discussion by identifying a few misconceptions about sex which have, like the bugaboos about masturbation, been shot down in recent years.

Misconception: *Genital size is related to sexual capability. The bigger the better.* This is not the case in either the male or the female. Generally speaking, size is irrelevant with respect to sensitivity or giving satisfaction to the mate. The vagina adjusts itself to the particular penis size. With regard to the female, muscle tonus of the outer portion of the vagina may be poor, but this can usually be corrected by suitable exercise.

By "suitable exercise," we mean vigorous contraction of the muscles in the pelvic floor, which can be brought about by imagining that one is attempting to "hold back" one's urine and feces. There is some reason to believe that such contractions should be held for approximately six seconds, relaxed for several seconds, with up to ten repetitions of this sequence one or two times daily.

Misconception: *The male is erotic; the female is basically reproductory.* The female can, if she wishes, consider herself basically and/or solely a species replicating mechanism. But she does not have to. A long and heavy-handed, male-dominated tradition has attempted to persuade her that erotic pleasure is for males. Yet, in addition to being capable of reproduction she is at least as capable of attaining erotic gratification as is the male. Speaking in quantitative terms, whereas the male is capable of a single orgasm which must then be followed by a recovery period, usually of at least 30 minutes in duration (three orgasms in ten minutes is something of a record and extremely rare), the female may desire and have multiple orgasms, from two to 30 or more, one following closely after the other. Subjective descriptions and physiological measures may indicate that each female orgasm in a series is as intense as the single one of the male. Clearly it is as ridiculous to say that having several orgasms in one episode is better than having one as it is to say that eating five eggs is necessarily better than eating one. But it is also ridiculous to underestimate the erotic potential of the female.

Misconception: *The female who does not reach orgasm as a result of "vaginal stimulation" is sexually more "hung up" than her sister who does.* This misconception is based upon old Freudian speculations on psychosexual development. They included the notion that at a relatively immature stage of development a female might experience a form of orgasm by manual or other stimulation of her clitoris. However, healthy females would pass through this stage, learning to obtain orgasm as a result of stimulation of the vagina by the penis during coitus. Masters and Johnson have observed many complete erotic response cycles under various laboratory conditions. They studied the effects of different types of sexual stimulation, including combinations of breast, anal, clitoral and vaginal stimulation. They noted that, physiologically speaking, orgasm brought on by fantasy or breast stimulation should not be called a fantasy or breast orgasm, but a sexual orgasm like any other.

If Masters and Johnson thought that their work would speedily bring an end to the question of "Whose orgasm is best?" they were mistaken. For example, psychiatrist Natalie Shainess (1966, p. 63) suggested that the women whose sexual response cycles Masters and Johnson studied were not really experiencing "authentic orgasm." She suggested that it would make more sense to view their responses as "possible pathologic responses to abnormal, persistent stimulation and irritation . . ." Whereas untold women undoubtedly have felt unnecessarily unhappy about themselves because the stimulation they received from a penis inserted into their vagina did not constitute a necessary and sufficient condition for their experiencing orgasm, if Shainess' ideas gain wide acceptance we will have a new Procrustean bed upon which women in the future can suffer. She has posited not just two types of orgasm, but a "spectrum of response." The woman most to be pitied is the one who is classified as suffering from "absolute frigidity." Moving along the spectrum one advances to "relative frigidity," where the woman is capable of some kind of erotic response under "very special conditions." Next in the hierarchy appears "clitoral orgasm," followed by "missed orgasm," "multiple orgasm," and finally, at the zenith, what Shainess prefers to call "authentic orgasm." Hopefully, none of our readers will feel compelled to measure themselves by this speculative spectrum, which is explained in some detail by Shainess in the reference cited. We wince at the prospect of humans suffering feelings of diminution as a result of having become convinced, for example, that a woman who experiences and/or desires more than one orgasm during the same sexual response cycle has not advanced to the stage of "authentic orgasm."

Further evidence that fascination with the matter of "vaginal" vs. "clitoral" orgasm has not died with the pronouncements of Masters and Johnson exists in the interesting article (1972) entitled "Opinion: Is There Any Difference between 'Vaginal' and 'Clitoral' Orgasm?" Personally, we see no reason to discount the reports of the many women who say that for them orgasms variously produced are variously experienced. Such reports do not discredit Masters' and Johnson's observations that *physiologically* "orgasm is orgasm"; nor do the physiological findings invalidate subjective experience. Some women are indifferent to vaginal penetration and stimulation. Others greatly prefer a large penis inserted deeply enough to bounce the uterus about. And so it goes.

Misconception: *The optimal position for coition is the man on top of the supine woman.* Actually this position is optimal for some couples, but the great majority of women in the Masters and Johnson research sample found the woman-on-top position more likely to permit optimal stimulation of the woman. They are prone to recommend a position in which the woman is partially on top of the man, but with most of her weight being carried by her own side. Thus, both have ample opportunity to move and neither is being pinned down or having to maintain a tiring position. If impregnation is desired, the optimal position is for the woman to assume a kneeling position with the upper body resting on the forearms, the buttocks thus being somewhat elevated. The man then mounts from the rear, and the ejaculated semen is encouraged to pool at the cervix, thus increasing chances of sperm reaching the uterus.

Misconception: *Impotent men are less masculine or have something physically wrong with them.* Impotency is very common, but it is not due to inadequate "masculinity" and is usually not due to a physical difficulty. Its cause is almost always psychological, and it can happen to men at any age. Of course such things as excessive fatigue, heavy drinking, and trying too hard to be a he-man can make any man incapable of adequate erection sometimes. If such an experience causes a man to panic, to make sex a test of his ego rather than a pleasure—and/or if his partner ridicules him—there is a good chance that after two such failures he will be impotent, at least with that particular woman. This and other problems of sexual adequacy can now be treated successfully by qualified psychologists, psychiatrists, obstetricians and gynecologists, and marriage counselors, thanks largely to the work of bold researchers and therapists who have put service to their patients first and foremost.

Misconception: *Show me a woman who is "frigid" and I will show you a woman who is . . .* (you fill in your favorite stereotype and we will call it a misconception). First of all we hope that in the very near future the word "frigidity" will no longer be used in this context. A young woman who finally worked up the courage to "admit" to her gynecologist that she had never experienced orgasm felt discouraged and betrayed when the (male) physician responded with surprised intonation "Why I always thought of you as such a *warm* person." In this particular case, subsequent investigation by a different physician revealed a slightly lower than usual thyroid activity in the particular woman. Shortly after administration of thyroxin, many of her little health complaints (e.g., constipation, feeling chilly when companions did not, orgasmic dysfunction) disappeared.

It is not our argument that the solution to problems of orgasmic dysfunction is necessarily to be sought in the female's physiology. It is our argument that whether or not a given individual reaches orgasm at any given time is determined by the balance of inhibiting and facilitating variables which exists at the time. For example, a woman may have a wonderfully warm, trusting relationship with her mate, have very favorable attitudes regarding her potential to give and to receive erotic pleasure, and still experience orgasmic dysfunction. In other words, despite the aforementioned psychosocial facilitators to erotic responsiveness, other inhibitors in her biophysical and/or psychosocial realms may prevent full erotic responsiveness. Perhaps the telling inhibitory factor in the hypothetical case would be adhesions between the clitoris and the clitoral hood, which give rise to pain upon stimulation of the region.

Suggested in Table 1 are some of the facilitating and inhibiting variables that may be at play in any given situation. According to this concept, it is the relative preponderance of facilitation or inhibition which determines whether or not a woman will experience orgasmic dysfunction. Viewed from such a framework, we have been able to "make sense" of many reports that defy the common stereotypes of what does or does not characterize an erotically responsive woman. Thus, virtually *anything* that tips the balance will work in some situations with some people. Thus, some therapists

Table 1. Examples of Variables that Can Influence Erotic Response

Facilitators	*Inhibitors*
love and affection for partner	indifference or negative feelings toward partner
healthy urogenital system	urogenital infections, adhesions, bruises, or wounds
"well-trained" erotic response pattern	"poorly trained" erotic response pattern
prior satisfactory erotic experience under similar circumstances	previous unpleasant sexual experience under similar circumstances
abundant supply of androgen	relatively little androgen
general sense of well-being and satisfaction with life	general depression
good muscular development and conditioning	poor muscular development and conditioning
reasonably well rested	fatigued
skillful erotic techniques	poor erotic techniques
feelings of security and intimacy	feelings of insecurity and/or lack of desired privacy

focus upon reducing psychosocial inhibitions and increasing psychosocial facilitation. Others take a more physical approach, manipulating different variables toward the same ends—enabling the woman to experience orgasm. We have dwelt on this topic at some length because it has been our impression that in the past women who desired to experience orgasm, but who could not, were inclined to feel hopeless because there *must* be something physically wrong. In contrast, today there seems to be a tendency for women in similar positions to feel unhappy because they are led to believe that something *must* be wrong with them psychologically.

Misconception: *Sexual release has various bad effects including lowering of physical performance—as in sports.* Actually there is a good deal of evidence that sexual stimulation and release can be beneficial in various ways to males and females, and there is evidently no evidence to the contrary. (See the reference by Hansen, 1967, for a brief discussion of the spectrum of symptoms that may result from prolonged sexual tension.) Obviously, sexual expression can be part of a pattern of psychopathology, but then so can eating and automobile driving, and no one seems to consider eating or driving the *cause* of the pathological pattern.

The long-standing and still existing claim that coitus and masturbation lower physical performance, as in sports competition, still leads some coaches to tell their athletes to sleep with "their hands on top of the covers" and to try to separate athletes from their wives at least one night before competition. One experimental study of this subject (Johnson, 1968) would seem to confirm the view that coitus some hours before testing does not lower muscular strength or endurance performance. Indeed, sexual release may have a worthwhile relaxing effect on overly tense athletes.

Misconception: *Interest in genital sex diminishes with the years and is lost in the aging process.* The peak years of sexual interest may very well be in the twenties. However, many clinicians have found that interest in coitus continues into the later years. Masters simply says that sexual interest and activity continue—even into the seventies, eighties, and nineties—so long as there is (1) reasonably good health and (2) an interested partner. This information is important with regard to the erroneous popular notion that sex is no longer a part of life as one grows older and one is something of a freak if he or she shows an interest in it.

Misconception: *The ideal in coitus is for the couple's orgasms to occur simultaneously.* Simultaneous orgasm is highly esteemed by some, but others consider striving for it pointless. In fact, such striving is likely to cause difficulty in that it requires rather precise timing and diverting effort. If a woman has multiple orgasms, with which of these should the male attempt to correspond? Many couples prefer that the man delay, retain his erection, and assure the woman full gratification before they turn their attention to the male. The reader who is interested in discussions of actual sexual techniques is referred to such sources as Ellis (1960), Ellis and Conway (1967), Belliveau and Richter (1970), Masters and Johnson (1970), and *Opinion: Does Emphasis on "Technique" Dehumanize Sex?* (1972).

Misconception: *The black male is superior, sexually, to the white male.* This misapprehension has given rise to a widespread fear among white males that the black is a superior sexual partner, and that the white female—including perhaps wives and daughters—would therefore prefer or be unable to resist the black. This fear has generated incalculable anxiety and hatred of the black by the white man because of the implied personal threat. *Actually, there is no evidence whatever that any race is superior to any other in terms of sexual vigor.*

One version of this misconception is related to the previously discussed misconception that, generally speaking, the larger the penis the more pleasure it is capable of providing a female partner. Informal, anonymous surveys with a number of university classes in human sexuality have indicated that: the notion (as far as we know, a misconception) that black males have larger penises on the average than white males is widespread; on the average, male students in these classes indicated that the "most desirable penis size" was "slightly larger" than the hypothetical average of all penis lengths in the world; ironically, female students indicated, on the average, that the "most desirable penis size" was "slightly smaller" than the hypothetical average size of all penises in the world! Obviously, without regard to race at all, any sexually repressed individual with little or no relaxed and happy sexual experience is likely to be a less satisfactory sexual partner than one who is experienced, is not sexually repressed, and who is not feeling guilty or sexually desperate. A relaxed, experienced and confident tennis player is likely to make a better partner than a beginner who is anxious about proving his ability.

Misconception: *The male is the primary sex.* In the cultural sense this has traditionally been true, but in the biological sense, all embryos are female in structure until the fifth or sixth week after conception. At this time, genetically male embryos produce testicular substances which suppress ovarian growth and give rise to male patterns. Without this testicular substance intervention (*e.g.*, if it is blocked experimentally), the fetus becomes female automatically (Sherfey, 1966). This kind of information plus evidence of superior biological ruggedness which presumably makes possible taking menstruation, and childbearing and -rearing in stride have led some authorities to a belief in the "natural superiority of women" (Montagu, 1953).

In speculating about the biological ruggedness of the female, people like Montagu are not implying that one sex is "better" than or superior personally to the other. They are simply saying that males and females are different in various ways over and above reproductory and related structures. For example, many investigators have noted that even a few hours after birth, male babies exhibit more muscular, "coping" behavior than females; and the females exhibit more preverbal "talking" behavior. From early infancy onward, males on the average seem to show greater interest in objects and in manipulating them than do girls. Girls show greater interest in people (Garai and Scheinfeld, 1968, p. 270).

Moreover, there is a good deal of evidence that females have a sharper sense of smell than males, but that males give off stronger bodily odors—an arrangement which smacks of Mephistophelean contrivance. Such differences can hardly be attributed to social conditioning and are apparently evidence of biological sex differences on a par with differences in maturation rate, hair distribution, voice, and so on.

In spite of such differences, the fact remains that males and females are very considerably more alike than unalike, and the door seems open as never before to better and happier understanding and communication between them.

Misconception: *A mark of a sexually educated person is his or her ability correctly to identify various types of sexual behaviors as either normal or abnormal.* The words "normal" and "abnormal" are commonly used in sexual contexts. Unfortunately, many times both the senders and receivers of messages dealing with normality, or the lack thereof, are not clear on how the words

4

are being used. The next time you catch yourself branding something or somebody as normal or abnormal, ask yourself "What do I mean?" Perhaps you mean "I approve of that" when you say something is normal in one context. In another you might mean "That is quite ordinary."

"Confusion over so-called normality is one of the most troublesome problems in sex education and counseling" (Johnson and Fretz, 1972, p. 68). Johnson and Fretz have written about five senses in which "normality" may be used. There is the pathological or *clinical* approach. The criteria for normality in this sense include: "freedom from disabling symptoms, primarily stress; and efficiency in adaptation. By these criteria, people who are unhappy, unsatisfied, anxious, self-defeating, and inefficient are 'abnormal'."

Then, there is the *moralistic* model in which "abnormal" is equated with "evil," with the breaking of an ethical code, perhaps even a Law of God. Overlapping with the moralistic are the *cultural* criteria for abnormality. Thus, coital positions which are ordinarily used in a given society are seen as "normal" by its members, but deviations from common practice are viewed as "abnormal." The Japanese have a proverb: "The nail that raises its head is hammered down."

A relatively modern refinement of the cultural model of normality is the *statistical*. Very often we are reassured to learn that 75% of the general population share our "abnormal" (in the moralistic sense) sex lives, thus enabling us to feel reassured of our "normality" in the statistical sense. And the competitive will be inflated to learn that only 1% have reached such limits as they have striven for and attained (perhaps number of sexual liaisons, or orgasms within a time limit).

Another sense in which the concept of normality/abnormality is often used in day-to-day life is the rather vague *personal* view. We often compare others to ourselves, and if we feel okay about ourselves, those who are similar are viewed as normal, or vice versa. Unfortunately, many people who feel okay about themselves may appropriately be thought of as "sexual fascists" (chauvinists) who are convinced that theirs is *the* true way to think, feel, and do.

Perhaps instead of facilely labeling behaviors as normal or abnormal, a sexually well-educated person will be more tentative in his or her judgments, and try to understand how others are using the terms at a given time.

For those who are weary of the futility of ritualistic prohibitions and of the negative emotional consequences of repression and guilt, there remains the possibility of changing the question from 'what is normal?' to 'what are the consequences?' It may be easier to determine when behaviors should be changed versus when consequences might best be changed; e.g., eliminating taboos on nonmarital sex activity or eliminating unwanted pregnancy via near-foolproof contraception. Whatever other benefits such a change in focus might have, it would very likely increase the self-acceptance and self-respect of the many now burdened with anxiety and guilt over being less than normal (Johnson and Fretz, 1972, p. 73).

Can you identify some additional important misconceptions and justify your claim that they are indeed misconceptions? (See McCary, 1971.)

REFERENCES

Aldrich, C. A., and Aldrich, M. M.: Babies Are Human Beings: An Interpretation of Growth. 2nd Ed., New York, Collier Books (paperback), 1962.

Benjamin, H.: The Transexual Phenomenon. New York, Julian Press, 1966.

Blau, A.: The clitoris. Part I. Eros, Autumn, 1962.

Belliveau, F., and Richter, L.: Understanding Human Sexual Inadequacy. New York, Bantam Books, 1970.

Bonaparte, M.: Female Sexuality. New York, Grove Press, 1962.

Calderone, M. S. (Ed.): Manual of Family Planning and Contraceptive Practice. 2nd Ed. Baltimore, Williams and Wilkins, 1970.

Clark, L.: When do women want intercourse most? Sexology, 43:519-21, March, 1968.

Diczfalusy, E., and Borell, U. (Eds.): Control of Human Fertility. New York, Wiley Interscience Division, 1971.

Drellich, M. G., and Waxenberg, S. E.: Erotic and affectional components of female sexuality. In Sexuality of Women. Edited by Jules E. Masserman. New York, Grune and Stratton, Inc., 1966, pp. 45-53.

Ellis, A.: The Art and Science of Love. New York, Lyle Stuart, 1960.

Ellison, A., and Conway, R. O.: The Art of Seduction. New York, Lyle Stuart, 1967.

Fiumara, N. J.: Ineffectiveness of condoms in preventing venereal disease. Medical Aspects of Human Sexuality, 6:146-148, October, 1972.

Ford, C. S., and Beach, F. A.: Patterns of Sexual Behavior. New York, Harper, 1951.

Garai, J. E., and Scheinfeld, A.: Sex differences in mental and behavioral traits. Genetic Psychology Monographs, 77:169-299, May, 1968.

Gebhard, P. H., et al.: Pregnancy, Birth and Abortion. New York, Harper, 1958.

Graves, E. R.: Sex psychology of the unmarried adult. In Men: The Variety and Meaning of Their Sexual Experience. Edited by A. M. Kirch. New York, Dell Publishing Co., 1954.

Green, R., and Money, J. (Eds.): Transsexualism and Sex Reassignment. Baltimore, Johns Hopkins University Press, 1969.

Greenblatt, R. B.: A guide to hormonal therapy. Medical Opinion, 7:22-26, September, 1971.

Guttmacher, A. F.: Babies by Choice or by Chance. New York, Avon Books, 1959.

Guttmacher, A. F.: Pregnancy and Birth. New York, Signet Books (paperback), 1962.

Hanson, D. D.: Physical manifestations of sexual conflict. Medical Aspects of Human Sexuality, 1:31-34, September, 1967.

Havermann, E.: Birth Control. New York, Time Inc., 1967.

Himes, N. E.: A Medical History of Contraception. Baltimore, The Williams & Wilkins Co., 1936.

Holland, N. H., Jurichs, R., and Clemans, G.: Detection of asymptomatic urinary tract infection in girls. Journal of the Kentucky Medical Association, 67:662-64 and 699, September, 1969.

Hoyman, H. S.: Should we teach about birth control in high school sex education? Journal of School Health, 38:545-56, November, 1968.

Israel, S. L.: Diagnosis and Treatment of Menstrual Disorders and Sterility. 5th Ed., New York, Harper and Row, 1967.

Johnson, W. R.: Muscular performance and coitus. Journal of Sex Research, 4:247-48, August, 1968.

Johnson, W. R., and Fretz, B. R.: What is sexual "normality"? Sexual Behavior, 1:68-73, June, 1972.

Kanner, L.: The clitoris. Part II. Eros, Autumn, 1962.

Kaplan, D. M.: Freud and his own patients. Harper's Magazine, December, 1967.

Keith, L., et al.: Laparoscopy for puerperal sterilization. Obstetrics and Gynecology, 39:616-21, April, 1972.

Kinsey, A., et al.: Sexual Behavior in the Human Female. Philadelphia, W. B. Saunders Co., 1953.

Maslow, A. H.: Motivation and Personality. New York, Harper, 1954.

Masters, W. H., and Johnson, V. E.: Human Sexual Inadequacy. Boston, Little, Brown and Company, 1970.

Masters, W. H., and Johnson, V. E.: Human Sexual Response. Boston, Little, Brown and Company, 1966.

McCary, J. L.: Sexual Myths and Fallacies. New York, Van Nostrand-Reinhold, 1971.

Money, J.: Paper presented before the American Association for the Advancement of Science, December, 1972, as quoted in Behavior Today, 4:1, January 8, 1973.

Money, J.: Sex reassignment. International Journal of Psychiatry, 9:249-282, 1970–1971.

Money, J., and Ehrhardt, A. A.: Man and Woman, Boy and Girl (Differentiation and Dimorphism of Gender Identity from Conception to Maturity). Baltimore, Johns Hopkins University Press, 1973.

Montagu, A.: Life Before Birth. New York, Signet Books, 1964.

Montague, A.: The Natural Superiority of Women. New York, Macmillan, 1953.

Neill, A. S.: Summerhill: A Radical Approach to Child Rearing. New York, Hart, 1960.

Neubardt, S.: A Concept of Contraception. New York, Trident Press, 1967.

Newton, N.: Breast feeding. Psychology Today, 2:34 and 68-70, June, 1968.

Opinion: does emphasis on "technique" dehumanize sex? Sexual Behavior, 2:63-65, January, 1972.

Raphaelian, H. M.: Signs of Life, A Pictorial Dictionary of Symbols: Religion, Art, Sex. New York, Anatol Sivas Publication, 1957.

Reimann-Hunzikir, R., and Reimann-Hunzikir, G.: Twenty years experience with vasectomized patients. Journal of Sex Research, 2:99-110, July, 1966.

Rock, J.: The Time Has Come. New York, Knopf, 1963.

Rubin, I.: When are women most receptive? Sexology, March, 1964.

Salzman, L.: Recently exploded sex myths. Medical Aspects of Human Sexuality, 1:7-8, September, 1967.

Shainess, N.: A re-assessment of feminine sexuality and erotic experience. In Sexuality of Women. Edited by Jules E. Masserman, New York, Grune and Stratton, Inc., 1966, pp. 56-71.

Sherfey, M. J.: The evolution and nature of female sexuality in relation to psychoanalytic theory. Journal American Psychoanalytic Association, 14:28-128, 1966.

Spock, B. M.: Baby and Child Care. New York, Pocket Books, 1957.

Spock, B. M., and Lowenberg, M. E.: Feeding Your Baby and Child. New York, Pocket Books, 1955.

Street, R.: Modern Sex Techniques. New York, Archer House, 1959.

Stopes, M. C.: Contraception. London, John Bale Sons and Danielsson, 1923.

Thomas, P.: Kama, Kalpa: The Hindu Ritual of Love. Bombay, India, D. B. Taraporevalva Sons, Ltd., 1959.

Williams, J. G. P.: Sex and sports. Sexology, October, 1963.

Ziegler, F. J.: Male sterilization. Sexual Behavior, 1:71-73, July, 1971.

3

Growing Up, Communicating, and Sex

Most North Americans grew up in households where the discussion of two main topics was taboo. One was money; the other, of course, was sex. Mark Twain once quipped "Where I was brought up we never talked about money because there was never enough to furnish a topic of conversation." Perhaps we could accept an analog to Twain's comment to explain the extreme reluctance to communicate about sexual matters. Although we haven't conducted this research, we suspect that great numbers of current day adults would be willing to grant considerable validity to the proposition that "there was never enough sexual activity (in the erotic sense) in our house to furnish a topic of conversation."

The more or less erotic aspects of sexuality in childhood have traditionally been taboo, to the extent that their very existence has been denied—in the face of virtually every healthy person's awareness that he or she had, regrettably perhaps, been fascinated by these topics, feelings, or even experiences in childhood. Freud established himself as one of the world's most hated men by demonstrating the profundity of the error of the traditional view. But even he hypothesized a "latent stage" of psychosexual development during which a child supposedly was not interested in sexual matters and had better not have them prematurely called to his or her attention by others. Although this notion has been put forward by opponents as a "scientific" argument against sex education, contemporary authorities have evidence that thoroughly discredits it (Gadpaille, 1970).

Psychoanalysis has contributed so much to what is known of human sexuality and the significance of pre-adult sexual stages for subsequent adjustment that the temptation was to write this chapter in terms of "psychosexual development" along Freudian lines. Such an approach would certainly have included some of the confused ideas about sexuality which children have. (How could it be otherwise when such interest is surrounded by such ignorance?) For example, ideas about oral impregnation and urethral birth are quite common among children, as are concepts of intercourse as "attack." However, it was decided not to approach the subject from this direction for several reasons, including the following.

Psychoanalytic findings and views have been expertly presented by many other writers, including their discoverers and creators (Freud, A., 1946; Freud, S., 1933, 1947, 1949, 1953; Hall, 1954; Hendrick, 1958; Mullahy, 1953).

The terminology of psychoanalysis tends to require considerable definition and discussion; and it seems fantastic or grotesque to those not more or less familiar with the subject. Consider "Oedipus situation," "penis envy," "castration anxiety," "id," "ego," "superego," and dream symbolism. There is the matter of the fundamental role that is played by the "unconscious mind" in psychoanalytic theories. Also, there would have been the task of disassociating our chapter from numerous discredited Freudian theories including that of "biology is destiny," which is so repugnant to contemporary "Women's Lib" people, among others. In brief, we do not feel up to trying to deal with all this in one little chapter, which must also include a discussion of the subject from quite a different point of view.

In this chapter, we mean to talk about growing up and sex in a somewhat different way than we have come upon before. Our intent is to discuss the subject in a way that will not require learning a new language or accepting a "new" dimension of mental life. We are concerned here with commonplace facts and events which are experienced by and mold males and females who grow up in our particular society—events that profoundly condition our attitudes toward ourselves and others, but which we rarely if ever think systematically about and almost never talk about.

In the preceding chapter we took into account briefly the male and female sex structures and their functions. *Let us now consider a little of what it means to grow up possessing one or the other of these structures and functions in our particular society.*

The personal experience of growing up as a sexual creature has meaning only with respect to the social context within which the individual lives. Our particular society happens to be curiously ambivalent concerning sex. On the one hand, it imposes a rigid set of specifications intended to regulate and generally restrict sexual behavior in the course of life. On the other hand, it subjects individuals of nearly all ages to intensive sexual stimulation via private conversation, the entertainment media, advertising, and so on. The net result tends to be an extraordinarily popular preoccupation with sex, co-existing with a generally uncomfortable and often negative attitude toward many facets of this dimension of life, particularly in the young and old.

Let us review our society's traditional specifications concerning how people are supposed to behave sexually.

In the course of life, people are expected to meta-

morphose through at least two and as many as four
stages of sexual behavior. That is, before puberty we are
presumed "innocent"—which is to say sexless except for
classification purposes. This may be termed the *"nonsexual"* stage of life. Then, after puberty, when the existence of sex can hardly be ignored or denied, we become *"asexual."* By asexual we mean a state of unex-
pressed sexuality which is presumed to last for the re-
mainder of life among those who do not marry and
among those married individuals whose mates become,
for any reason, sexually disinterested or incapacitated.

The third possible stage in life is the sexual one. By
traditional prescription in our culture, individuals who
enter into monogamous marriage are the exclusive pos-
sessors of a "sex life." The unmarried, if virtuous, neither
seek nor accept opportunities for sexual expression. And
finally, married or unmarried, the elderly are presumed
to revert to the nonsexual state, except again for classification purposes.

Now, of course, as everyone knows, childhood is not
really "innocent" of sex; most adolescent youngsters and
unmarried adults do not confine themselves to indirect,
sublimated, or otherwise "socially acceptable" manifestations of their sexuality; the married, having at last
been granted sex, do not by any means always know
what to do with it; and older persons do not necessarily
outgrow the whole business and lapse into wisdom, at
least not voluntarily. Still, failure to meet the sexual behavior specifications of one's stage in life is to be
childish, immature, peculiar, "bad," immoral, perverted,
illegal and/or just plain silly. Especially in childhood
and youth, the almost inevitable deviations of the
healthy from the code make people feel guilty—in some
cases terribly, even traumatically, so. Still, the young
are led to believe that all decent people live strictly by
the code. No one ever admits to them that an entirely

satisfactory adjustment to the sex code is possible only among the chronically very ill and perhaps the quite elderly.

In the course of growing up, the young person is always subjected to pressures that tend to make happy adjustment to himself or herself as a sexual creature most difficult if not impossible. Frequently, the first specific sex education is that associated with the parent's pulling and perhaps slapping the infant's hands away from the genitals, thereby beginning the second- or tenth-class citizenship status of those structures among those of the body. Soon the cultural pressure goes on to implant in him and her the realization that one body part is especially objectionable, somehow "bad," unmentionable, and so dirty that touching it requires careful scrubbing of the hands. It must always be carefully covered up, not touched, and treated in public as though it did not exist. It is probably no exaggeration to say that this pressure aimed against the basic biological self presently forms itself into one of the elemental substrata of the mind. The words associated with this part of the body are "not nice," not to be used by good children. Certainly the associated attitudes of rejection and ineffability are profoundly complicating factors in future sex adjustment and efforts at constructive sex education (Ellis, 1954, 1958).

There is, too, the biological pressure to which we must be grateful for the survival of the species and which tends to make this objectionable part of the individual involved in virtually everything he or she does. Then, as we have indicated, there is the pressure of the sexual preoccupation of older children and the adult world, manifesting itself in many ways, including private conversation and ubiquitous popular entertainment and advertising. And finally, as the child grows older and these several pressures converge on him or her full blast, still another pressure is imposed which is unique to the present day in our tradition in that it used to apply mainly to young men about to go into combat. We have come to realize that today, which may well be the twilight of the human race, there is that feeling of urgency among a great many young men and women—and a reluctance to die without having experienced "sexual love."

We may deplore all or most of these pressures but they are very real, and together they generate a fantastic adjustment problem for every reasonably intelligent individual. It could easily be argued that an understanding of child psychology and human behavior, generally, must begin with a deep appreciation of what it means to be a highly sexual creature growing up in the context of a *sex-centric* society, which is at the same time profoundly *anti-sexual* . . . and threatened from day to day with extinction.

Compromising and reconciling of the divergent biological and psychosocial pressures associated with sex is a problem which must be dealt with throughout most of life. This rather incredible task may be viewed as a kind of common denominator in the general sex adjustment situation. The variables in the numerator deal with change—rapid change at such times as puberty and marriage—and handling the day-to-day consequences of the sexual "double think" that is implied in the dynamics of the entire situation. A simple example can illustrate this Orwellian concept.

Some children were tumbling on a lawn. One little girl succeeded in standing on her head for an appreciable period of time. Suddenly the child's young and attractive mother, clad in tight, revealing, black party dress, charged onto the scene and whacked her daughter's bottom all of the way back to their apartment entrance for standing on her head "and showing herself and her underpants that way." How long after that, one wonders, would the child begin to notice that her mother-goddess built her own life around various forms of sexual display, including the artful displaying of her body? How much difficulty would the child encounter in future efforts to compromise the *nonsexual, asexual,* and perhaps, finally, *sexual* specifications of sexual behavior at the various levels of her mental functioning, conscious and unconscious? Subsequent conversation with the mother revealed that she saw nothing incongruous in her own behavior. This little anecdote summarizes and typifies one large part of the informal sex education of virtually all our children: adult preoccupation with sex, hand in hand with adult persecution of childhood sexuality, "innocent" or otherwise. Innumerable additional examples of sex-related "double think" could be cited from daily observation; but the reader can doubtless fill in and elaborate endlessly from personal experience.

In the early years, beginning long before interpersonal communication reaches a verbal level, children are swept up in some of the stronger currents of their culture's stream. One of these currents has to do with how people feel about their bodies and their bodily functions. In later years individuals rarely remember just how they came to feel as they do about such things as nakedness and "being seen" naked or in undercloth-ing; about their excrement and the act of defecation (many girls and women prefer painful constipation to "being heard" in a school or other public toilet); about the oral cavity (which we are led to believe is teeming with germs that must be attacked frequently with ger-micidal washes and pastes, and which is likely to emit a foul odor and perhaps a more or less poisonous saliva); about our germ-ridden and stinking skin; or about sex, the sexual structures and their secretions, maleness and femaleness—and sexual self-stimulation. Still they "know" without the slightest doubt that some things and some behaviors are "bad"—too "bad" even to be talked about. And in our projective tests of sex "attitudes," in which people could feel free to comment on how the sexual structures looked to them, we have seldom had girls or women describe the appearance of female sex structures in favorable terms. Quite the contrary. The fantastic sales of oftentimes dangerous vaginal perfumes attest to the desperate need to do something about those unfortunate structures. The male structures don't tend to make out very well with males or females, either. In sum, our impression is that people do not find a basic aspect of the "self"—the body—by any means totally likeable, attractive, trustworthy, or acceptable.

Let us now consider some of the more obvious problems that highly sexual creatures encounter in the course of growing up in a sex-centric, sex-rejecting society.

Life would be much simpler for girls if, in the course of progressing through their nonsexual and asexual phases of life, they had no sex to cope with at all. Girls are expected to act as though they have no real sex drive, no thoughts of sex whatever, except to a degree in matters of clothing, certain home chores, perhaps, and the lavatory they may enter. Many have commented that they would have been happy to enter a convent so as to escape the sex and sex related confusions and problems of being a healthy young female. As though escape were possible! For many girls are virtually doomed to be sexually "precocious" in one may or another.

There are two kinds of female sexual precocity, biological and moral (Johnson, 1973). Biological precocity may mean extremely early arrival of menstruation, puberal body hair, or such early arrival of ovulation that motherhood is possible in childhood. Biological precocity also may mean the less drastic early maturing of those relatively few girls who are young women while their classmates are still children, and who must find ways of adjusting, under the suspicious eye of parents and teachers, to both worlds. Moral precocity has reference to *any* evidence of sexual interest, other than certain kinds of self-decoration and display, prior to marriage. Thus, being members of the sexually propagating human race and being subjected to a chronically sex-laden environment, they are bound to violate the traditional non- and a-sexual moral codes in both thought and deed—and to be severely punished, by themselves if not by others, for their violations. Interestingly, early maturing and sexually aware boys are more likely to be encouraged than darkly labeled "precocious."

There is an increasing tendency to make elementary menstrual education available to little girls who are presumed old enough to begin menstruating. This is certainly a step forward because mothers still frequently neglect the menstrual education of their daughters with all that this implies for a natural function being a traumatizing "curse." In consequence of such basic instruction, which usually expands somewhat beyond menstruation, young females generally know more about academic sex than young males; and our local studies of hundreds of first year college students indicate that females often know more about various details of male sex anatomy and physiology than males do. Males usually find this state of affairs humiliating, if not depressing, because we males tend to think that *we* own sex. More importantly, perhaps, is the lack of communication between the sexes about sex, for it assures that they will continue to be strangers to each other.

Males have no comparably obvious developmental event like menstruation to demand a degree of sex education. We should not underestimate our indebtedness to the companies which market products making possible at least a semi-graceful disposal of menstrual flow. Their advertising has encouraged a popular acceptance of at least a little sex education for girls. Unfortunately, no one has yet discovered a commercial value in any exclusively male function at puberty which might give an impetus to comparable sex education for boys. So the boys are usually on their own. This is in spite of the fact that many men consider their first "wet dreams" among the most terrifying experiences of their lives, brought on, they may conclude, by their masturbating. Other developments at and around puberty are difficult for boys to handle, too.

For their part, men find it fairly easy to adjust to menstruation as a normal female function which reasonable women should be able to deal with without undue fuss or commotion. Women do not tend to share this rather light-hearted attitude. At one point in an older, widely used film on sex education, a father has just been told by mother and daughter that the youngster has begun to menstruate. Everyone is very happy. The father chuckles and in a deep Santa Claus voice says something like: "Well, well, our little girl is growing up!" The women in class almost invariably find this noble effort absurd and even angering. As a matter of fact, their comments concerning what it means to contend with the first arrival and thereafter the threat of, or actual arrival of unexpected menstruation, from adolescence to menopause, have been profoundly impressive. We continue to marvel at the training in stoicism of those girls and women who still keep up appearances in spite of their too small, misshapen shoes and heat-holding, tight girdles—all in the name of "femininity." As Reich (1971) has described so convincingly in his *Greening of America,* young people today in great numbers are having nothing to do with such patterns of sexuality. But by comparison with problems that menstruation *can* pose, the wearing of "feminine" footwear and "foundation garments" may seem like relatively small matters.

Of course, some women wisely learn to accept menstruation as a necessary condition of womanhood, but this does not mean that they learn to like it. How could they? Bleeding has always meant "sickness" or injury and in this special case, something of a "curse." At a lower level of abstraction it is likely to mean a stained skirt or other intense embarrassment. Moreover, the menstruating woman is not likely to be the "self" that she likes most—or that others like most. (Few would go so far as Father Morice [1905, p. 971] who wrote of the Dené Indian belief: "A menstruating woman is the very incarnation of evil, a plague to be avoided at all costs . . ." This *is* extreme. Still, sometimes it seems . . .) At best, menstruation is a complete bore, and a great many women are chronically outraged by it. Thus menstruation is likely to be added to the estrangement from self that earlier sexual conditioning has begun.

That most girls and women discover sexual self-stimulation somewhere along the way has tended to be unthinkable to men. Masturbation, to males, is an evil, a guiltful, anguish-causing, exciting evil inherent in having a penis. As with males, each individual female tends to believe that masturbatory behavior is beneath good people and is, indeed, a wickedness that only she is guilty of. She cannot imagine that respectable women, her mother, her teachers, or her friends or classmates could possibly do such a thing. In fact, as with many males, she may be under the impression that she invented the behavior. The gestapo of her mind must torture her on the rack, and she is likely to blame unexplained developments like pimples, feelings of fatigue, emotional upset, and various misfortunes on her secret play. Worst of all, perhaps, she is likely to fear that the behavior may cause an infection requiring treatment—and her guilt will be known. Part of a letter from a former student may illustrate this point.

I was profoundly uneasy about masturbation and a nurse's punishment of my masturbatory bathing activity. Later I was sure that I was one of those who masturbated excessively, and that this was symptomatic of nymphomania if nothing else. I was sure that it would interfere with successful marital adjustment, and my husband should never know. Hence it took three years and much new sex education to even get up the nerve and self-belief to tell him how I did it so that I could teach him for gratifying foreplay. To tell him before would imply that I did actually masturbate, ugly creature. Finally, it took months of sexual activity with my husband and the sex education before I could tolerate his manipulation of my genitals without all the massive resistance and shame and denial of it, in that this was just masturbating, repeating that awful thing I did. The guilt carried over to totally block heterosexual sexual release.

She went on to plead for a frank, honest, positive sex education which would free girls of the horrible guilt, fear, and self-depreciation—perhaps the *coup de grâce* to emerging sexuality—so often brought on by simply being human.

A psychologist could easily describe this entire situation as the contrivance of some ingenious and diabolical experimentalist in, perhaps, terms like these: Arrange a most severe punishment for a certain behavior. But then, make the same behavior so rewarding that the experimental animal cannot quite resist it. Then observe the avoidance, frustration, desperate action, and subsequent anguish of the animal as the punishment built into the experiment is administered.

The discussion of the basic anatomy and physiology of the human male did not tell us much about what it means to be a male in the course of growing up. Without pretending to cover the subject thoroughly, let us talk a little about that now.

In infancy, the male learns, somehow, that probably the most objectionable part of him is his penis. (Of course his inevitable tendency to be something of a "Dennis the Menace," to resist domestication, to scrap, clown and adventure are all in that objectionableness too.) The penis is not like the arms, legs, fingers and toes in that it does not at a certain age respond automatically to one's will. On the other hand, it is not like the nose or ears which can be counted upon to remain relatively still. The penis is more like a fairly well trained work dog which, generally speaking, carries out its routine chores but can never really be counted upon to be responsive to its "master's" will. In fact it is disconcertingly mindless but willful.

In childhood, the penis is used for urination (or for something which is supposed to make the unfortunate function seem nicer—like "tinkle," "pee-pee," "wet" or "number one"). But it also gives rise to pleasant sensations when stroked or fondled, whereupon it is likely to rise. It is also likely to rise when the boy is sleeping, a fact which can be embarrassingly obvious when Mom rousts him in the morning for school. It may rise disconcertingly when a boy or a young man is doing some rhythmical activity such as riding a bicycle, riding a horse, or (horrors!) dancing with a girl. Restlessness in a class at school may give rise to an erection. The willful penis may rise for no reason that its "owner" can discern. Worst of all, it seems to some, it can refuse to rise to an occasion which the cerebral cortex evaluates as being appropriate.

In due course, males learn that stimulation of the penis causes increasingly pleasing excitement, and eventually orgasm is obtained. Kinsey put the age of this discovery at around fourteen. However, like the onset of menstruation, there is considerable variability in this respect. Some little boys chance upon orgasm early in elementary school, and they may not even associate the experience with "sex" until some time later. On the other hand, some boys do not discover orgasm before the late teens, and a few do not discover it at all.

To this day, somehow it slides into the minds of many if not most boys that sexual self-stimulation has some dire effects upon their health, their appearance, and their physical prowess. It tends to undermine the personality generally. Pimples on the face may be taken as a signal to the world that one masturbates. Masturbation, one comes to believe, chips away at one's manhood, weakens one, has a corroding effect upon the nervous system. Very possibly, as the old medical books said and as some physicians and other professional people claim even today, it affects one's sanity. Of course, as has been pointed out earlier, all this is nonsense, but it is still a source of intense apprehension among young people. We recall a situation in which a seventh grade boy changed overnight from being an eager, happy, well-organized "good student" to the reverse of these things. It finally came out that a classmate had informed him that the new dark hairs on the backs of his fingers and wrists proved that he masturbated. The other boy got this bit of "information" from his father who felt it his duty to terrorize his sons concerning this behavior.

This little incident illustrates a very important point concerning masturbatory behavior. That is, although it is harmless physiologically speaking, if the individual is convinced that it is harmful to him, it can, for psychosomatic reasons be harmful. After all, the great physiologist Walter Cannon (1957) accepted "voodoo death" as physiological breakdown brought on by extreme fear over having violated a tribal taboo, and although we are not aware that anyone has gone so far as to die over masturbating, it has certainly been one of our strongest and most vindictive tribal taboos (Johnson, 1970, 1973).

Another very important point concerning masturbation is that although harmless in itself, it can be symptomatic of various things. Obviously, in a healthy person it can be symptomatic of a deprivation of heterosexual expression (Ellis, 1958). In married women it can be symptomatic of a husband's failure as a lover. In children, it can be symptomatic of some adjustment problem—just as excessive eating or excessive reading can be symptomatic of a desperate effort to find *something* satifying to do with life. For example, an English teacher in one of our sex education classes asked what she should do about her son who "lies in the tub and masturbates all of the time. I'm always catching him at it." Inquiry disclosed that the boy's neuromuscular development was somewhat slow, and he had therefore failed to learn many basic physical skills. He couldn't run well, could not throw and catch balls nor climb ropes or trees. Deprived of such normal childhood satisfactions as these and the interpersonal relationships that ordinarily accompany physical play, he had to find his satisfactions where he could. After a few weeks in the University of Maryland's *Children's Physical Developmental Clinic,* where he was taught to use his body with skill and confidence, his range of satisfactions in life was greatly expanded and he spent far less time in the tub.

For much of her life the female is expected to be, somehow, a graceful composite of the Virgin Mary and Racquel Welch. While playing this nonsexual erotic role in the manner of Candy (Southern and Hoffenberg, 1964) she has to make some very concrete decisions. Following is a possible series. Young women must decide whether they will engage in sexual intercourse or will not. If their answer is no and they stick to this decision, further choices in this series are unnecessary. This particular problem is solved. If, on the other hand, they choose to participate in coital relations further choices are then to be made.

One of these choices has to do with whether or not to use some form of contraceptive. If the choice is not to insist upon this, pregnancy is to be expected sooner or later. If the choice is to insist on this, the threat of pregnancy is greatly reduced, but is of course not entirely eliminated. Many girls depend trustingly upon the male to furnish this equipment. Unfortunately for them, many males dislike using "rubbers" and some still take great pride in "knocking up" (*i.e.*, impregnating) girls. Moreover, if the girl does decide to see to her safety by means of using a contraceptive of her own, there is a very good chance that unless she and her date have been very frank with each other, he will accuse her of having planned for sex all along and raise the question of "promiscuity." Moreover, we have known girls to go through more than one abortion before becoming willing to admit to themselves that they anticipate coition on dates and should therefore provide for their protection by contraception. Incidentally, what a bind females tend to be in! If they refuse to engage in sexual relations, they are likely to be called "frigid," but if they do engage, the label is likely to be "slut." This is a game called "you lose." Thank goodness girls are refusing to play this game much any more.

But to continue, if pregnancy does occur, the victim must choose among several possible courses of action.

The first possibility is to go ahead and have the child without benefit of a husband. This continues to be an extremely unattractive prospect for most women in our society where it is considered a most blatant affront to the specification of asexual behavior and is very likely to be dealt with accordingly. Although the girl's own parents may turn on her like tigers, sometimes both the girl "in trouble" and her family are amazed at the mutual support given in facing this sort of problem.

The more popular choice is still marriage, at least for a sufficient period to rescue the respectability of the mother and the legitimacy of the child. This simple solution is not always available, however. The male may suddenly vanish from the area or there may be difficulties establishing paternity. Marriage that is forced upon couples by an unwanted pregnancy certainly does not tend to be off to an ideal start; for lifetime contracts are not best made under duress, particularly by the very young, inexperienced, and frightened. The prospects for the child are likely to be bleak. Perhaps when we as a society become wise concerning our own welfare we will know that no child's prospects can be permitted to be bleak.

Another possibility is for the mother to have her baby and then turn it over to some organization for adoption or rearing in an institution. Some people consider this the only suitable course, and the associated suffering of the mother is sometimes referred to as proper payment for her sinful behavior. In one case a junior high school girl became pregnant. The boy, also virtually a child, was most willing to marry her. But her parents forbade this, requiring instead that she continue to attend school, even though quite obviously pregnant, until refused admission. She had the baby which by then she desired to keep, but her parents took it from her, putting it up for adoption. By this time her behavior had become quite psychotic.

Then, there is also induced abortion as a solution for unwanted pregnancies. In Canada this is likely to be a desperate measure of the first magnitude, particularly for individuals of limited means who cannot visit one of the countries where legal abortions happen at this point in history to be available. If an illegal, non-medical abortion is resorted to, the pregnancy is commonly well advanced by the time an abortionist can be located (if one is located at all). His qualifications and "clinical setting" may be highly questionable. Even though most induced abortions are successful in the sense that the woman lives and the act remains a secret, there is always the very real possibility that she will be made to feel the full impact of society's grimly negative attitude.

And finally, there is suicide and there is infanticide.

We are both fathers of young girls and we and their mothers intend that they will know about this series of choices and the implications of each for the next. Without question, in our society vaginal coitus among the young and desperate is full of danger for all concerned. It is for this reason that practically every leader we know in the sex education field urges sexually active teenagers, especially early teenagers, to find their sexual release in solitary masturbation, mutual masturbation, and other gratifying but innocuous ways—but not in vaginal coitus. Experience has shown that unless mother insists upon putting the pill in teenage daughter's mouth each day, the young cannot be counted on to use contraception even if it is available. But then, nor can lots of older persons. (Incidentally, the use of oral contraception is generally medically contraindicated for girls who have not yet stopped growing in height, or at least for those who have not grown to a height with which they will remain satisfied. As mentioned earlier, one of the functions of estrogen is to hasten maturation and cessation of growth of the long bones of the body which largely determine body height.)

Most people would probably agree that the time they have spent making love, pursuing and being pursued,

and so on, is among the happiest and most intense of
their lives. Unfortunately, certain venomous things are
injected into this important aspect of life by some traditional sex attitudes. We have already, in a superficial
way, taken into account the antisexual conditioning that
is begun in infancy and tends to carry over and assert
itself subsequently in various ways even in marriage.
Another difficulty to be considered is the way in which
men and women commonly feel about being "male"
or "female" and about the sex that they are not.

Everyone knows that there is still a greater sexual permissiveness accorded to males than to females. Virginity
is still more highly prized if not always required in girls,
although after a certain age it may seem rather pathetic;
but in men it is likely to be a source of ridicule after a
certain age. Thus, in addition to whatever psycho-
biological pressure the young man may be under, there
is also this very real traditional pressure to "prove his
manhood," as the saying goes, particularly perhaps,
while he is in military service. Now, of course, the information in the foregoing sentences is news to no one,
and the popular male image is precisely in these terms.
It is simply one of our folkways. However, what is unfortunate and sometimes quite terrible about it is a traditional psychology which justifies in many men's minds
their behaving or feeling that they should behave as
sexual marauders. As a matter of fact, we have known
many men who viewed women not so much as fellow
human beings as more or less stubborn guardians of
vaginas. To their minds, any approach that would gain
them access to the vagina is legitimate; and to "knock
a girl up" is a very special achievement. Give the girl
gifts, caress her sensitive spots, get her drunk, slip some
alleged aphrodisiac into her drink, promise her anything, use physical force (perhaps with the help of
friends), claim sterility—even marry her. In considera-

tion of our traditional antisexual morality, it seems almost incredible that such behavior is widely accepted (when one's own daughter is not involved) as red blooded masculinity, even by many women, and is boasted of among men. But then, if sex out of marriage is illegal and/or immoral it must be quite an achievement to beat the game—and perhaps to win out over "a woman." On the other hand, women are doubtless not any more altruistic in their feelings toward men than men are toward women. However, before they find refuge in marriage, women are usually less capable of inflicting injury upon men, who tend to be stronger, incapable of impregnation, and likely to be equipped with a certain amount of predisposition toward what we have called sexual marauding. We have rarely heard as bitter diatribes uttered against any group, including hippies, straights, Blacks, Whites, wartime enemies, Catholics, Jews, WASPS, capitalists and communists, as we have against women by men.

However, the two sexes merely usually undertake to attack and exploit each other in different ways. The female assault is likely to be along acquisitive, status-seeking lines and more as Franklin Roosevelt described the daily harassment he received while President: "Nibbled to death by ducks." Oscar Wilde put it this way: "The history of women is the history of the worst form of tyranny the world has ever known. The tyranny of the weak over the strong. It is the only tyranny that lasts."

Of course not all male thinking about women is vagina oriented. There is a tendency when not in the heat of actual or contemplated seduction for men to think of other things, especially when considering marriage and motherhood. This is not to say that men try to insist upon virginity in prospective wives as much as they used to, and some will even say that they would prefer wives who "know what sex is all about." The fact remains, however, that few men take any pleasure in hearing of their wives' previous sexual experiences, be they solitary (unthinkable!), homosexual, or heterosexual. Quite the contrary. The woman who is (foolishly?) honest about her previous sexual interests and activities is likely to dismay her mate, lead him to question her "virtue" and his own sexual preeminence with her, and provide him with ammunition for future controversies. The new wife becomes the lover; but merging with this is a wife image and a mother image, neither of which tend to be predominantly a sex image. Many a man has fallen into this trap: For a girl to be attractive as a prospective wife, she must resemble mother; but sex thoughts and mother thoughts just aren't supposed to go together.

Much has been written about the sex conflicts in marriage which tend to reduce the frequency of love making, to bring some women to look upon their husband's sexual demands as legalized rape, and to encourage impotency and orgasmic dysfunction in large numbers of people (e.g., Ellis, 1954; Freud, A., 1946; Masters and Johnson, 1970).

After all, what is to be expected after perhaps twenty years or more of intensive nonsexual and asexual conditioning? Does anyone seriously believe that a ceremony of a few minutes' duration is going to cleanse the mind of negative sex attitudes and instill it with sexual wisdom and the skills of intimate interpersonal relationships with a person, a stranger, of the "opposite sex" whose psychosexual background is so incalculably different?

In our chapter entitled "The Polar Icecap of Human Relations," there is a discussion of marriage as an ultimate challenge in human relations. However, it is important to realize that all sex problems in marriage are by no means due exclusively to traditional attitudes and faulty education. After all, whether or not problems are due to a rejectionist attitude toward nonsymbolic sex, the fact remains that circumstances of modern life tend to limit opportunities for leisurely, playful lovemaking in marriage to only the least opportune times of day. First there is early morning. Some people, doubtless a very small minority of biological sports, are fresh, alert, full of life and potentially passionate shortly after they wake up. We suspect that most such individuals are males, because the level of circulating androgens in males tends to be highest after a night's sleep. At any rate, these individuals are rarely married to people with kindred metabolisms. Others, probably the great majority, have a hard time climbing up out of sleep, glimpse the day ahead with foreboding if not dismay, and view their coffee more as an injection than a beverage. Then, late at night after children and television have been put to bed, another opportunity arises. People tend to forget that sexual intercourse to climax is likely to be something of a muscular feat that is not encouraged by fatigue, low physical fitness, a stomach full of food, or a circulatory system full of alcohol—any more than it is encouraged by a head full of antisexual attitudes, guilt feelings, hostilities toward the mate, or confusions as to how the devil the game is supposed to be played anyway.

In brief, many factors—including indoctrination concerning one's own body and sex, mate's body and sex, and sexual intercourse, plus circumstances of life, and confusion as to just what one's role is in marriage—converge upon happiness in marriage as though a society officially and romantically dedicated to it were bent upon destroying it.

As something toward which young people are pointed as they grow up, it is important to consider just what meaning marriage has today and what meaning it is likely to have tomorrow. Historically it has usually meant a kind of symbiotic relationship between man and woman. Each sex grew up knowing pretty much what its role in marriage would be, and preparation for that role was made along the way, usually from early childhood. One of the woman's well known functions was to bear children who were also of great importance to the family. Generally speaking we tend to think of marriage in about these same terms today—in spite of the fact that circumstances have so changed that men and women do not really need marriage as they once did. For example, large numbers of women who have graduated from high school or college and who have received training for business or a profession take a dim view of wasting this training and spending the rest of their lives "keeping house." Many are not at all attracted by the idea of interrupting a career in order to have children, a twenty-year commitment per child, or of saddling themselves with the task of being simultaneously career woman, wife, mother, and housekeeper. For their part, men no longer really need the services of "a wife" as they did in the past. In other words, it is likely that increasing numbers of people will choose not to marry or will demand relatively easy termination of childless marriage. Imbalance of numbers of eligible males and females in some areas can make monogamous marriage impossible. It is for such reasons as these that realistic sex education cannot confine itself to preparation for traditional marriage and family life. Realistic sex education attempts to take into account whatever the future may hold.

The matter of having children is an interesting one also. Here again, historical function has been lost; and the question should be raised and dealt with: Why have children today? In the past, children, especially boys, were of great economic importance to the family. A fruitful woman could produce children who would become free labor, sickness and old age insurance, and perhaps a fighting force for the family. Children mean none of these things to the modern family. In fact, economically speaking, they are all outlay with no return whatever on the dollar. With Social Security, Medicare, and the like, who *needs* children? (Of course they have meaning for the future of the community, but we have never once heard parents or prospective parents give this as their personal reason for having children.)

This change in the meaning of children is a matter of great interest to us for various reasons, including the fact that in our professional lives we have spent a great deal of time working with children, their parents, and their teachers. (Indeed, for quite a few years now the senior author, his wife, and hundreds of his students have conducted a clinic for children with various types of developmental disturbances and disorders, and with their parents. Years ago, the junior author was one of those student clinicians.) Our distinct impression from all of this and from casual day-to-day observation is that for the most part parents do not understand children, have no training in how to deal with them (to qualify as a taxi drixer or traffic policeman one must demonstrate basic competency, but nearly everyone is assumed competent, without training, for politics and parenthood, two of the most complex jobs imaginable), spend a great deal of time feeling hostile toward them, view them with suspicion and seek ways of getting rid of them via TV, schools, camps, jobs, and marriage. Have you watched mothers with their children in the department and grocery stores? Such language is generally reserved for enemies, and such blows would mean a jail sentence if inflicted on an adult. Indeed, some American Indians, including the Sioux and Hopi, who would not dream of striking their children in anger, have asked why the white man treats his children as enemies. It is well known among public health officials that physical abuse of children by their parents is an extremely common cause of childhood morbidity and mortality (*Battered Babies*, 1969; Murdock, 1970).

When people have children on purpose, it is often in something like the same spirit that motivates their going out and buying a puppy, and young girls are still encouraged to feel quite good about themselves when they declare that they want to get married and have six children. Some people decide to have a child because they are lonely, their life being empty and that kind of thing, just as many marry to fill a vacuum in their lives. Those who look upon having a child—or getting married for that matter—as such a substitute for personal therapy are often precisely those least qualified for parenthood, if parenthood is viewed as being something more than just producing a child. As professional educators of demonstrated interest in and concern for children, we feel qualified to raise the question concerning children: What do children mean today as opposed to what they meant in the past?

In their book *Marriage: East and West,* the Maces (1960, p. 301) conclude that it is possible for us to exercise wisdom in discarding what is no longer of value in marriage and family life:

. . . and in preserving that which is essential to our highest well-being. The break-up of the old type of family life, which has served the human race for countless ages, is now inevitable . . . We may ask, in fear and trembling, what we are to put in its place. The answer is that we do not know and cannot know as yet. But what is important is not the institution, but the values that the institution expresses and enshrines. The loss of the institutional form is inevitable. It can be replaced in time by another, more suited to the strange new life that will be the destiny of our children and our children's children. But the loss of the values—the true values that stand for man's dignity and worth—would be disastrous.

Albert Einstein once said something to the effect that everything has changed in recent years except our ways of thinking about them. Here again in matters of sex, marriage, and the having and rearing of children, there is clearly a need for careful thought concerning things that, due to changing circumstances, have lost much of their former meaning, but that surely have as profound, if more or less different, meaning for human beings today.

In this chapter we have undertaken to discuss some things of immense human meaning which are within almost everyone's experience—but which are not talked or even thought much about in a systematic way in the course of growing up and growing older. The traditional expectation of how people are "supposed to" behave sexually in the course of life is outlined; and then some of the problems are noted which highly sexual creatures usually encounter in the course of growing up and trying to deal simultaneously with society's conflicted and inconsistent specifications of sexual behavior, their own biological selves and enormous sexual stimulation in day to day living. The problems associated with supposedly being *nonsexual* and then *asexual* creatures growing up in a *sex-centric, sex-rejecting* society are seen to be key considerations in the weird dynamics of the situation. The spirit of urgency occasioned by the threat of modern warfare is also noted as a factor in the sexual behavior of the young. Finally, marriage and the having of children are commented upon as aspects of the general sexual behavior picture, and a question is raised concerning the profoundly altered meaning that both have for human beings today as opposed to human beings in the past.

It seems reasonable to conclude that many of our most serious communications problems stem from, or at least are re-enforced by, our ways of dealing with our sexuality, especially during childhood and youth. These are some of the main communications problems that we have in mind, which traditional sexual attitudes and practices engender, even guarantee.

1. *Communication with self.* From earliest childhood we learn that there is an unspeakable, dirty, unacceptable part of ourselves, our sexual anatomy, physiology, thought, and language. It seems incredible that psychologists and psychiatrists have made so little of this fact since they are so interested in such things as self-acceptance, body image, self concept, and mental health.

Recently, students in one of our university sex education classes were asked to keep a private diary of their activities, thoughts, and feelings relative to the course and the subjects to which it pertained. This diary was to serve as a basis for a term paper with the inelegant title "Where I've Been, What I've Done, Thought, and Felt, and Where I'm At Relative to the Course Human Sexuality and Educating About It." The papers included numerous testimonials on how their sex education experiences had improved their communication. Pertinent to communication with self, for example, one student reported that it was reassuring to realize, as a result of course activities, "that many other people suffer from these small hang-ups or problems which may not be serious but only personally aggravating and bothersome." This student was no longer propagandizing himself with "The Fallacy of Uniqueness." It was just such a sense of relief that undoubtedly contributed to the popularity of the famous Kinsey reports.

Another student wrote, "I think the health education course in human sexuality has had enough influence on my thought processes to contribute to my own personal development as an individual." We classify this influence on "thought processes" under "communication with self," because thinking is basically talking with oneself. Yet another student who apparently felt better about the way she talked with herself at the end of the course wrote, "As I reflect, while looking through the diary I have kept for the past three months, I cannot help but feel a wonderful insight has enlightened me. Although I am unable to identify this insight specifically, it can be described as an accumulation and processing of ideas, feelings, facts, and data dealing with human sexuality which I have obtained within and out of the Health Education class."

2. *Communication with older persons such as parents and teachers.* At a certain point, the young begin to see through the sex hypocrisy. They begin to notice the discrepancy between what adults tell and otherwise communicate to them about sex and what adults actually think, feel, talk about, watch, and do about sex. Could this be the beginning or one of the beginnings of the credibility gap that exists between the young and their elders? (The senior author proposed this idea a few years ago in a talk at the annual meeting of the American Orthopsychiatric Association; and a young psychiatrist questioned whether this kind of communication problem might lie at the perhaps unconscious root of youthful protest which was then expressing itself at many universities. The young have very good reasons for distrusting those who are older.) The latency period which Freud perceived is probably more accurately viewed as the time when kids in Victorian-influenced societies are old enough to begin seeing through the sham; and sex goes underground. Perhaps a certain sexual nihilism is generated by this gross violation of faith?

A student in a university sex education class wrote ". . . I can see how this course has enabled me to speak more freely at home. As I mentioned before, my mother does my typing for this course and we now discuss things that previously we would never think of talking about. It seems odd that you can live under the same roof with someone for twenty-one years and never really know her. Even though my mother and I are fairly close we had never talked about sex before. This course, however, has finally knocked down the barriers. I have an even greater love for my mother now and my whole idea of love has changed." Among the spin-off benefits of such improved rapport is the opportunity for better understanding of menopause, which many mothers of university students are experiencing.

3. *Communication with the aging.* Elderly persons are mistakenly presumed automatically returned to a nonsexual second childhood. To repeat, an active sex life can continue as long as there is reasonably good health and an interested partner (Rubin, 1966, 1967). Older people are simply not a race or species apart as they are so often treated. Continuing sexuality is but one of many possible bridges to better communication with other generations, interest in fun and good fellowship being others (see de Beauvoir, 1972).

Several years ago a student in one of our sex education classes conducted an unusual term project. He contacted members of a local senior citizens' club and interviewed the aged men and women individually. He questioned them quite specifically about their sexual behavior, attitudes, desires, and the like. Only after getting launched into the project did this student really believe the reports he had read in conjunction with the course about the existing sexual potential in aged humans. He was also very surprised at how few of the club members declined his request for an interview, and how eager they were to communicate about sexual matters with a person who was two generations younger than they, and who certainly did not "look like" a scholar (physically, he resembled the original model for the stereotype of a "jock-type-phys-ed-major").

4. *Communication with the other sex.* Is it reasonable to expect sex education activities to facilitate communication between the sexes? Experience with literally thousands of university and other students and with hundreds of parents has assured us that it can. Individuals have frequently reported improved communication not only with members of the opposite sex with whom they might have been sexually involved, but with members of the complementary sex (isn't that better than saying "opposite sex"?) in general.

REFERENCES

Battered babies. Canadian Medical Association Journal, *101*: 98, November, 1969.

Cannon, W. B.: Voodoo death. Psychosomatic Medicine, *19*:182, 1957.

de Beauvoir, S.: The Coming of Age. New York, G. P. Putnam, 1972.

Ellis, A.: If this be heresy. The Realist, February, 1962.

Ellis, A.: Sex Without Guilt. New York, Lyle Stuart, 1958.

Ellis, A.: The American Sex Tragedy. New York, Twayne, 1954.

Freud, A.: The Ego and the Mechanisms of Defence (1936). New York, International, 1946.

Freud, S.: Three Essays on Sexuality (1905). London, Hogarth, 1953.

Freud, S.: Five Introductory Lectures on Psychoanalysis (1910). London, Hogarth, 1947.

Freud, S.: New Introductory Lectures on Psychoanalysis. New York, Norton, 1933.

Freud, S.: An Outline of Psychoanalysis. New York, Norton, 1949.

Gadpaille, W. J.: Is there a too soon? Today's Health, *48*:34-35, 70-71, February, 1970.

Hall, C. S.: A Primer of Freudian Psychology. New York, Mentor, 1954.

Hendrick, I.: Facts and Theories of Psychoanalysis. 3rd Ed. New York, Knopf, 1958.

Johnson, W. R.: Masturbation. SIECUS Study Guide No. 3. (1855 Broadway, New York, N.Y.) 1973.

Johnson, W. R.: Masturbation in medical counseling in sex education. *In* The Adolescent Experience: A Counseling Guide to Social and Sexual Behavior. Edited by J. P. Semmens and K. E. Krantz. New York, Macmillan, 1970.

Johnson, W. R.: Awakening sexuality of girls. Sexual Behavior, March, 1973.

Jones, E.: The Life and Work of Sigmund Freud. New York, Basic Books, 1957.

Mace, D., and Mace, V.: Marriage: East and West. New York, Doubleday, 1960.

Masters, W. H., and Johnson, V. E.: Human Sexual Inadequacy. Boston, Little, Brown and Company, 1970.

Morice, A. G.: Canadian Dené Archaeological Report. Toronto, 1905.

Mullahy, P.: Oedipus: Myth and Complex (A Review of Psychoanalytic Theory). New York, Hermitage House, 1953.

Murdock, C. G.: The abused child and the school system. American Journal of Public Health, 60:105-109, January, 1970.

Reich, C. A.: The Greening of America. New York, Bantam Books, Inc., 1971.

Rubin, I.: Sexual Life after Sixty. New York, Signet Books, 1967.

Rubin, I.: Sex life after forty and after seventy. *In* An Analysis of Human Sexual Response. Edited by Ruth and Edward Brecher. New York, Signet Books, 1966.

Southern, T., and Hoffenberg, M.: Candy. New York, G. P. Putnam's Sons, 1964.

4

Modern Sexual Customs in
Historical Perspective

IT has been contended that history is a pack of lies
that men agree to call the truth. Certainly the bias of
historians; the emotions of witnesses; and the complex-
ities, irrationalities, and improbabilities surrounding
events combine to make "history" a most precarious and
dubious report on things past. Then too, there is the
matter of prehistory, that great bulk of human existence
which preceded recorded history. We can little more
than speculate about the origins of many sexual customs
and events, such as male and female circumcision, the
invention of the phallic gods, the fall of the early matriarchies, and the subjugation of women.

Still, the fact remains that the history of our official
sexual attitudes, morality, and laws is nearly as traceable
as the history of the rules of football. Of course, the
football rule books will not tell you much of what actually happened in games played from year to year, but
they do tell you what, officially, could and could not be
done and what the penalties were for violations. Similarly, the sacred writings of the Judeo-Christian tradition and certain well-established events such as the
separation of the Anglican Church from Roman Catholicism and the Puritan influence upon our official stance

concerning sex tell much of the story of how we came to be as we are with regard to sex attitudes, laws, and morality.

The discussion that follows represents an effort to review some of what seems to be known of the history behind our attitudes, laws, and customs concerning sex and the sexes. The coverage is broad, and it draws on information from other cultural traditions to make certain points. However, perhaps the key things to be noted are as follows.

1. Sex has always played a major role in human affairs and has been prominent in customs, religions, art, moralities, and laws.

2. Our standards, attitudes, and laws are derived mainly from the Old Testament Jewish patterns. In those, sex was highly regarded from the points of view of both reproduction and pleasure, but it was subjected to strict regulation, mainly in the interests of propagation of the chosen people.

3. The second major influence upon our official sexual tradition was that of the early Christian fathers who adopted the Jewish sexual regulations almost in toto, but added to these a highly negative attitude toward both sex and nearly all women.

4. The Judeo-Christian sexual tradition was transmitted in intensified form to America by the Puritan fathers of the seventeenth century, and through them that highly regulating and antisexual pattern became, and is today, the official sexual morality and legal structure of this part of the world.

Turning now to the general discussion, one can only speculate with regard to the prehistoric factors that resulted in the dominance of males. However, their physical superiority for various activities and freedom from the periodic restrictions and weaknesses imposed

by femininity and motherhood on women were doubtless influential considerations. Simone de Beauvoir has
suggested that as man rose above the animal level and
began to exercise control over nature by means of tools,
woman continued to be more closely bound to her animal nature and her body because of her maternal functions; and the "biological and economic conditions of
the primitive horde must have led to male supremacy"
(1953, p. 65). Bertrand Russell has speculated that
agriculture introduced the subjugation of women—as
well as serfdom, human sacrifice, and the despotic em-
pires which succeeded each other from the first Egyptian dynasty to the fall of Rome (1955, xx). Because of
her reproductory function (*i.e.*, producer of laborers
and fighters who were also the likely providers in sickness and old age) and her utilitarian value as worker,
a woman was economically valuable in an agricultural
society—however else she may have been valuable.
And thus, it seems, women came to be regarded as
property—valuable property with the special and highly
prized capacity for procreation, but property nonethe-
less. Among the early Jews, the husband could send his
wife away if she did not please him (Exodus 21:8-11);
women were booty in war (Leviticus 27:1-7); and repeatedly it is made clear that woman's real value depends upon bearing children. Sarah and Rachel were
barren so they "gave" their handmaids to their husbands
in order that they might have children by them (Genesis, 16 and 30). David took it as a measure of the Lord's
greatness that he could make a sterile woman fertile
(Psalms, 113:9). And conversely, the Lord punished
Michal in the most dire way when she criticized David
for dancing nude before the Arc: he made her infertile
(Samuel, 2:6). In the ten commandments, women are
classed with material possessions, servants, and domestic
animals:

Thou shalt not covet they neighbour's house, thou shalt not covet thy neighbour's wife, nor his manservant, nor his ox, nor his ass, nor anything that is thy neighbour's (Exodus, xx, 17).

Symbolic of the status of sex and especially of masculinity, the male phallus or penis became a very common symbol of power as well as pleasure, and numerous representations of it made of stone, bone, and clay have been found, some of which date back many thousands of years. Scott insists that "The study of phallicism is the study of religion . . . no one who neglects the study of phallic worship can hope to secure any adequate understanding of the origin of religion" (1953, p. v). Today, people tend to be offended by assertions of this kind. When evidence to this effect came to our attention, each of us was in his turn shaken as well as incredulous; for we, as have been most other people, had been led to believe that religion is good and sex, for the most part, bad. There was to our minds no possible relationship between the two except that the one was against the other. Subsequent years of experience in sex education work with a wide range of ages, subcultural backgrounds, and geographical locations in North America have led us to realize that this continues to be a very common reaction. Therefore, be forewarned: if in your own sex education efforts you deal with the history of our present "official" sexual customs and mores, you are likely to encounter considerable hostility, at least initially, from some of your students. We have found that most become able to view the evidence objectively, and subsequently resynthesize their badly shaken frames of reference into what they perceive as being a more satisfactory view of the realities of human sexuality.

Investigation of the relationship between matters sexual and religious leads to the realization that at the root of most if not all of the world's religions there is to be found close association, if not deliberate identification, of the sex organs or their symbolization with deity, for "The worship of the reproductive organs representing the fertilizing, protecting, and saving powers of nature was very widespread and in accord with basic human aspirations" (Knight and Wright, 1957, p. 195). In Shiva worship (Hindu religion), on the day of creation when the gods, Brahma and Vishnu, sprang forth into being from nonbeing, they were bewildered by their own birth, but presently "they found shining beside them a resplendent Lingam (phallus) of huge dimensions whose base or top they could not see." Stupefied by the magnificence of the phenomenon of the luminous Lingam, they attempted to determine its size, but years of diving for its base and flying for its top resulted in failure to reach either end (Thomas, 1959, p. 113). The present day Lingayats are most puritanical by Western standards, but always carry their god-symbol with them—the carved Lingam or phallus.

The ancient peoples in and around the base of our own tradition also associated religion with sex. Baal-Peor, the phallic God of the Moabites and Midianites ". . . claimed from man the sacrifice of circumcision and from women the sacrifice of her maidenhead" (*i.e.*, by penetration by a phallus) (Scott, 1956, p. 134). Yahweh or Jehovah, too, required circumcision. The Old Testament makes it clear that sex and reproduction were of enormous importance to the early Jews, and the phallic nature of the religion is abundantly evident. Thus, there is the covenant with God of circumcision (Genesis 17: 9-14; Jeremiah 9:25) and endless preoccupation with sex-related matters such as: going forth and multiplying; excluding men with cut off or injured genitals from the Lord's congregation (Deut. 23:1); specifying punishments for wasting the male's precious seed of life;

and declaring the uncleanliness of both menstrual blood (Leviticus 12 and 20) and semen (Leviticus 15:16).

Bible translators substituted the word "thigh" for penis. "It was the universal custom for anyone making a vow to place his hand upon either his own sexual member or upon that of the other person concerned. Than the penis, the representative of Yahweh, no higher testimony could be given or asked. Thus when Abraham asked his servant to swear to him, he said: 'Put, I pray thee, thy hand under my thigh [penis]; and I will make thee swear by the Lord, the God of heaven and the God of earth' (Genesis 24:2)" (Scott, 1956, p. 148).

It was not until sex and sin had become closely associated in the minds of Christians that direct representations of the generative organs were disguised in symbolic form, the phallus became the phallic symbol; and the concept of obscenity led to the alteration of many original texts and pieces of art work as indicated above with reference to the Bible. (See especially Goldberg, 1958; Henriques, 1960; Knight and Wright, 1957; Raphaelian, 1957; Scott, 1956; Thomas, 1959.) Moreover, as Christianity moved northward into Europe, it had no easy time "cleansing" religion of sex; for the pagan peoples had so tended to identify the one with the other that setting the two apart into warring factions was almost an impossibility. So the converts learned to do what the earlier Christians had long since learned to do: worship openly at one shrine, secretly at the other. Significantly, many early churches contain art work and ornaments depicting male and female genitals and out-and-out sexual activity which would to later Christian eyes be most blasphemous, but which reflected the magnitude of the task of purging sex from places of worship. Helpfully, the tendency for artists the world over to abstract reality in their representations provided a vehicle for the retaining of sex in disguise in places of worship and elsewhere. Thus, as the antisexual influence of the Christians spread, it was a natural step for sexual representations to go underground, as it were, into symbolism; and sex symbolism replaced direct sexual representation in ornamentation, art, and architecture (Goldberg, 1958; Henriques, 1960; Knight and Wright, 1957; Lewinsohn, 1958; Scott, 1956).

A few years ago, an ardent church-goer who was also an ardent student of symbols wrote to us of his examination of his church.

The church I attend is of very plain design. The group feels that symbolism is to be avoided as diverting from the main purpose of the church. However, the building contains a 'chancel' which is concave in design, representing, I believe, a 'secure' place for the most holy of the structure, and obviously derives from the security of the female (womb) in the antiquity of the race.

The stained glass windows contain various objects such as lilies (resurrection), wheat in shock and field (seed, generation, the source of life—eventually the union of the sexes in regeneration), and finally one innocuous lamp!

And he goes on to describe the lamp which has a spout, at the base of which are two round objects, one on each side; and the handle is a direct continuation of the phallus to the testes. From the spout there issues a cloud, and the female object, the oil vessel, is covered but easily opened for impregnation. The obvious symbolism, he concluded, is that wisdom is derived from a knowledge of the symbols of the race, continued in all of our institutions; and he asked what nobler association with religion than the creating and renewing of life?

Presumably the symbolism which has made possible the retaining of sexual representation even in sacred places provides satisfaction without requiring direct confrontation with sex. In an effort to discover the extent to which the mind defends itself against recognizing the reality behind sex symbols, the senior author trained two bright graduate students, a man and a woman, both regular church-goers, in deep trance hypnosis. Independently of each other, they were then asked to look at a picture of a famous old sex symbol which thinly disguises the representation of the penis and female sex structures by portraying them as a "bird" sitting on "eggs." Neither out of the trance nor in the very deep trance, which would be followed by posthypnotic amnesia, did these subjects give evidence of recognizing the sexual element in the picture. But when they were asked to dream about the picture and describe the dream as it took place—only then was there clear-cut evidence that the sexual symbolism was not actually lost on them (Johnson, 1967).

According to many students of the subject, the Christian cross may be taken as an example of how respected sexual abstractions of long standing became an effective disguise for sex association gone underground. For example, Goldberg has pointed out:

The cross, from time immemorial a symbol of the creative forces in union, was early brought into the symbolism of Christianity, where it has ever grown in importance. And the Christian, mindful only of its relation to his Savior, does not see in it the symbol of the saving grace of generation (1958, p. 204).

This same idea of sacred union of male and female in the creative act has also been reflected in religions of the Far East. The great god Siva of India was divided into male and female and became the Reproducer. Brahma, the great Creator of the Hindu religion, is depicted as being female on the left side and male on the right. The sacred Cross theme appears over the genital region of Brahma's body, that religion not tabooing and repressing sex; but the arm of the cross on the female side is in the form of a loop to represent the female sex structures. Apparently, travelers to the Orient have seen and misunderstood the depictions of the half male, half female god; the symbolic labia-loop *is* at right angles to the perpendicular. Apparently they supposed that the horizontal loop of the symbolic cross was a depiction of actual female sex structures. Perhaps this is the reason why a surprising number of men have been firmly convinced that "Oriental women are built different."

At any rate, it is suddenly popular these days to say that sex is beautiful, "A gift of God," as some ministers like to say. It is an interesting test of acceptance of sex on anyone's part to see how he or she reacts to the idea that sex is and always has been very much a part of his or her religion and sacred ornamentation. Is it discomforting to learn that Easter eggs and the jolly Bunny who somehow manages to lay them are fertility-sex symbols which have held over from pagan days?

The Ancient Greeks could deal directly with sex in a manner that would shock later generations. They saw nothing obscene in Aristophanes' *Lysistrata,* in which the Spartans' wives refuse to sleep with them until they forego warfare. At one point, the Athenians tease the sex-starved Spartan peace-makers by pretending to believe that they see spears hidden under their clothing. At another point, the women's talk about "an eight-inch penis" is translated slyly as "thing"; and we read "If they refuse to give you their hands, bring them whichever way you can"—where the Greek literally translated is "drag them by the balls" (Loth, 1961, p. 50). Somewhat ironically, the fairly well-cleaned-up King James version of the Bible was produced in Shakespeare's time, but he, too, was to be "cleaned up" two hundred years later by Bowdler.

When children become interested in sex, their prime

motivation is certainly not the desire to procreate. Similarly, it is likely, if not certain, that early man highly prized woman long before he associated her with the economics or politics of offspring production. Thus the famous Venus of Willendorf and other statuettes were carved from stone by cave men who were obviously concerned with depicting uniquely female characteristics in grossest form—and as with most present day restroom art work, nonessential features of the anatomy such as face, arms, and feet are all but ignored (Henriques, 1960; Lewinsohn, 1958; Seltman, 1955). However, from very early times the woman's procreative powers were associated in men's minds with the great creative powers of nature, the source of crops, plenty, and security—Mother Earth, Nature. Still, she, like Nature herself, could be unpredictable, prone to whimsey, sudden anger, and unexpected harshness. She became a goddess who could grant favors if properly besought.

Perhaps this association of woman, sexual pleasure, fertility, and the great forces of nature is why sex was so much involved in the religions of the ancients. If men liked something, they assumed that the gods had similar tastes; and so gave them such things as food, tools and weapons, incense, flowers, and sex to win their favor (Scott, 1956, p. 47). There were religious sexual orgies (Partridge, 1960), temple prostitution (Lewinsohn, 1958, p. 27), sex in spring and autumn festivals, fertility rites, and so on. Holy places were decorated with realistic portrayals of the sex organs and sexual activity, and later with much more abstract symbolizations of these (see especially Raphaelian, 1957, p. 24). By such activities, people hoped to bring themselves in harmony with and encourage the creative and other forces upon which they depended for food, strength, offspring, and luck.

Of course, it has been argued by many that in the incomparable sex act, at orgasm, both male and female make their closest contact with the divine, "The Sacred Fire," and that this is essentially a profoundly religious experience (Goldberg, 1958). Incidentally, Goldberg's explanation of temple prostitution among various of the ancients makes that institution more plausible than it might otherwise be:

> In those times and places where the institution of temple priestesses was established, society did not look upon it as prostitutional. Quite to the contrary, it was the most respectable and pious vocation a woman could select, or have selected for her by her parents or guardians. Nor did the temple priestess view herself as a prostitute. She saw herself a servant of the god, possibly bringing more joy and gladness to the divinity than to herself (1958, p. 75).

At any rate, so important was the role of the woman, especially as fruitful, nurturing Mother, that impressive evidence, beginning with Bachofen (1861) and Morgan (1891), has been presented in support of the theory that prior to our own and other patriarchal traditions, there were matriarchal—not merely matrilinear (*i.e.*, property being passed through the female rather than male line)—traditions (see Bebel, 1904; Choisy, 1962; de Beauvoir, 1953; Eisler, 1950; Lewisohn, 1958). Many modern writers simply take the early matriarchies for granted. Buckminster Fuller (1968), for example, does this as he traces the evolution of sex roles during the pre-agricultural, agricultural, and industrial eras. He goes on to state that women have now taken over the fundamental ownership and control of modern industry —due to the earlier demise of their husbands—and that by the twenty-first century, womankind will have assumed full management of "Spaceship Earth." Full circle after so many thousands of years?

Be that as it may, the Great Mother was called Ishtar

in Babylonia, Astarte among the Semitic peoples, Gaea, Rhea or Cybele by the Greeks (not the terror associated with the sacred Grove of the Mothers in the Oedipus at Colonus). Male gods were subordinated to her (de Beauvoir, 1953, pp. 68-70).

> The Great Mother of protohistory was adored under the image of a snake or of a woman with a reptile's head . . . the serpent of the Bible represents the "heathen" worship of the Great Goddess which the Jewish patriarchy had to drive out of Asia Minor. The substitution of patriarchy for matriarchy is one of the most important events in history, if not the most important . . . It was brought about by . . . Nomads . . . Semites . . . Mongols . . . Aryans . . . One or another of these invaders, and sometimes all of them, conquered the peaceful matriarchy populations (Choisy, 1962, pp. 84-85).

On the basis of available historical documents and modern day behavior, it seems that the general outline of the patterns of sexual behavior in our historical tradition and the evolution of the male-female picture are reasonably clear. But of course since we do not really know all the details of modern sexual behavior or its meaning to humanity, it seems most presumptuous to profess a detailed knowledge of the sex-related situation among those people at the roots of our tradition or even along its course. As an analogy, consider Malinowski's comment about his conversations with fellow ethnologists on the subject of sex and kinship among primitive peoples:

> I become at once aware that my partner does not understand anything in the matter, and I end usually with the feeling that this also applies to myself (Lewinsohn, 1958, p. 15).

Every indication is, however, that generally speaking, from the beginning or our own partriarchal tradition the status of woman has surely been that of "second sex," to use de Beauvoir's term. For example, Plato thanked the gods for eight favors bestowed upon him: first that he had been born a free man rather than a slave; and second, he was a man and not a woman. For their part, male Jews pray: "Blessed be Thou, our God and Lord of Hosts who has not created me a woman;" and the Jewish women pray at the corresponding place: "who hast created me after Thy will" (Bebel, 1904, p. 79). Among the ancient Jews, women had few rights, wedlock was marriage by purchase, and strictest chastity was demanded of them. After all, she was largely responsible for Adam's folly, and on the authority of Jehovah himself, blood was unclean and woman had, thus, chronic uncleanliness attached to her (Smith, 1953, pp. 107, 117-18). Bearing a child must be followed by atonement.

Economic and other utilitarian reasons led the ancient Jews to place a great premium upon begetting children, although in later years they were to suffer from over-population.

It was sinful to abstain from marriage and unlawful to live childless in the marital state. Jehovah had created the universe and He desired it to be filled with living beings. For centuries the polygamy of the heathen world had been accepted by the Jews, and insofar as a man could afford wives and concubines he was expected to deliver his seed in making them fruitful (Henry, 1955, p. 494).

"Seed" was not to be wasted; masturbation and other intentional loss of semen were unpardonable sins—according to some authorities, the worst of sins (Taylor, 1954, p. 246). Recall the Biblical story of Onan who was struck dead by God for spilling his seed on the ground instead of performing his duty of inseminating his dead brother's wife. Incidentally, early in the Christian era this story was misinterpreted to the masses by clerics who were eager to convince their flocks that masturbation was prohibited by the Bible. To this day, onanism and masturbation are equivalent words (Taylor, 1954, p. 57).

Economic considerations also undoubtedly influenced male-female relationships of the Greeks and their attitude towards sex. Unlike the Jews, the Greeks were under pressure to restrict population and even customarily resorted to infanticide, especially female, when population threatened to exceed food supply. Whereas the Jews considered wasting their seed a grave sin, the Greeks regarded homosexual unions socially acceptable; and, as a matter of fact, in Plato's *Symposium* we find that certain cultured Athenian gentlemen considered the noble love of youth for youth a higher form of love than that of male for female. Under these conditions, in which children were important but only up to a point, it is not surprising that women took a like course of seeking an ideal of "love" which might not necessarily be fruitful; and the Island of Lesbos (with which we associate "Lesbian love") became more famous in history than it would otherwise have been because of love poems that Sappho of Lesbos addressed to other women. In Greece women were of three kinds; *hetaerae* for "spiritual" as well as, perhaps, physical companionship; prostitutes for sensual pleasure; and wives to provide sons and domestic labor. (See Lewinsohn, 1958, on *hetaerae*.)

Indications are that the Romans had a very high regard for their sex lives, and many considered prostitution an essential institution for preserving marriages in which the man, for some reason, did not consider himself adequately satisfied sexually at home (Lewinsohn, 1958, p. 70). Apparently, too, they had a considerable lightheartedness concerning sex. Ovid's book, *The Art of Love,* is often taken to be something of a reflection of the times. For example, Humphries has written:

Yet how brightly and clearly, with evocative skill far beyond that of the most dutiful and self-conscious researcher, he portrays the social life of ancient Rome! . . . Ovid dearly loved his time, and perhaps that is why we can see it so illumined . . . Every age probably regards itself as unique in its sexual sophistication . . . If we take Ovid as a typical spokesman, we should have to conclude that the keynote was elegance (*Ovid*, 1957, p. 6).

Witness Ovid's lines:

Always our nature insists on things denied and forbidden . . .
He is a countrified lout, who objects when his wife does some
    cheating,
    Yes an ignorant lout, blind to the ways of our town . . .
Why take a beautiful wife, if all you want is a pure one?
    Every natural law says you can't have it both ways.
Don't be a fool; let her play; put off that glooming expression;
    Don't be too much of a spouse, always demanding and stiff
(1957, pp. 74-75).
    Love on the sly delights men; it is equally pleasing to women.
        Men are poor at pretense; women can hide their desire.
    It's a convention, no more, that men play the part of pursuer.
    Women don't run after us; mousetraps don't run after mice
(1957, p. 113).

At any rate, the women of Rome were not property or slaves but had, instead, legal status, could own property and deal directly in politics. It was still "a man's world," but women could involve themselves sufficiently in it to elicit complaints like Cato's famous:

If, after the example of his ancestors, every head of a family kept his wife in proper subjection, we would not have so much public bother with the whole sex.

By the time Christianity became the official religion of Rome, the empire was in decay. Oftentimes its fall is

attributed to the corruption of morals of the population
—although just as psychiatrists are usually unable to
specify just what caused the illness of any given func-
tionally psychotic patient, it would seem rash to attempt
to pinpoint the exact cause of the illness of an entire
nation. However, Lewinsohn has reflected the view of
many historians who believe that circumstances reached
a point where children were a burden rather than an
economic asset, and therefore the population fell below
a critical level as people avoided having children. Moreover, the spreading asceticism which encouraged sexual
abstinence (infanticide, abortion, and contraception
being forbidden) is believed to have been a very real
factor in encouraging this supposed drop in population
(Lewinsohn, 1958, p. 101). On the other hand, it has
more recently been proposed that Rome fell because of
lead poisoning of its aristocracy, its leaders, which resulted in their becoming mentally defective. Archeologi-
cal information reveals that well-to-do Romans took to
keeping their wine in bottles, the inner surfaces of which
were coated with lead. Wine was drunk from childhood
and small amounts of lead gradually accumulated within
the body; and lead poisoning, it is argued, incapacitated
the prospective leadership. (*Lead Among the Romans*,
1966.) It is nice to have bits of information like this
around to hand to simple-minded "historians" who attribute the fall of nations to "immorality"—the violation
of the sex codes of the not-yet-arrived-on-the-scene
Puritans!

Be that as it may, it was within the context of the
Roman Empire, which was so influenced by Greece,
that Christianity was born. The new religion was to be
the vehicle which transported the Jewish sex laws and
sexual morality northward into Europe, to England, and
finally to North America where they are the basis of our
present-day sex laws and the accepted sexual morality.

It is interesting that few if any of the "great teachers" of history have taught us, by example or otherwise, how to handle the relationships of marriage in a very satisfactory way. Most of what they had to say concerning sex had to do with specifying what kinds of behavior are forbidden and/or indicating how to keep the women in line. Socrates is supposed to have married for the somewhat cynical purpose of demonstrating that a man could remain wise in spite of having a wife. Plato eschewed marriage. Gautama, who was to become the Buddha, fled from his marriage. Mohammed, who married fourteen times, specified in the Koran that husbands should, at their own discretion, beat their wives to maintain what they considered order. Gandhi, who after years of feeling guilty for the strong sexual appetite which eventually he blamed for the death of one of his children, was grateful to God when sexual decline made possible his final vow of chastity, even though married (Pacion, 1971, p. 81).

For his part, Jesus did not marry and evidently gave little direct indication of his views on sex. However, unlike many of his influential followers, He did not spend time denouncing women or sex. He concerned himself with attempting to improve human relations of every kind including those with harlots and adultresses; and the Gospels evidently contain no demand whatever that sexual abstinence be practiced. If meeting vital human needs required a miracle, Jesus is reported to have produced it. The same gentle concern can certainly not be said of all of the Church Fathers who followed. St. Paul said that it is best not to marry, but that if a person is, unlike himself, so unfortunate as to need sex, then marriage is preferable to fornication. There is his famous comment, "It is better to marry than to burn."

But a few quotations from early church leaders who

profoundly influenced subsequent Christian thought will give some indication of the Christian attitude toward women and sex which emerged. (It is recognized that such men as those quoted here wrote, too, of brotherly love, love of God and kindness and charity— as, for example, in some of the beautiful lines in St. Paul's Epistles. However, we are concerned here with sex attitudes.)

Peter: Ye, wives, be in subjection to your own husbands . . . (I Peter, 3:1)
Paul: The husband is the head of the wife, even as Christ is head of the Church (Ephesians, 5:23); Man . . . is the image and glory of God, but the woman is the glory of man (I Corinthians, 11:7); Let the woman learn in silence with all subjection. But I suffer not a woman to teach, nor to usurp authority over the man, but to be in silence (I Timothy, 2:11 and 12); Let women keep silence in the churches; for it is not permitted unto them to speak; but they are commanded to be under obedience, as also saith the law. And if they will learn anything, let them ask their husbands at home, for it is a shame for women to speak in the church (I Corinthians, 14:34 and 35). (See Bebel, 1904.)

To the molders of Christian ideology, woman became the devil's worst temptation. Tertullian wrote:

Woman, you are the devil's doorway. You led astray one whom the devil would not dare attack directly. It is your fault that the Son of God had to die; you should always go in mourning and rags.

St. John Chrysostom: "Among all savage beasts none is found so harmful as woman." St. Thomas declared that woman is only an "occasional" and incomplete being, a kind of imperfect man. "Man is above woman, as Christ is above man" (de Beauvoir, 1953, pp. 97-98).

With this background it is almost surprising that in the sixteenth century the council of Macon decided that women do, after all, have a soul—although the decision was by a majority of only one vote (Bebel, 1904, p. 52). But even though granted a soul, women must suffer for the sin of Eve. In modern times when anesthetics were first used in childbirth, the Church was enraged since the Bible said that woman should bring her young forth in sorrow. Fortunately, Victoria was Queen of England at this time, and decided to seek the relief of chloroform in her seventh delivery—and thus set a new precedent (Taylor, 1954, p. 208).

St. Augustine, the Fifth Century Bishop of Hippo in North Africa, wrote many treatises upon sin and evil which profoundly influenced all subsequent Christian thought and practice. According to his famous *Confessions,* in his youth he was extremely fond of his devout and saintly mother who, for her part, frowned on his wild living and maintaining of mistresses. Of course he was torn between desire for "purity" and sexuality. After his conversion under the influence of Paul's writings, he viewed his past mode of life in darkest colors; and his later teaching and writing undoubtedly reflected the violence of his reactions and conditioned his attitude toward sex (Smith, 1953, p. 249).*

But St. Augustine had to wrestle with a very difficult theological issue. This was his problem: God, who is good and just, not only punished Adam and Eve but their blameless offspring through ages without end for the original sin of disobedience. How could a good God be perpetually cruel? And how could Adam's uncleanly

* Compare: "Thus, though his boyhood was evil and his manhood fraught with many ill-deeds, he became, when his hair began to grow thin, a model of kindly wisdom, never wantoning it save with much discretion . . . truth to tell, his desires no longer pricked him, and that is enough to make the Devil himself calm and sober from heel to headpiece" (Balzac in *Droll Tales*).

or sinful state be transmitted afresh to his posterity? St. Augustine found the solution to both problems in sexual intercourse. Adam's sin of disobedience led to God's requiring people to propagate sexually, in lust, in self-interest and in pleasure—that is, in sin. And people can continue to exist only by engaging in sin, continual reinfection, and guilt (Smith, 1953, pp. 249-50).

No wonder then that avoidance of intercourse by discipline, celibacy, or even self-emasculation was deemed desirable in the interests of salvation. Marriage was no excuse.

There is no material difference, wrote St. Augustine, between the *copula carnalis* of man and wife and the *copula fornicatoria,* or physical union with a whore. Both are sinful . . . And two hundred years later, Pope Gregory, who officially imposed celibacy on the priesthood, endorsed St. Augustine's doctrine; even marital intercourse was never free from sin . . . The disobedience and undiscipline of the generative organs are the proof of original sin (Lewinsohn, 1958, p. 98).

On the other hand, in spite of espousing and teaching a highly antisexual attitude, it was Christianity, too, which in a special way elevated a woman to a new idealized status—even perhaps beyond that of any of the pagan goddesses—not as a sex figure, of course, but as virgin, wife, and most of all as revered, comforting, forgiving Mother. Her importance grew as the severity of the Papistic doctrine increased the need of the people for a kindly loving mother. This aspect of the attitude toward sexless woman is, of course, symbolized by the Holy Virgin Mary, wife of Joseph, unblemished Mother of Jesus (Goldberg, 1958, p. 205ff). Only Jesus and, as of about a hundred years ago, his Mother have been born of a clean, that is "immaculate," sinless, conception.

During the Middle Ages the Church converted several millions of Europeans, and in so doing introduced them to a drastically altered and in ways inverted perspective, biologically and traditionally speaking, not the least important aspect of which was concerned with sex. According to the ascetic ideal, the sexual activity of the married was, if possible, restricted to procreative purposes and otherwise it was limited to particular days of the week, perhaps two or three, and it was forbidden for extended periods, such as the forty days of Lent (Taylor, 1954). The ideas of the sinfulness of sexual intercourse, woman as temptress, the glorification of virginity, continence, and purity of thought as well as deed —these and other refinements of control and restriction of the sex drive were superimposed upon a pagan tradition in which sex had been a natural and pleasurable function that was somehow related to fertility, creativity, the great forces of nature, and to religion. Such fundamentally conflicting points of view represented by the two traditions, Christian and pagan, are not readily synthesized by a single mind, and indications are that those simple-minded, magic-minded, superstitious country people reacted as moderns do when they are under pressure and torn, psychologically speaking, in two or more directions at once. That is, indications are that they squirmed and, in surprising numbers, developed symptoms of mental illness.

G. Rattray Taylor writes:

In the early part of the Middle Ages what we chiefly find is frank sexuality, with which the Church at first battles in vain. Then, as the Church improves its system of control, we find a mounting toll of perversion and neurosis. For whenever society attempts to restrict expression of the sexual drive more severely than the human constitution will stand, one or more of three things must occur. Either men will defy the taboos, or they will turn to perverted forms of sex, or they will develop psychoneurotic symptoms (1954, p. 19).

Taylor likens Medieval Europe to a vast insane asylum and in support of his contention cites evidence of

widespread hysterias, hallucinations, incubi (male demons which ravish women at night) and succubi (female demons of like inclination for males), compulsive
behavior, convulsions, witchcraft, and other symptoms
of mental disturbance. He does not attribute these
things to the Christianity of Christ, but to the sexually
obsessed church Fathers who wrote many years after
Christ and whose associating of sexual pleasure with
damnation led them to distorting and falsifying of
scriptures and all manner of violent measures in order
to stem the tide of what they considered to be evil
(Taylor, 1954, p. 56). Since church and state were intimately associated, church authority and the inquisitions
were backed by civil law and might (*e.g.*, the death of
Joan of Arc).

Popular notions of knightly love during the later
Middle Ages are not generally borne out by the written
record. De Beauvoir points out that the period has been
regarded as platonic; "but the truth is that the feudal
husband was guardian and tyrant, and the wife sought
an extramarital lover; knightly love was a compensation
for the barbarism of the official mores . . ." (1953, p.
100). Bebel says: "Imaginative romancers, together
with calculating people, have endeavored to represent
the Middle Ages as particularly 'moral,' and animated
with a veritable worship for woman. . . . The contrary is
true. This period contributed to destroy whatever
regard possibly existed for the female sex. The knights,
both of country and town, consisted mainly of rough,
dissolute fellows, whose principal passion, besides feuds
and guzzling, was the unbridled gratification of sexual
cravings. The chronicles of the time do not tire of telling
about the deeds of rapine and violence, that the nobil-
ity was guilty of . . ." (1904, pp. 63-64). Behavior of
this kind certainly did not represent the ideal of behavior that the Christians had brought with them, the

ideal being much more accurately portrayed in the popular legends of the period which, expurgated, have reached us.

At any rate, by this time the sexual tradition of the ancient Jews, as modified by the Christian fathers, was well established as the criterion of male and female behavior in Europe and in England. Some of these modifications were of enormous significance. For example, "sins of the father" no longer meant ancestral errors generally which later sons must expiate. It now meant the act of generation specifically which guaranteed being born in sin (Lewinsohn, 1958, p. 98). On the other hand, some changes doubtless were of less significance, and some even may be viewed as liberalization. For example, circumcision was no longer required. Saint Paul had taught:

For in Jesus Christ neither circumcision availeth any thing, nor uncircumcision; but faith which worketh by love (Galatians, 5:6).

Sixteenth Century England was of special historical importance with regard to our sex tradition. In the first place, Henry VIII pulled away from the Church of Rome, establishing himself as head of both civil and ecclesiastical law. Prior to that time sex-related as well as "spiritual" and moral concerns were the responsibility of the church; and it may well be the long precedent of church preeminence in such matters that accounts for the belief of some modern theologians that churches have something special to say to legislators with regard to sex-related laws which will apply to everyone, not just their own following. Of greatest significance, however, is the fact that Henry's drawing ecclesiastical and civil laws together under his control provided the model followed to this day in North America. Thus, there has never been a separation of church and state with regard to sexual matters. There is a long tradition which, contrary to our legal philosophy generally, permits intrusion of government into the private sex lives of the people.

In the second place, Sixteenth Century England produced Puritanism. Most people are brought up on a rather steady diet of Puritan glorification. However, there is a saying that we'd all be much better off if, instead of the Pilgrims landing on Plymouth Rock, Plymouth Rock had landed on the Pilgrims. In their quest for the True way which would influence God favorably in their undertakings, the Puritans sought to return to the fundamental teachings of the Old Testament and the early Christian Church fathers, and it was their conviction that everyone should live by that revealed Truth. The Puritan tradition has been especially influential with regard to our official sex attitudes, laws, and language, and our taboos concerning nudity, "dirty" words, and pornography—that portion of obscenity which is concerned with sex. *

Typically, the Puritan mind of today sees nothing incongruous or unreasonable about attributing the "decay of public morals" almost exclusively to such things as sexual and other permissiveness, nudity, live or pictorial, genitals on doll babies, "dirty" words especially in print, breast feeding where it might be "seen," or even in the unclothed genitals of animals. (A few years

* "Obscenity" is the broader term meaning "that which may not be portrayed upon the stage," that is, in public. In other words, that which offends you or the governing body may be defined obscene. "Pornography" means depictions of whores in pictures or writing, or more loosely, frank depictions of sexual activity. We tend to define sexual depictions obscene as well as pornographic, and try to protect the young from it. The French do not define sexual depictions obscene, but they attempt to protect their young from depictions of violence (*e.g.,* warfare) which they define obscene.

ago a man received thousands of dollars in contributions when he announced a campaign in the United States to pass laws which would require the covering of the genitals of all animals which might be seen by the public. He was joking but his supporters were not.) And typically, too, the Puritan mind of today as of yesteryear is prepared to persecute without mercy any such threats to public morality, which is to say violation of revealed Truth. As we shall see in the chapter on sex laws, the Puritan sex laws are indeed punitive and thousands of people are in jail for long terms for violating them. Apprehension concerning the quite viable Puritan spirit is what has led some persons to anticipate strong reactionary movements against sex education and to warn that those who believe in an enlightened sex education must act now or run the risk of losing the opportunity for years to come. Californians were warned in advance.

It must be admitted that the Puritan mind is consistent. The enemy, sex and the flesh, is clearly identified and attacked so as to protect society from temptations of thought and deed. And who are the Puritans among us? Officially and in our dealings with the young we continue to wear the mask of a Puritan society—as we wallow most inconsistently in verbal and pictorial incitements to sex. The most remarkable thing about the Greek god Janus was that he was unaware that he had two faces which looked in opposite directions.

We are also especially puritanical with regard to the sexuality of handicapped persons (especially perhaps mentally retarded; see Johnson, 1967 and 1969), the elderly (see Lief, 1971 and Rubin, 1965), and animals. In *Opus 21*, Philip Wylie (1949, p. 92) has a fine discussion of animal sexuality in which he has one person point out that dog owners impose upon their animals their own Puritan sex ethic; whereas if they are left alone, pups and even adult dogs do all of the things that in people would be called "sinful, immoral and perverse."

Second person: "They do not."
First person: "Perhaps yours didn't. Perhaps whenever you saw in your pups a symptom of any sort of sex activity—you yelled at them. Pulled them apart. Swatted them with a switch . . ."
Second person: "I never used a thing but rolled newspaper!"

It has been our intent, here, to outline the basic theme of the Judeo-Christian sexual tradition and to suggest something of its progress from its source into the present day. We have seen what every healthy person has discovered personally in the course of his or her own life, namely that human interest in sex is irrepressible and demands some kind of expression, direct and open if possible in both behavior and art, indirect and covert if necessary. This is likely to remain the situation until such time, as Orwell suggested, as neurologists develop ways of eliminating the orgasm. Since sex and religion have been fundamentally intertwined throughout history, it does not seem possible that any religion could have survived which denied at least the symbolic representation of sex. As we have seen, our own major religions have made the necessary concessions; and even today it is not an uncommon sight to see ministers elaborating upon sin, the matter of being born in sin and the avoidance of sin—as they stand before the altars covered with phallic symbols, all unrecognized but some very thinly disguised (see especially Raphaelian, 1957). And at the verbal level: in the marriage service we may hear "With my body I thee worship." Huxley has written "Worshipping with the body—that's the genuine phallicism. If you imagine it has anything to do with the unimpassioned civilized promiscuity of our advanced young people, you're very much mistaken indeed."

(1928, p. 127). Huxley may well have been correct at that time, but we note what may be considered an increase in genuine phallicism of some young people these days.

In hymns, we sing such things as:

> And He walks with me and He talks with me
> And He tells me I am His own. And the joy we share
> As we tarry there, none other has ever known.

The language of sex and religion are often undeniably interchangeable. (For numerous additional examples, see any Baptist hymn book.) Thus, the question is, of course, not whether there will be sexual expression in the future, but what forms this expression might best take. *This is the fundamental problem of all sex education.*

In all such considerations, it is important to bear in mind that the past is still very much with us. It affects our attitudes toward such things as our sex, our "maleness" or "femaleness," and our bodies and their functions; and it affects our sexual behavior, our familial relationships, our child rearing, our notions of right and wrong, our laws, our education, the dynamics of our mental functioning, our language, and our health. But since our own way of looking at this entire matter is the only one that we know, we are inclined to assume that our way is the natural way—obviously the natural way for human beings—in spite of the fact that "our way" has sometimes amounted to our carrying on a campaign of psychological warfare against ourselves. Thus it is that we need some awareness of how our way came about if we are to understand our dilemma and something of the circumstances responsible for it. Perhaps then we can hope to restructure the situation; to evolve a more realistic kind of sex education, more realistic sex laws and sexual morality, and a more workable and humane pattern of sexual behavior. To emphasize that we have a long way to go before we can hope to achieve a healthy pattern of sexual behavior within a humanistic morality and humane framework of laws, it seems to me that a quotation from Taylor's book, *Sex in History*, makes a particularly suitable conclusion to this discussion.

If I have done my work properly, it will now be clear to the reader how muddled and arbitrary our system of sexual morality is. In fact, it is not in any consistent ethical sense a morality at all. It is essentially a hodge-podge of attitudes derived from the past, upon which is erected a shaky and inconsistent system of laws and social prohibitions. Some of these fragments from the past date from before the introduction of Christianity; some are magical in origin, others are based on faulty sciences; yet others have grown up by reinterpretation of old laws, originally passed with quite a different purpose (1954, pp. 295-96).

REFERENCES

Bebel, A.: Woman Under Socialism. New York, New York Labor News Press, 1904.

Choisy, M.: Psychoanalysis of The Prostitute. New York, Pyramid Books, 1962.

Cole, W. G.: Sex and Love in The Bible. New York, Association Press, 1959.

De Beauvoir, S.: The Second Sex. New York, Alfred Knopf, 1953.

Dingwall, E. J.: The Girdle of Chastity. New York, The MaCaulay Co., 1931.

Eisler, R.: Man Into Wolf (An Anthropological Interpretation of Sadism, Masochism, and Lycanthropy). London, Spring Books, 1950.

Fuller, B.: Goddesses of the twenty-first century. Saturday Review, *51*:12-14 and 45-46, March 2, 1968

Ginsburg, R.: An Unhurried View of Erotica. New York, Helmsman Press, 1958.

Goldberg, B. Z.: The Sacred Fire (The Story of Sex in Religion). New York, University Books, 1958.

Henriques, F.: Love in Action. New York, E. P. Dutton, 1960.

Henry, G. W.: All the Sexes. New York, Rinehart, 1955.

Huxley, A.: Point Counter Point. New York, Avon Books (Originally Harper), 1928.

Johnson, W. R.: Hypnotic analysis of the recognition of a sex symbol. Journal of Sex Research, 3:229-31, August, 1967.

6

Johnson, W. R.: Sex education and the mentally retarded. Journal of Sex Research, 5:179-85, August, 1969.

Johnson, W. R.: Sex education of mentally retarded children. Sexology, 33:410-14, January, 1967.

Knight, R. P., and Wright, T.: Sexual Symbolism (A History of Phallic Worship). New York, The Julian Press, 1957.

Lead among the Romans. Time, 88:79, September 23, 1966.

Lewinsohn, R.: A History of Sexual Customs. New York, Harper, 1958.

Lief, H. I.: Interview: sex in older people. Sexual Behavior, 1: 72-74, October, 1971.

Loth, D.: The Erotic in Literature. New York, Julian Messner, Inc., 1961.

Mannix, D. P.: The Hell Fire Club. New York, Ballantine Books, 1959.

Ovid: The Art of Love. (Translated by Rolfe Humphries.) Bloomington, Indiana University Press, 1957.

Pacion, S. J.: Gandhi's struggle with sexuality. Medical Aspects of Human Sexuality, January, 1971.

Partridge, B.: A History of Orgies. New York, Bonanza Books, 1960.

Raphaelian, H. M.: Signs of Life. New York, Anatol Swas Publ., 1957.

Rubin, I.: Sexual Life after Sixty. New York, Basic Books, Inc., 1965.

Russell, B.: Human Society in Ethics and Politics. New York, Simon and Schuster, 1955.

Scott, G. R.: Curious Customs of Sex and Marriage. London, Torchstream Books, 1953.

Scott, G. R.: Phallic Worship. Westport, Conn., Mental Health Press, 1956.

Seltman, C.: Women in Antiquity. New York, St. Martin's Press, 1955.

Smith, H. W.: Man and His Gods. Boston, Little, Brown and Co., 1953.

Taylor, G. R.: Sex in History. New York, Vanguard Press, 1954.

Thomas, P.: Kama Kalpa or The Hindu Ritual of Love. Bombay, India, D. B. Taraporevala Sons & Co., 1959. (Obtainable from Marlboro Book Co., N. Y.)

Walton, A. H.: Aphrodisiacs: from Legend to Prescription. Westport, Conn., Associated Book Sellers, 1958.

Wylie, P.: Opus 21. New York, Rinehart and Company, Inc., 1949.

5

The Language Barrier

A Note on Language as a Factor in Sexual Behavior and Sex Education

It is a sobering if not startling experience to become even partially aware of the extent to which the criteria for evaluating sexual behavior today are under the control of ancient prescriptions.

In the four chapters that follow, we have undertaken to expand upon some of the implications of our historical tradition for modern circumstances. This chapter has to do with language not only as a vehicle of thought, but also as a major conditioner of thought, influencing sexual attitudes and practices. Although nonverbal communication is of great importance historically and in interpersonal relationships, verbal language is here focused upon as being perhaps the major means whereby the past is conveyed into the present and adults communicate with each other. The next chapter, "There's a Law Against It! A Note on Sex and the Law," is concerned with directing attention to some of the problems associated with attempting to live by the rules of a long-gone game. In the third note, "The Three Faces of the Clergy," sexual morality is viewed in the light of its history and transformation. The final note, "The Polar Icecap of Human Relations: A Note on Modern Marriage," represents an effort to examine some of the problems that beset an old "institution" in modern times.

In recent years, there has been a growing awareness of the need to consider language an important dimension of human health and health education—that is, a dimension comparable in significance to physiology, microbiology, sociology, psychiatry, and so on (Johnson and Belzer, 1962; Johnson, 1968, 1969). Decades ago, a neuropsychiatrist (Campbell, 1937) argued that physiological studies of animals have little or no relevance to human beings because such studies cannot take into account the life-long conditioning role of language in human physiological processes. In any event, language is an impressively critical factor in the sex education aspect of the broad field of health education. Let us examine, briefly, its acute and chronic roles in impeding communication about sex and in perpetuating highly negative and inappropriate sexual attitudes and practices. (For other perspectives, see Canan, 1968; Haslam, 1967; Hayakawa, 1968; and Kirkendall, 1966, 1968.)

To begin with, there is the obvious problem that language concerning sex reflects and helps greatly to maintain the peculiar Judeo-Christian-Puritan attitude toward sex. Thus, our profoundly conflicting sex attitudes are manifested in a fascination with and rejection of the language of sex. Verbal and nonverbal language then feed back like mirror reflecting mirror, perpetuating the curiously pejorative or depreciatory worship of sex. In what other area is language such a barrier to thought, communication, research, and education? How does one teach a subject, the language of which is forbidden or offensive—even, oftentimes, when confined to the sterile, white, medical terminology of a long-dead language, Latin? Among other things, the teacher or counselor must reckon with the problem of having to com-

municate with people by means of words that are emotionally charged—very possibly for the teacher or counselor as well as for his audience. We need pause to consider that these sex-related words are capable of giving
rise to measurable psychophysiological upset in varying
but marked degrees. Generally, *emotional upset lowers
the level of functioning intelligence.* The greater the
upset, the greater the drop in available thinking ability.
The individual therefore is likely to be less able to cope
with sex-related problems than with other problems of
concern to him for reasons of the emotionally charged
language, not to mention reasons of ignorance and irrational attitude.

To illustrate how language blends in with the other
factors that bar the way to realistic sex education, consider the relatively tame word "prurient." This is not
even a "dirty" word, but is associated darkly with "obscenity," as in "that which appeals to the prurient interest." One of us once asked an interdenominational group
of clergymen what they thought of having literature
that appeals to "prurient interest" available to young
people. Apparently all present thought this a very bad
thing and their feelings about it were noticeably strong.
They were then asked what the word "prurient" means,
and they were startled to realize that their strong feelings about the word could not be translated readily into
words. It was a negative verbal stimulus without intellectual content.

Our language has come to us out of the past and, like
a great conveyor belt, automatically brings the verbal
past to us by way of written and spoken words. So automatic is this process that we generally fail to notice it at
all and suppose that our feelings and behaviors concerning sex are somehow "natural" to mankind. Little do we
suspect the influence of this great conveyor belt of language in this whole business. When we do submit the

conveyor belt to historical scrutiny, what a shock it is to learn that our standards of "naturalness" as crystalized in our sex laws, attitude, and morality are, as we have noted earlier, creations of: (1) the ancient, struggling Jewish people of the Middle East who could not possibly have anticipated today's circumstances or needs; (2) the sex-obsessed, sex-hating, woman-hating early Christian church fathers; and (3) the Puritan tradition which began in the Sixteenth Century and has as one of its salient features an intensive effort to cleanse the language of sex. We are still diligently at work on this language purification problem.

Of course, there is a history behind the verbal attitudes of Canadian and American Anglos. In pre-Christian England, Anglo-Saxon language was used by rich and poor alike. With the appearance of Christendom on the British Isles, Latin became the language of the educated. Later, after the Norman conquest of England, French was used as the language of the courts and legal transactions. Thus, the minority in power used Latin and French, while the vulgate (the common people) used common (vulgar) English. People seem more or less to equate might with right. Our Anglo cultural ancestors who aspired to be mightier (more proper) strove to eliminate vulgarity from their language. Contemporary parents and teachers are wont to play the role of aspiring aristocrats, trying to ensure that the children with whom they are concerned develop into members of the proper class. (Older readers may recognize why we have called this "The Maggie and Jiggs Syndrome," with parents and teachers playing Maggie roles and the kids trying their best to retain their souls as Jiggs.)

Various authors have discussed the problem of our "dirty, four-letter" words associated with sex and other bodily functions. Unlike their respectable but foreign counterparts, these were standard English words of daily use a very few centuries ago. Edward Saragin (1962) and others (Ellis, 1960; MacDougald, 1961) have demonstrated that our attitude toward these words represents a gross hypocrisy which the Puritan tradition makes seem "natural," but which deprives us of some extremely useful, direct, and universally understood means of communication. Incidentally, modern circumstances are forcing the issue of word usage in some rather surprising, and disconcerting, ways. Public health nurses in our classes tell us that their effectiveness on the job is not infrequently seriously hampered by their inability to employ such words as "piss." Large numbers of the people with whom they work know no other word for this universally understood but publicly unutterable onomatopoeia-ism. This is also an unpublicized but grave problem in the schools of many cities. Routine, standard words to many pupils are sharply, even painfully offensive to their teachers. The pupils, well chastised, learn a proper word substitute—and they are ridiculed or worse at home. We may recall, in this general connection, that the authorities at Berkeley did not feel free to bring the full weight of the law upon the protesting students until certain impolite words were paraded about on a placard, thus establishing by association the ill-repute of the entire effort.

We would not like to defend the proposition that humanity knows any less about male bovine excrement because the popular and more parsimonious term for it is unacceptable in polite conversation. (An interesting thing is occurring these days. It seems that more and more people are feeling free to use the term "bullshit," but fewer and fewer have even seen any!) However, there is a whole list of sex-related behaviors and conditions whose dark labels contribute to our ignorance and frequent irrationality, for example, the so-called perversions. The ineffable deity of the ancient Jews had very strict rules about people being fruitful and about wastage of the male's seed. The attitude thereby engendered, plus the limited usability of the dark verbal labels involved, do make us surprisingly ignorant of and unable to think rationally about these behaviors. In fact, we remain hopelessly befuddled concerning them and continue to tolerate laws which belong in museums of preternatural history. Consider the matter of "sodomy" as a case in point. Everyone knows that by definition, sodomy is a very bad thing, deserving of rather harsh punishment. Unfortunately, there is no way of knowing what the word means when you hear that someone committed it—except that something sexual happened, probably other than vaginal coitus with the man on top. Similarly, one of the few accurate definitions of "prostitution" is that it is, of course, bad—and thereby inaccessible to objective scrutiny, and it is certainly not to be talked about in the classroom except as an item in a list of social pathologies.

The same kind of situation works a unique hardship with regard to control of the wonderfully named "venereal" or goddess-of-love diseases. For example, during and following World War I, neither the United States Army nor the public health authorities could make any progress in the control of syphilis because almost no one, including medical doctors, was willing to use the word. VD was recognized to be associated with coitus long before the respective bacteria were identified—which is to say that these diseases have traditionally been viewed as a punishment for sexual transgression. Thus, syphilis and gonorrhea are "dirty words" and most people still cannot view them merely as dangerous communicable diseases. Only when it gradually became possible to use such words and thereby to educate people on the subject did progress on combating the diseases occur following World War II. Present day public health authorities report that the subject has again become taboo to a surprising extent, and that this is surely a factor in our current failure to reverse the upward trend of the disease. Typically, society demonstrates its ability to tolerate the problem, but not the language associated with it.

With regard to sex, among other things, people in our tradition have spent much of their time living in a make-believe world composed of words. Revelation of this fact in statistical terms was the great shocker of the Kinsey reports. For example, we attempt and pretend to adjust to a sex-centric world, which is simultaneously a profoundly sex-rejecting world. Moreover, we pretend to adjust to the nonsense that childhood is a period of nonsexuality and that after childhood nice people do not permit sex to "rear its ugly head," unless marriage occurs, after which people live happily ever after. We also pretend that older people are not sexual creatures. Like children, they are led to believe that their sexuality is a mistake, that they should "act their age" and be content to live in a word-world that is, as far as they are concerned, conveniently free of sex. This illusory word-world is more real than the "real" world to our official view and perhaps to most people including educators, it would seem.

It seems that one of the most pernicious effects of language is the barrier it helps to maintain between various groups of people in our society whose successful functioning together requires good communication. The American Indian tribes lived in relative isolation from each other so that language differences were not terribly important. The tribes we're talking about, our tribes, are rubbing shoulders every day, using the English language for the most part—and not communicating. The groups we're referring to include parents and children, teachers and pupils, and males and females. The barrier is erected in part by parents when they forbid the use of certain language by their children and require the use of certain "polite" language, particularly when speaking with adults but presumably at all times. Teachers and other adult authority figures continue this language control and supervision.* So far so good. But children soon learn that adults do not believe in or observe their own rules. It is all a big fake, a make believe, another Alice in Wonderland episode. They soon retaliate against this infringement upon their freedom of speech (and thought) by appearing to play the game as required while in secret and with other little villains they do what all readers of this book found a way to do at least once in a while: they curse, grovel in "dirty" words, write them, draw pictures about their content, and the like. In due course the retaliation continues. They become part of a sub-tribe of teenagers which among other things evolves its own baffling, irksome language which stakes out the territory of the ins and the outs.

It is interesting that students of adolescent psychology who really want to communicate with the young begin by learning and using naturally the language of the young—or of any other estranged group that interests them. Folk singer Pete Seeger summarized what anthropologists and linguists have known for a long time: "If you learn another human being's language, you can learn a little of his soul" (Haslam, 1967, p. 191). If we would communicate with children and the young, perhaps we must learn to penetrate the language barrier.

Consider also communication between the sexes. At least in mixed company, women are trained to use "po-

* A 35-mm. slide program, "Breaking the Language Barrier" (Teacher Training Aids, 27 Harvey Drive, Summit, New Jersey), may be helpful in breaking language barriers and in helping to desensitize people to slang and "vulgar" words.

lite" language and come by tremendous criticism if they curse. In fact, if a single woman does some discreet love making now and again, her reputation is likely to be less damaged than if she is indiscreet in her use of language. Still, a young woman made the following observation at a workshop. She had become close friends with a small group of fellow graduate students, male and female; and she and the other girls noted that when they relaxed and made appropriate use of "cussing" and "dirty" words as the males habitually did in order to express themselves as adequately as possible, communication between the sexes improved tremendously. She insisted that this was not a matter of the women "lowering themselves" or of "talking dirty to talk dirty," but rather a utilization of the vernacular of the day which females usually pretend not to use. This young woman's statement was at first upsetting to a number of those present, but in time most agreed that this was a small price to pay for improved communication between the sexes.

Some relatively recent developments may illustrate the difficulty of bringing language into harmony with current facts. The following observations may serve as examples.

It has been only little more than half a century that respectable college women could participate in sports. Consequently, it is not surprising that our language related to this female behavior has not yet developed adequately for effective communication. To be called a "female athlete" is not likely to be taken as a compliment. Traditionally, when a boy has played hard and aggressively, it been said that "he is playing like a man." When a girl plays well, hard, and aggressively—which is to say successfully—what can one say she is playing like? "A man"? Hardly. But then playing "like a woman" does not seem quite right either.

Every year a great deal of youthful behavior is controlled by the expression, "get married and have children"—even though the order of these events is often reversed. The cold fact of the matter is that marrying and the having of children have lost most of their historical functions. Marriage is, for growing numbers, a convenience rather than a near necessity, and modern circumstances have rendered children economically valueless and very possibly an unmitigated nuisance. Blue Cross and Social Security are much more reliable. However, we continue to think and talk of "marriage" and children as though these awesome changes were not taking place under our very noses.

We also continue to use the words "male" and "female" and "masculine" and "feminine," as though present day male and female roles were the same as they have been, traditionally. Just how is a growing boy supposed to act as opposed to how a girl is supposed to act? Just what are "masculine" as opposed to "feminine" behaviors that they should evince? We are not prepared to say, but many of the traditional criteria do not seem very applicable and the language of sex roles has yet to catch up.

The increased education of women along with increased encouragment for them to *think* has led to a variety of language confusions. For example, is it a compliment for a woman to be told that she "thinks like a man"? How would a man feel if he were told that he thinks like a woman? Due to the conveyor belt of language, we tend to have surprising difficulty recognizing that thought and language do not necessarily have a sex and that our concern is more likely to be with the *quality* of communication, its rationality, clarity, and so forth; and that this can come from a disciplined, objective mind regardless of the sex of its possessor.

An interesting contrast may be seen when we compare the conveyor belt word "wife" with the largely non-conveyor belt word "secretary." Whereas "wife," in consequence of being an ill-defined role today, is an ill-defined word, "secretary" has a definite meaning in relation to a specific function. There is little question in any experienced person's mind what is expected of a good secretary. But the well-trained and excellent secretary commonly steps daily from her well-structured, clearly defined office role and becomes lost in the ambiguities of the wife role when she goes home. She knows who and what she is when on the job.

Similarly, when a woman is a prostitute, she knows quite accurately what her role is and how she is to play it—just as her customer does not have to wonder about the nature of his visit. Like the competent secretary or dental hygienist, she is trained to do her job—just as females used to be trained effectively for "women's work." The wife, on the other hand, generally has no such clear-cut idea of her role in or out of bed. In fact, a sexually sophisticated wife or one who attempts to become such may be suspected or rejected by her husband for lacking in "virtue" or proper modesty.

When people marry, they generally are being wedded to a symbol delivered to them in considerable part on the great conveyor belt of language. The husband feels that he has a right to expect the wife to exhibit certain kitchen behavior, bathroom behavior, living room behavior, and garden behavior. This expectation is quite rigid, and although it is inevitably violated in actual practice—which is to say in real life—its violation exacts its cost in suffering on the part of both male and female. For both accept the same symbol and really expect about the same behavior of "a wife." The wife is often more disillusioned than her husband by her own failure to come pretwisted to the dimensions of what she considers the wife symbol to be. This is not a happy situation either, since the symbol-ideal as commonly conceived, is all but impossible to achieve today. The wife, too, marries a symbol constructed of words—the dominant, aggressive, achieving, mature, providing, understanding, inexhaustibly-sexual-but-out-of-the-home-infallibly-restrained, masculine male. (There's a nice trick for anyone. Can you define "masculine" in a way that is appropriate today rather than to Wyatt Earp's or King Solomon's day?)

Of course, the husband expects certain masculine behavior of himself, because the conveyor belt sets his word-structured, self criteria too, and he is naturally profoundly undermined by his almost inevitable failure to "measure up" to the symbol. It seems of little importance that few besides professional athletes and actors—viewed from a distance—do measure up.

The language associated with rape provides an excellent example of how words can influence behavior and health. Some girls are severely emotionally upset for extended periods following rape. Others are not, even though the circumstances and physical injury of both groups are comparable. What makes the difference? It is a well-known fact that what is *said* about rape in the presence of the girls before and after it happens is what makes the difference. If a girl has grown up hearing rape described in catastrophic terms, and if after being raped people (and she herself) *talk* about what a terrible thing has happened, how she will never be the same, is shamed for ever, will not be able to marry, and the like, there is a very good chance that she will become emotionally upset to the extent of requiring psychiatric help for a considerable period of time. If, on the other hand, rape has not been talked about in these extreme, unrealistic terms in the home, and if it is treated as an unfortunate experience, perhaps on a par with being hurt in an automobile accident, the girl has to deal only with the actual physical injury and not with emotional trauma built into the *word* rape. Now of course this example is not to justify rape or to underestimate possible injury, but to illustrate how parents and others can profoundly alter, worsen, and complicate the meaning of sexual experiences by the way in which they choose to talk about them in the presence of the young. It should be noted also that whether or not girls are seriously emotionally upset by "molestation," by being confronted by exhibitionists, or being seen by peeping Toms depends largely upon how attitudes and expectations are molded by language. Some girls are profoundly shaken by an exhibitionist's suddenly presenting his genitals in a public place. Others laugh about the same experience.

A final point is that sex education is complicated by the fact that there is a conspicuous lack of basic information concerning its broad subject matter. This would not be so bad, especially now that research on sex is becoming socially acceptable and progress is being made, were it not for the fact that numerous widely known and used words create an illusion that when we use them we know what we are talking about, or that others know what we are talking about. We have reference here to such words as promiscuous, obscenity, precocious, homosexuality, impotency, frigidity, masturbation, masculinity, femininity, sodomy, sin and, of course, love. Were it not such a travesty of communication, it would be amusing to hear a class composed of advanced undergraduate and graduate students discuss, for example, "promiscuity"—only to find that when forced to a definition they discover that the word has many meanings to them. Using the same word merely makes them think they are talking about the same thing. Kirkendall (1959) has elaborated on this point, showing how being specific about the meaning of such words as intercourse and copulation can improve communication. About the only defense against this kind of confusion is to try to train students to start by admitting that promiscuity, homosexuality, love, and all the rest are *words*. They are words capable of any definition. We then attempt to see what the evidence permits us to say about them and reach some kind of agreement as to just what we intend to mean by them.

In this discussion we have examined briefly some of the ways in which language serves as an incredible, self-perpetuating, adaptation-thwarting barrier to useful and accurate communication and rationality concerning sex and sex-related matters. Our sexual ignorance, conflicting attitudes, and strange behaviors would seem to place us in the throes of a subtle, pervading, societal masochism. Perhaps we need look to our language behavior for some of our therapy.

REFERENCES

Campbell, D. G.: General semantics: implications of linguistic revision for theoretical and clinical neuropsychiatry. American Journal of Psychiatry, 93:789-807, January 1937.

Canan, S.: Talking about sex by not talking about sex. ETC: A Review of General Semantics, 25:154-162, June, 1968.

Ellis, A.: An impolite interview whith Albert Ellis. The Realist, May, 1960.

Haslam, G. W.: The language of the oil fields. ETC: A Review of General Semantics, 24:191-201, June, 1967.

Hayakawa, S. I.: Semantics and sexuality. ETC: A Review of General Semantics, 25:135-153, June, 1968.

Johnson, W. R.: Psycholinguistics: something new in health education. J. Amer. Assoc. for Health, Physical Education and Recreation, March, 1968.

Johnson, W. R.: Magic, morals and health. School Health Review, November, 1969.

Johnson, W. R., and Belzer, E.: Language and health. Journal of School Health, 32:134, April, 1962.

Kirkendall, L. A.: Semantics and sexual communication. ETC: A Review of General Semantics, 23:235-244, June, 1966.

Kirkendall, L. A.: Talk, non-talk and double talk about sex, ETC: A Review of General Semantics, 25:222-234, June, 1968.

MacDougald, D., Jr.: Language and sex. *In* the Encyclopedia of Sexual Behavior. Vol. II. Edited by A. Ellis and A. Abarbanel. New York, Hawthorne Books, 1961.

Sagarin, E.: The Anatomy of Dirty Words. New York, Lyle Stuart, 1962.

6

There's a Law Against It!

A Note on Sex and the Law

WE HAVE considered how the codes of sexual behavior of an ancient people became solidified into the remarkably enduring tradition of sexual morality and law within which we live today. The rules which the Jews formulated into laws and incorporated into their religion continue to be the principal ones whereby we judge our present sexual behavior: our own sexual behavior and that of others. We have also observed how King Henry VIII of England, in withdrawing the territory over which he reigned from the Church of Rome and setting himself up as not only the secular but also the clerical ruler of England, initiated a long process of incorporating church law into civil and criminal law—a process the results of which evidently have more or less been taken for granted until fairly recently.

The intent of this chapter on the law is (1) to illustrate the continuity of this powerful tradition from its ancient, tribal, Middle Eastern origin to the present which endeavors to abide by its prototype, and (2) to see how that tradition is working out today in terms of its legal aspects.

Kinsey has summarized our sexual-legal tradition as follows:

Jewish sex codes were brought over into Christian codes by the early adherents of the Church, including St. Paul, who had been raised in the Jewish tradition on matters of sex. The Catholic sex code is an almost precise continuation of the more ancient Jewish code. For centuries in Medieval Europe, the ecclesiastic law dominated on all questions of morals and subsequently became the basis for the English common law, the statute laws of England, and the laws of the various states of the United States. This accounts for the considerable conformity between the Talmudic and Catholic codes and the present statute law on sex (Kinsey and others, 1953, p. 483).

The Puritan fathers equated crime and sin and carried the spirit of the Judeo-Christian moral codes farther in their laws than the countries of Europe had. As Gore Vidal has pointed out:

When the Cromwells fell, the disgruntled Puritans left England for Holland. To put it baldly, they departed not because they were persecuted for their religious beliefs, but because they were forbidden to persecute others for *their* beliefs. Holland took them in, and promptly turned them out. Only North America was left. Here, as lords of the wilderness, they were free to create the sort of quasi-theocratic society they had dreamed of. Rigorously persecuting one another for religious heresies, witchcraft, sexual misbehavior . . . the Puritans made adultery and fornication criminal offenses even though no such laws existed in England, before or after Cromwell's reign (1965, p. 234).

And they set the pattern of legislation which North America was to follow. Legal reformers are still trying, with very modest success, to find ways of getting the government out of the business of trying to shepherd people in the paths of sexual "righteousness."

Many authors have pointed out serious problems associated with enforcing sex laws today that were designed in response to circumstances of a distant time and place. For example, G. W. Henry, a medical specialist, has written:

If the present laws in the United States against various sexual practices were enforced, the majority of the population would be classed as sex offenders . . . Our laws decree that all sexual activity, except vaginal coitus between husband and wife, and solitary masturbation in privacy, is illicit. This means that the single, the divorced, the widowed and the wives of husbands who are impotent, have no legitimate sex outlet except through involuntary or self-induced orgasms. Some of the more rigid religious codes would make sexual activity solely procreative. Opposed to this is the reality of illicit sexual activity in which the majority of the population have at some time engaged (1955, pp. 379-80).

Kinsey has made very much the same protest concerning both the unreasonableness and non-enforceability of the sex laws:

They are too completely out of accord with the realities of human behavior, and because they attempt too much in the way of social control . . . it is inconceivable that the present laws could be administered in any fashion that even remotely approaches systematic and complete enforcement (1953, p. 262).

The consequently capricious enforcement which these laws now receive offers an opportunity for mal-administration, for police and political graft, and for blackmail, which is regularly imposed both by underworld groups and the police themselves (Kinsey and others, 1953, p. 20).

The legal problem in the United States is vastly complicated by the fact that there are so many inconsistencies in the sex laws from state to state (see Tables 2 and 3). For example, it is possible for a man legally to be put to death in the state of Texas for having sexual intercourse with a female to whom he is not married who is under eighteen years of age, whereas in the state of Delaware, if the female is over seven years of age and consents the male has not committed a crime. (For a discussion of special problems associated with the psycholegal aspects of rape, see Caprio and Brenner, 1961.) Almost (but not quite) all states prohibit sexual relations with animals ("And if a man lie with a beast, he shall surely be put to death: and ye shall slay the beast." Leviticus, 20:15). Thus, acts which are punishable by as much as twenty years of imprisonment in some states are legal in neighboring regions. "Bestiality" is common among males in rural communities, and laws against it are invoked occasionally. However, virtually no females have been legally prosecuted for having sexual relations with animals, although such behavior certainly occurs (Kinsey and others, 1953, p. 508).

In Indiana and Wyoming, "heavy petting" with a girl under twenty-one years of age is "sodomy" and calls for a prison sentence of ten or more years. In New Jersey, "heavy petting" is lewdness or carnal indecency and can bring a penalty of three years in prison. In Michigan the penalty is five years. Ohio tolerates cunnilingus but punishes fellatio. In the state of Arizona the maximum penalty for fellatio and/or cunnilingus is five years in jail, and that for anal intercourse is twenty years. But if a couple in the "Four Corners Region"* who desire to engage in such sports merely step across the border from Arizona to Colorado, they may proceed without being outside the law.

Whereas adultery is apparently all right in ten states, it is punishable by a fine of $10 in Maryland, $1,000 in Texas, and by both a stiff fine and up to five years in jail in a number of other states. In most states, unmarried adults who engage voluntarily in sexual intercourse are committing the crime of fornication, and they can be fined $10 in Rhode Island or $500 in Texas, or they can be jailed for thirty days in North Dakota.

Penalties for homosexual acts are severe in most states, and in some they are as severe as those for serious

* The "Four Corners Region" of the United States refers to the region where New Mexico, Colorado, Utah, and Arizona meet.

Table 2. A Comparison of Minimum and Maximum Penalties for Certain Sex Offenses in Pennsylvania and Other States

Offense	Pennsylvania Penalty	Greatest Maximum Penalty in Other States	Least Maximum Penalty in Other States
(1)	(2)	(3)	(4)
1. Sodomy	Minimum: determined by sentencing judge, but may not exceed one-half statutory maximum. Maximum: 10 years and/or $5,000 fine or Under Barr-Walker Act: 1 day to life.	Life imprisonment (Colorado, Georgia, and Nevada)	Not a crime (New Hampshire and Vermont)
2. Rape	Minimum: determined by sentencing judge, but may not exceed one-half statutory maximum. Maximum: 15 years and/or $7,000 fine or Under Barr-Walker Act: 1 day to life.	Death (Alabama, Arkansas, Delaware, Florida, Georgia, Kentucky, Louisiana, Maryland, Mississippi, Missouri, Nevada,	5 years and/or fine (Rhode Island)

		North Carolina, Oklahoma, South Carolina, Tennessee, Texas, Virginia, & West Virginia)	Death when victim under 18 years (Texas)	If victim over 7 years of age and consents, not a crime (Delaware)
3.	Statutory Rape	Minimum: determined by sentencing judge, but may not exceed one-half statutory maximum. Maximum: 15 years and/or $7,000 fine.	Death when victim under 18 years (Texas)	If victim over 7 years of age and consents, not a crime (Delaware)
4.	Incest	Minimum: determined by sentencing judge, but may not exceed one-half statutory maximum. Maximum: 5 years and/or $2,000 fine or Under Barr-Walker Act: 1 day to life.	50 years (California, New Mexico)	3 years (Oregon); other than father-daughter, $500 and/or 12 months (Virginia)

Adapted from: *The Dangerous Sex Offender*. A Report of the Panel of Medical Advisors on Health and Welfare to the Joint State Government Commission. Harrisburg, General Assembly of the Commonwealth of Pennsylvania, 1963, pp. 22-23.

crimes of violence. Homosexual behavior is likely to involve mouth or anus, and is therefore penalized under sodomy statutes which may not include the word "homosexuality." As with masturbation, there is a long history behind our attitudes and laws concerning homosexuality, neither of which has extinguished either behavior at any level of society. Death is the penalty specified in the Bible: "And the Lord spake unto Moses, saying, If a man also lie with mankind, as he lieth with a woman, both of them have committed an abomination: they shall surely be put to death; their blood shall be upon them" (Leviticus 20:13).

Interestingly, there is apparently no comparable biblical statement regarding women. However, it is common knowledge that although there are large numbers of women homosexuals, almost none are ever arrested and fewer still convicted. In New York City, the Kinsey investigators found only three arrests of females on homosexual charges during a ten-year period and all of these cases were dismissed. Curiously, in that same period, there were tens of thousands of arrests and convictions of males on charges of this kind (Kinsey and others, 1953, p. 485). Various explanations in addition to the biblical one have been proposed to account for the discrepancy between the treatment of male versus female homosexuality. However, this is only one of many differences in the law as it applies to men versus women. Thus, generally speaking, prostitutes are punished and their customers are not. (The matter of sexual inequality before the law, which usually but not always works to the disadvantage of females, is an extremely important one. Although it is beyond the scope of our little book, serious students are referred to Kanowitz, 1969.)

Perusal of Table 3 will reveal more than discrepancies among states. If you reside in one of the United

States, examination will tell you something of the legal implications of various sexual acts where you live—as of 1972. Have there been changes in your state since this Table was prepared? How do you feel about the change or lack thereof?

Rather typically, when a man is convicted of making homosexual advances, he is institutionalized in a place where perhaps three-fourths of the inmates are active if not exclusive homosexuals. This could hardly be considered an ideal environment for discouraging the behavior. And thus a young man at the height of his sexual capacity and by no means a confirmed homosexual can be shut off for extended periods of time from all but homosexual contacts. Speaking at a meeting of the Society for the Scientific Study of Sex, a prominent lawyer described the common police practice of "entrapment," whereby pairs of plain clothes officers encourage men in such places as subway urinals to make what can be interpreted as a "homosexual advance." The arrest is then made, the hidden officer serving as witness to the advance.

Such enthusiasm for enforcing the law has sometimes reached the point where the violation is created so that an arrest may be made; and of course opportunities for "shaking the victim down" are obvious. Moreover, young hoodlums have utilized the law's position on homosexual acts to seek such contacts with males and then blackmail, assault and even murder them—and then escape all punishment themselves by pleading self-protection from "indecent sexual advances" (Kinsey and others, 1953, pp. 20-21). Military men and school boys have reported doing this kind of thing, knowing themselves safe from retaliation by the law and feeling the victim somehow deserving of most vicious treatment. However, although the biblical stance against homosexuality continues officially in almost all states,

Table 3. State Penalties for Consensual Sex Offenses

State	Adultery	Cohabitation	Fornication	Crimes Against Nature†	General Lewdness
Alabama	up to 6 months and/or $100 up	up to 6 months and/or $100 up		2-10 years (a, b, c, d)	up to 12 months and/or up to $500
Alaska	up to 3 months or up to $200	1 to 2 years and/or up to $500		1-10 years (b)	3-12 months or $50-$500
Arizona	up to 3 years	up to 3 years		1-5 years (a) 5-20 years (b, c)	1-5 years
Arkansas		$20-$100		1-21 years (a, b, c)	
California	up to 1 year and/or up to $1000			up to 15 years (a) not less than 1 year (b, c)	up to 6 months and/or up to $500
Colorado					
Connecticut	up to 12 months and/or up to $1000			up to 12 months and/or up to $1000 (c, d)	up to 6 months and /or up to $1000
Delaware	up to 1 year and/or up to $500			up to 3 years plus up to $1000 (a, b, c)	sentence at the court's discretion
District of Columbia	up to 1 year and/or up to $500		up to 6 months and/or up to $300		up to 90 days and up to $250
Florida	up to 12 months and/or up to $1000	up to 60 days and/or up to $500	up to 60 days and/or up to $500	up to 1 year (under common law) (a, b, c)	up to 60 days and/or up to $500
Georgia	up to 12 months and/or up to $1000		up to 12 months and/or up to $1000	1-20 years (a, b) 1-5 years (c)	up to 12 months and/or up to $1000

Hawaii*	(men) 2-12 months and/or $30-$100 (women) 2-4 months and/or $10-$30		1-3 months or $10-50	up to 20 years and up to $1000 (a, b, c)	up to 1 year and/or or up to $1000
Idaho	3 months-3 years and/or $100-$1000	6 months and/or $300	6 months and/or $300	not less than 5 years (a, b, c, d)	6 months and/or $300
Illinois	up to 1 year and/or up to $500	up to 6 months and/or up to $200	up to 6 months and/or up to $200		
Indiana	up to 6 months and/or up to $500	up to 6 months and/or up to $500		$100-$1000 (a, b, c) up to 2 to 14 years	$5-$100 up to 6 months
Iowa	up to 3 years or up to 1 year and up to $300	up to 6 months or up to $200		up to 10 years (a, b, c)	up to 6 months or up to $200
Kansas	up to 1 month and/or up to $500			up to 6 months and/or up to $1000 (a, b, c)	up to 6 months and /or up to $1000
Kentucky	$20-$50		$20-$50	2-5 years (a, b, c)	up to 1 year and/or up to $200
Louisiana				up to 5 years and/or up to $2000 (a, b, c)	up to 5 years and/or up to $1000
Maine	up to 5 years or up to $1000	up to 5 years or up to $300	up to 60 days plus up to $100	1-10 years (a, b, c, d)	up to 6 months and up to $25
Maryland	$10			up to 10 years and/or up to $1000 (a, c, d) 1-10 (b)	up to 60 days and/or up to $50
Massachusetts	up to 3 years or up to $500	up to 3 years or up to $300	up to 3 months or up to $30	up to 5 years or $100-$1000 (a) up to 20 years (b, c)	up to 3 years or up to $300

Table 3. State Penalties for Consensual Sex Offenses
(Continued)

State	Adultery	Cohabitation	Fornication	Crimes Against Nature†
Michigan	up to 4 years and/or up to $2000	up to 1 year or up to $500	up to 5 years or up to $2500	up to 5 years or up to $2500 (a, d) up to 15 years (b, c)	up to 1 year or up to $500
Minnesota	up to 1 year and/or up to $1000 (doesn't apply if female unmarried)		up to 90 days or up to $100	up to 1 year and/or up to $1000 (a, b) up to 90 days or up to $100 (c, d)	up to 90 days or up to $100
Mississippi	up to 6 months and up to $500	up to 6 months and up to $500		1-10 years (b, c)	up to 6 months or up to $500
Missouri	up to 1 year and/or up to $1000			not less than 2 years (a, b, c)	up to 1 year and/ or up to $1000
Montana		up to 6 months and/or up to $500		not less than 5 years (a, b, c)	
Nebraska	up to 1 year	up to 6 months and up to $100		up to 20 years (a, b, c)	up to 90 days or up to $100
Nevada				1-6 years (a, b, c)	up to 1 year and/ or up to $1000
New Hampshire	up to 1 year		up to 1 year or $50	up to 1 year (a, b, c, d)	up to 1 year and/or up to $200
New Jersey	up to 3 years and/or up to $1000		up to 6 months and/or up to $50	up to 20 years and/or up to $5000 (b, c)	up to 3 years and/ or up to $1000

State					
New Mexico				2-10 years and/or up to $5000 (a, b, c)	up to 6 months and/or up to $100
New York	up to 3 months and/or up to $500			up to 3 months and/or up to $500 (a, b). up to 1 year and/or up to $1000 (c, d)	
North Carolina		up to 6 months and/or up to $500		up to 10 years and/or any fine (a, b, c)	
North Dakota	1-3 years or up to 1 year and/or up to $500	30 days-1 year or $100-$500	up to 30 days and/or up to $100	up to 10 years (a, b, c, d)	1-5 years and/or up to $1000
Ohio		up to 3 months plus up to $200		1-20 years (a, b, c)	
Oklahoma	up to 5 years and/or up to $500			up to 10 years (a, b, c)	up to 5 years and/or up to $5000
Oregon					
Pennsylvania	up to 1 year and/or up to $500		up to $100	up to 10 years and up to $5000 (a, b, c)	up to 1 year and/or up to $500
Rhode Island	up to 1 year or up to $500		up to $10	7-20 years (a, b, c)	up to 1 year and/or up to $5000
South Carolina	6 to 12 months and/or $100-$500	6-12 months and/or $100-$500		5 years and/or not less than $500 (b, c)	sentence at the court's discretion
South Dakota	up to 5 years and/or up to $500			up to 10 years (a, b, c)	up to 1 year and/or up to $2000
Tennessee				5-15 years (a, b, c)	

Table 3. State Penalties for Consensual Sex Offenses
(Continued)

State	Adultery	Cohabitation	Fornication	Crimes Against Nature†	
Texas	$100-$1000	$50-$500	$50-$500	2-15 years (a, b, c)	$50-$200 and/or 1-6 months
Utah	up to 3 years	up to 5 years (polygamous co-habitation only)	up to 6 months or up to $100	up to 6 months and/or up to $299 (a, b) 3-20 years (c)	up to 6 months and/or up to $300
Vermont	up to 5 years and/or up to $1000			1-5 years	up to 5 years or up to $300
Virginia	$20-$100	$50-$500	$20-$100	1-3 years (a, b, c)	up to 1 year and/ or up to $1000
Washington	up to 2 years or up to $1000	up to 1 year and/ or up to $1000		up to 10 years (a, b, c, d)	up to 90 days or up to $250
West Virginia	not less than $20	up to 6 months and/or not less than $50	not less than $20	1-10 years (a, b, c)	up to 30 days and/ or not less than $50
Wisconsin	up to 3 years and/or up to $1000	up to 1 year and/or up to $500	up to 6 months and/or up to $200	up to 5 years and/or up to $500 (a, b, c)	up to 1 year and/or up to $500
Wyoming	up to 3 months plus up to $100	up to 3 months plus up to $100	up to 3 months and up to $100	up to 10 years (a, b, c)	

NOTE: In many states, the violations must be proved to be "open and notorious."

* Effective January 1, 1973, consensual sex between adults is legal under the revised Penal Code.

† Key: a. Oral intercourse (fellatio, cunnilingus) b. Anal intercourse c. Sex with animals d. Sex with the dead

From Rhodes, R.: Sex and sin in Sheboygan. *Playboy*, 19:188-89, August, 1972. Reproduced by permission.

174

a more humane, less persecutory, more accepting, "do your own thing" attitude has been growing in recent years.

One of the most remarkable developments in the history of American sex-related law was the passing of the so-called "Comstock laws" of 1873 which are concerned mainly with censorship. Anthony Comstock's mind was a kind of precipitate and concentrate of the Puritan tradition as it relates to sex. His intense and single-minded conviction and perseverance overwhelmed judges and legislators, and fired the wit of H. L. Mencken.

Comstock embodied some of the severer aspects of the Judeo-Christian-Puritan sex tradition. He was absolutely convinced of the necessity of his long-lasting assault upon the "obscene" in art and literature and his tightening and extending of previous censorship laws. To him obscenity was a "poison to soul and body, and anything remotely touching upon sex was to his mind obscene" (Broun and Leech, 1927, p. 265). Moreover, although ideas on this subject were changing in the period following the Civil War, Comstock continued to be convinced that masturbation caused idiocy, epilepsy, locomotor-ataxia (actually caused by syphilis), and other dire ailments. His fight and his laws were to save people, especially the young, from disease, death, and damnation. The obscene encouraged masturbation, among other things, and all the rest followed. Although he carried much of the fight alone, there was an army of supporters (including representatives of such groups as the Y.M.C.A.) behind him whose own super-egos, having been created by the same tradition, were of the same substance if not of the same vigor, militance, and self-assertiveness. Legislators often found themselves in the position of having to be for him so as not to appear to be on the side of vice and obscenity. At the trial of one man who had been brought to justice by Comstock for circulating obscene literature, the Assistant District Attorney began his remarks to the jury by saying: "Now gentlemen, this case is not entitled 'Anthony Comstock against D. M. Bennett' . . . it is the United States against D. M. Bennett, and the United States is one great society for the suppression of vice" (Broun and Leech, 1927, p. 89).

This whole matter of just which pornography* should be considered obscene, and under what circumstances pornographic and/or obscene material may be produced or possessed, has been and will continue to be a source of major legal and social controversy. Relatively recently, and somewhat off center stage, pornography has been used in educational and therapeutic contexts. Marriage counselors, psychotherapists, and so forth have used pornography to help some of their clients. A motion picture film entitled "Touching" has been made as an aid in the rehabilitation of persons suffering from paraplegia and quadraplegia. It shows a male paraplegic and his girl friend engaging in a variety of noncoital erotic activities. This film has been shown to many hundreds of regular university students in classes on human sexuality with entirely favorable feedback.

Both of us have used "stag films" in our university classes to help attain various educational objectives. In one class a student investigated the availability of pornographic material in the city of his residence. In presenting a report of his project to the class, he exhibited two "stag films." The nature of the forthcoming presentation was announced ahead of time, so that anyone who wished could skip that meeting. Student evaluations included such remarks as:

* Remember, "pornography" refers to erotic portrayal (whore's writing or other depictions) and "obscene" refers to what may not be exhibited in public.

Surprisingly enough, my reactions to the pornography were not very strong. I had previously been exposed to pictures and films and they left me with *no* feelings. They were just there . . . I was upset and felt sympathetic toward Peter (the student presenting the project), when a lot of people were talking about not attending his class. To me, this was a sign of immaturity and I was surprised when the ones that were doing all the talking came to that class—late.

On March 16 the project on pornography was given. The week previous to this, when I heard that we were going to have a stag movie, I thought it was neat because I had never seen one. However, as the week progressed I heard comments from the other girls in the class that they didn't think they would go because of a fear of being grossed out. Then I started to become apprehensive, although I still planned to see it. However, when I viewed the first stag movie, my first reaction was that it was no different than some scenes in movies at the theatre. I found the stag movies became boring very quickly. The second film became boring also, and I had no feeling of embarrassment watching it. The thing which really got to me about the movies was the insensitivity of the act which was expressed, especially where one would be sitting on the sidelines watching.

The presentation on pornography was socially educative for me, in that as a female I was banned from seeing the much talked-about, shocking "stag movies." Now I have seen one. I was not repulsed, I was amused by the photography, the actors, and the male psychology behind the plotless enactments. The lesbian activities were the only parts that bothered me. They were dull and monotonous. Other girls in the room were repulsed by the movies, but I was more horrified and more offended by the movies shown a week or so later on illegal abortion.

(Interestingly, although some students have reported that *others* in their class had experienced strong negative feelings, no one has reported that this was true of himself/herself.)

In 1972, the senior author of this book presented a talk at a large national convention. The subject was, "Can pornography be educational?" The slides used to illustrate the talk were very specific (genital play, masturbation, coital positions), but were shown to illustrate

how such material may shed light upon artistic, historical, medical, and scientific matters of obvious educational value to at least some groups. If there was negative audience response, it was not expressed then or
later—and the audience included the officer in charge
of the city's vice squad.

Because of a national Criminal Code, people in Canada have an easier time ascertaining just what sexual
activities could get them into trouble with the law than
do their south-of-the-border neighbors. A summariza-
tion of the provisions of that Criminal Code is presented in Table 4. Even in Canada, however, the tech-
nicalities of the law are complex enough to confuse
most mortal minds. For example, although "acts of gross
indecency" are legal when engaged in between two
consenting adults in private, some people would be surprised to learn that if more than two persons are present
when a "grossly indecent act" is performed, the perform-
ers were not in private. *Mélange* lovers beware!

Canadian law relative to a few sexual topics has undergone some fairly recent revisions. For example,
homosexual relations between *two* consenting adults
in a private location are no longer legally prohibited.
Efforts to enforce the laws against the kinds of sexual
activities in which homosexuals engage have led to
such grave problems and corruption that England and
a few of the United States have undergone similar legal
reformations.

In 1969 the dissemination of contraceptive information and supplies became legal in Canada for the first
time. Prior to this, such information and supplies were
actually widely available, as the law was "honored in
the breach."

There is unquestionably a mounting wave of opinion
in the United States and Canada which favors a revamp-
ing of the current sex laws. The following is expressive

Table 4. Sexual Offenses in Canada under the Criminal
Code and the Punishment Therefor
(*Tremeear's Annotated Criminal Code*, 1971)

Offense	Section	Type of Offense*	Punishment (Maximum)
Rape	143 & 144	Indictable	Imprisonment for life and whipping
Sexual intercourse with female under 14	145(1)	"	"
Incest	150(2)	"	Male—14 years and whipping
Buggery or Bestiality (does not apply to acts in private between husband and wife or any two consenting persons over 21 years of age)	155 & 158	"	14 years
Parent or guardian procuring defilement of female under 14	166	"	"
Attempted rape	145	"	10 years and whipping
Assault by male on male with intent to commit buggery	156	"	"
Indecent assault by male on male	156	"	"

Table 4. Sexual Offenses in Canada under the Criminal Code and the Punishment Therefor (*Continued*)
(*Tremeear's Annotated Criminal Code*, 1971)

Offense	Section	Type of Offense*	Punishment (Maximum)
Abducting of female with intent	248	"	10 years
Procuring, pimping, etc.	195(1)	"	"
Indecent assault on female	149(1)	"	5 years and whipping
Sexual intercourse with female of previously chaste character 14 or more and under 16	146(1)	"	5 years
Sexual intercourse with feeble-minded, insane, idiot, imbecile	148	"	"
Gross acts of indecency (does not apply to acts in private between husband and wife or any two consenting persons over 21 years of age)	157 & 158	"	"
Parent or guardian procuring defilement of female 14 or more	166	"	"
Householder permitting defilement of female under 18	167	"	"

Conspiracy to defile	408(1)(c)	"	2 years
Seduction of female between 16 and 18	151	"	"
Seduction under promise of marriage of unmarried female under 21 of previously chaste character	152	"	"
Sexual intercourse with step-daughter or female ward	153(1)	"	"
Sexual intercourse with female employee under 21 of previously chaste character	153(1)	"	..
Seduction of female passengers on vessels	154	"	"
Corrupting children	168	"	"
Making, publishing, distributing, etc. obscene sexual matter, unless service to public good is established	159 & 165	Indictable or Summary	"
Immoral theatrical performance	163 & 165	Indictable or Summary	"
Indecent acts	169	Summary	6 months or fine of not more than $500.00 or both (s. 722)

Table 4. Sexual Offenses in Canada under the Criminal Code and the Punishment Therefor (*Continued*)
(*Tremeear's Annotated Criminal Code*, 1971)

Offense	Section	Type of Offense*	Punishment (Maximum)
Being clothed (or unclothed) so as to offend public decency or order	170 (1 & 2)	"	"
Prostitute or night walker	175[(1) (c) & (2)]	"	"
Sexual offenders loitering near schools, etc.	175[(1) (c) & (2)]	"	"
Keeping, inhabiting, being present in, etc. a "common bawdy-house"	193	"	"
Transporting person to bawdy-house	194	"	"

* The Canadian "indictable offense" is roughly equivalent to a "felony" in the United States. An offense punishable as a "summary conviction" is similar to a "misdemeanor" (although in the United States there is oftentimes no clear-cut distinction in severity of punishment between felony and misdemeanor).

of this view, which was given great impetus by such works as the Kinsey reports.

As sex moves out of the realm of a taboo and is accepted as a legitimate subject for scientific investigation, we may begin to ascertain on the basis of something other than prejudice what is "good" or "bad" sexual behavior from the social point of view. Until our criminal laws on the subject of sex are redrafted not only in the light of what we think ought to be, but also in terms of what is and what can be, we shall no doubt remain what we are now—a nation the overwhelming majority of whose citizens are at least technically sex criminals (Kinsey and others, 1953, p. 226).

However, rules once formulated and used tend to acquire a strength and inertia which are highly resistive to change. Everyone who has observed the battles of athletic coaches that have raged over even minor changes in the rules of their sports cannot but have been impressed by this phenomenon of durability. How much more difficult to change laws, especially sex laws, the questioning of which can so readily be interpreted as immoral or even irreligious and worthy only of attack. Ask legislators who have introduced bills to abolish existing sodomy laws!

Still, widespread feeling of a need for reform has been growing as public awareness of the pointless legal tangle that it is caught up in has gradually grown. Perhaps there will presently be test cases which will establish that "sin," where it does not disturb the public order, is not the concern of the state. This conception is implicit in our idea of the "free society." More likely, the coming generations of legislators will fail to comprehend the reticence of their immediate predecessors on these matters. Just a few years ago, we imagined that the only way significant legal reform in this area would occur would be for the judiciary to declare specific laws unconstitutional. We could not envision politicians standing for election on platforms that included, even by implication, the repeal of anti-cunnilingus or anti-fellatio laws. But as we move into the "Age of Aquarius," this does not seem to us an unlikely prospect at all. But not tomorrow!

REFERENCES

Broun, H., and Leech, M.: Anthony Comstock. New York, The Literary Guild, 1927.

Caprio, F. S., and Brenner, D. R.: Sexual Behavior: Psycho-Legal Aspects. New York, The Citadel Press, 1961.

Henry, G. W.: All the Sexes. New York, Rinehart, 1955.

Kanowitz, L.: Women and the Law: The Unfinished Revolution. Albuquerque, University of New Mexico Press, 1969.

Kinsey, A. D., Pomeroy, W. B., Martin, C. E., and Gebhard, P. H.: Sexual Behavior in the Human Female. Philadelphia, W. B. Saunders Co., 1953.

Rhodes, R.: Sex and sin in Sheboygan. Playboy, 19:129-30, 186-90, August, 1972.

The Dangerous Sex Offender. Harrisburg, General Assembly of the Commonwealth of Pennsylvania, 1963.

Tremeear's Annotated Criminal Code. 6th Ed. Toronto, The Carswell Company Limited, 1971.

Vidal, G.: The City and the Pillar Revisited. New York, E. P. Dutton and Co., Inc., 1965.

7

Three Faces of the Clergy— and of Society

A Note on Sexual Morality

A MINISTER participating in a recent sex education gathering commented that students no longer go to clergymen for counseling, and that if clergymen want to get involved in student affairs and problems they must go to the students. He went on to say that modern circumstances have forced the clergy out of the pulpit and into the world—"and we have found it a very sexual world indeed!" He and his colleagues were impressed that being in the midst of the game is quite different from calling the plays from the sidelines.

Clergymen—the professional "moralists" of our society —have undoubtedly become increasingly involved in human affairs including those associated with sex. They, like most socially concerned persons, are enormously preoccupied with the question of sexual morality, for by and large the pat answers of the past just do not seem to be *the* answers any more. What are the answers? What from the perspective of the middle of the game (or of the battlefield) does the clergy have to say about moral sexual behavior?

In the course of our many dealings with clergymen of

various denominations and faiths, it has occurred to us
that with regard to views on sexual morality they provide a thumbnail sketch of the diversity of view *of the
society at large.* Unlike the situation in the past when the
discrepancy between supposed-to-be behavior and actual behavior usually went unnoticed except among the
high and the low of society and *a* "sexual morality" ruled
supreme, today is something else. In spite of what statements of public officials, school authorities, and the laws
might lead one to believe, in point of fact, our society
no longer has *a* morality and people can no longer refer
complacently to "what society accepts," as though there
were some agreed-upon standard of acceptability. Nor
can they go around branding things "immoral" just because they used to be.

Our society does not have *a* rulebook of morality that
is undergoing change. It has three rulebooks, at least
two of which are undergoing change. Just as each face
of the clergy wears an expression of more or less confident virtue or at least an expression of questing after the
Truth, society's three faces represent persons who are
sure that their view is most reasonable and "moral." It is
most important to bear in mind *the conviction of right-
ness* of each group. In brief, it is as though three very
different Indian tribes were to camp together, call themselves one tribe—but cling to their separate very different customs and taboos while being confident that: "of
course the whole tribe does things our way and thinks
our way and condemns the things we condemn."

(It is noteworthy that the clergy is not being differ-
entiated here on the basis of the particular church group
involved, but on the basis of the conviction of the individual clergyman. True, certain groups such as the
Quakers, have come forward with something resembling
position statements on the subject of sexual morality.
However, by and large a liberal Baptist more closely

resembles a liberal Catholic, Unitarian, or Jew than he or she does a traditionalist Baptist.)

What are the three faces of the clergy that would seem to provide a model of the major faces of our society as a whole concerning sexual morality? At one extreme there is a relatively small group of *traditionalists* who believe that the rules laid down by the Old Testament Jews and the early Christian Church fathers are and always will be the only true rules, and their observance represents sexual morality.

At the other extreme is a relatively small group of clergymen whom we call the *liberal humanists*. They believe that these rules inherited from the past have little or no relevance to the present day. This group takes a more or less anthropological view of morality, pointing out that the words "morality" (ideal behavior) and "mores" (actual behavior) derive from the Latin for "customs"—which is to say that if one considers fifty different cultures he or she will find fifty different sets of customs, mores, and moral codes. To the liberal humanists, our official morality is derived from just one more cultural tradition and is no more sacred or morally "right" in an absolute sense than are the large numbers of others. They believe that "sexual morality" depends upon the particular circumstances and the meaning that the particular sexual behavior has for the persons involved and other members of the society.

The third, the middle group of clergymen, is quite large. It represents the vast majority we have known. Those in this group believe in and are loyal to most of the traditional rules of their church, but they tend to deny the sex-sin association or at least to de-emphasize or minimize it. In general, they believe in bending the old rules here and there in the interests of human happiness and justice if they believe that no individual or social harm will come of doing so. For example, they are

willing to take a new look at masturbation and homosexual and conclude that these are not sins after all. They
are more likely to view such behaviors as symptoms of
adjustment problems. Individuals in this large middle
group tend to feel obligated to at least try to compromise
traditional views with modern scientific psychological
and sociological developments. We call them the *neo-
traditionalists.*

When the traditionalists hear the liberal humanists
express their views about sexual morality they tend to
be quite sure that they are joking. Fellow clergymen
could not possibly hold such outlandish and, by definition, "immoral" views. On the other hand, to the traditionalists, the neotraditionalists make some sense in that
they agree to the basic validity of the Judeo-Christian-
Puritan rules and regulations. They just let themselves
be swayed by popular pressures, thereby betraying a
certain lack of fiber and determination to hold the line,
and a tendency toward a weak-kneed form of moral
relativism. But at least they're in the same ball game.

For their part, the liberal humanists tend to become
embarrassed when they hear their traditionalist colleagues discuss sexual morality. They cannot believe
that "thinkers" of today can be admitting to such outdated views. To them, the ancient Jewish mythology is
of a piece with that of the other mythologies, and to
adhere to it is similar to arguing for a return to the veri-
ties of the ancient Greek or Egyptian mythologies.

The issue of premarital sexual intercourse provides
a good example of the difference in moral positions of
the *traditionalist, neotraditionalist,* and *liberal humanist.*

To the traditionalists, there is simply no argument.
Coitus out of marriage is bad, sinful and properly illegal.

To neotraditionalists, coitus out of marriage is highly
suspect, dangerous, guilt-producing, and on the whole
they take a dim view of it. But under certain conditions,

especially within well-established engagements and more especially when marriage must be postponed for various urgent reasons, they cannot see too much harm or too much to condemn. Sex relations before marriage can, conceivably, help in preparation for marriage under certain conditions. However, just what those conditions are best determined *post facto.*

To liberal humanists, traditional views of premarital sexual intercourse are not useful in dealing with the dynamics of actual situations. They are like the rules of an unplayed or forgotten game which have only occasional and fortuitous application to the present game. They are mainly concerned with the quality of the human relationship within which the sexual behavior occurs, and duration of the relationship is of no particular significance. They are likely to report having seen much good as well as ill come of sexual relationships—in as well as out of marriage. Some liberal humanist clergymen have given sermons to young women on the subject of how sexual relationships can be both beautiful and responsible without regard for marital status. All in all, traditionalists cannot see how liberal humanists can call themselves either Christians or clergymen. For their part, the neotraditionalists consider the liberal humanists extremists who upon maturing will, of course, move closer to the middle, neotraditionalist position.

Homosexuality provides another issue to illuminate the three main faces of the clergy—and, we gather, of the society at large. To the traditionalist, homosexuality is sinful and unnatural. The scriptures are quite clear on this point. To the neotraditionalist, homosexuality is essentially unnatural if not sinful, but more importantly it is symptomatic of a disturbance, an illness. The victim needs sympathy, help, and understanding, and should if possible be cured. To the liberal humanist, homosexuality means nothing in and of itself. Its meaning to the individuals involved is what matters. If homosexuality is symptomatic of isolation from the other sex, fear of the other sex, or self-hate, the individual very probably needs professional counseling, certainly not punishment or rejection. If, on the other hand, it is simply a matter of preference in the reasonably well-adjusted noncoercive individual, he or she should be completely free to live in his or her own way without harassment, pressure to change, or any form of mistreatment or discrimination. We are under the impression that many neotraditionalists are now shifting toward the liberal humanist view concerning homosexuality.

In spite of rather dramatic differences in view among the clergy concerning sexual behavior, we have gained the distinct impression that their views are much more alike with regard to two areas: childhood sexuality and "pornography" for the young. With regard to these, there seems to be a distinct shift of the liberals toward a more conservative view. There tends to be a "gut feeling" that there is something intrinsically wrong, unwholesome, "perverted" and anti-social about, for example, homosexual or heterosexual sex play by children and the exposing of young eyes to "hard core" pornography in verbal or pictorial form. Thus, a rather "far out" liberal humanist minister has stated that, although he is totally opposed to censorship in all forms, he could not help being against young people reading the likes of the novel *Candy*, and it has seemed to us that the more liberal clergymen with whom we have worked have found it especially difficult to bring themselves to advise parents and teachers concerning the usual masturbatory and sex play activities of their children. But even this is changing. Still, the cultural tradition has made it much more possible to view adults as sexual and sex-interested creatures than to view children as such.

On this point our thesis that the three faces of the society and of the clergy are quite similar breaks down to some extent. Some leading students of human sexuality go farther than any clergy we have known in their relaxed view of childhood sexuality and pornography. These days a good many psychologists, sociologists—and we suspect some clergy—take the position that since *there is no evidence* of "clear and present danger" in childhood sex play, or in children's viewing of even "hard core" pornography, efforts to suppress both the doing and the viewing should be abandoned. Suppressing, they claim, merely drives the doing and the viewing underground and guarantees continued exaggerated interest, and perhaps self-defeating guilt feelings. They also claim that efforts to suppress sexual interest and expression help to guarantee the communication barrier, which tends to exist between the younger and older persons. Doing and viewing are two of the chief preoccupations of many of the very adults who condemn this behavior in children.

Many people, including perhaps most educators, who are steeped in the traditional morality are as shaken by the expressed views of some liberal humanists as they would be if laws were to be proposed *requiring* drunken driving. For their part, liberal humanists feel that they are proposing changes in outlook that are comparable to altering small town, model T Ford traffic regulations of fifty years ago to fit the super highways of today and perhaps the super highways of tomorrow.

It is typical of a system of morality that individuals absorb it unthinking in the process of growing up—in much the same fashion that they absorb their country's language, and their family's and community's or tribe's prejudices and taboos. The whole system of values comes prepackaged and is submitted to question by only occasional gadflies who tend to be perceived, like Socrates, as enemies of society. The liberal humanist, whether clergy or not, tends to be so perceived—but less than he was only a few years ago.

A rather unique feature of being alive today is the fact that more and more people are in the uncomfortable position of having to think about the validity of their values, including those associated with sex. Increased knowledge and its dissemination, and growing freedom to talk about sex seriously are giving the thinking apparatus something to work with. Unfortunately though, and painfully for many, the situation contains many overtones of the sacrilegious, for it is of the essence to the believer that he or she believe totally, and not question or think. What an ineffable boon, the peace of mind born of unexamined conviction! Thus, typically, the teacher of sex education begins with the basic subject matter of reproduction and then is almost immediately confronted with the "question of values." In the school situation this usually means trying to present an overwhelming case in favor of the traditional morality without daring to subject that morality to objective scrutiny.

Still, as we have seen, large numbers, perhaps most, of our professional moralists, are no longer finding the traditional position tenable, and in such key matters as masturbation, homosexuality, out-of-marriage sex, abortion, censorship, and sexual morality generally, are "departing the faith." They are thereby cutting the floor out from under the traditional morality's chief lay agents, the teachers. It is easy enough to dismiss the arguments of crazy, irreligious, free-thinking, and probably divorced psychologists, but when entirely respectable clergymen begin talking this way . . . ! !

Our impression is that the clergymen in the middle

ground, the large number that we have termed the neo-traditionalists, are the least comfortable of the three groups with their position. The traditionalists know they are right, and like the Irish who continue to pray for the early conversion of the Jews, they pray that the true light will again come to the minds of erring revisionists. The liberal humanists tend to be characterized by a spirit of adventure, to feel freed of what they consider the intellectual straight-jacket of the ancient rule book, and they tend to look to the challenge of the future when new and, it is hoped, better sexual codes will emerge. Paul Woodring's comments on the subject would tend to appeal to them:

> . . . the older sexual morality, based as it was on a combination of religion, tradition, and fear of pregnancy and disease, is no longer effective with the younger generation. The new code must . . . be based on a clear recognition of the fact that most of the educated and enlightened people living today look upon sexual desire as biologically, socially, and psychologically normal rather than as something evil, dirty, and shameful (1968, p. 63).

For their part, the middle ground group, the neo-traditionalists, are typically in a state of conflict because their aspiration is to effect a compromise among apparently irreconcilable forces and positions: the old codes, the new knowledges, and the scientific attitude. They tend to see the need for new codes, but they want them based on the old ones, and thus some observers are convinced that they have taken it upon themselves to square the circle. Their religious training having been sullied by a more or less liberal education places them in the position of trying to worship in shrines of warring gods, and so it would appear to be with huge numbers of our better-educated population.

What seeming paradoxes emerge! The Genesis Church of San Francisco describes itself as "a traditional church in doctrine and belief," but then goes on to say "Genesis believes in the celebration of human love in all its expressions and in the affirmation of the value of each person's God-given sexuality." Genesis means business. It has just opened (1973) America's first museum of erotic art, featuring the famous or infamous Kronhausen collection!

Bertrand Russell has commented that people would rather die than think—and they do all of the time. This is demonstrably true. But there is an element, a growing element, within the clergy—and within the society— which is claiming that it is moral, ethical, and necessary to think and talk openly about sexual morality. A minority would seem to demand a continued mindless observance of an ancient, tribal system of taboos. Still, the minority group's position is that of the officialdom of the nation, that of the laws of the several states, and certainly that of the vast majority of the nation's schools.

At any rate, it is useful to those interested in sexual morality and sex education to know that the clergy of the United States and Canada have at least three quite visible faces, not just one, on the subject of sexual morality—and so do the nations at large.

REFERENCE

Woodring, P.: Some thoughts on the sexual revolution. Saturday Review, 15:62-63, January 20, 1968.

The Polar Icecap of Human Relations

A Note on "Modern" Marriage

THERE is a great deal of literature on marriage available to interested students of the subject. There are statistical analyses of it; there are diatribes against it and apologies for it; there are pointed comparisons concerning how wives behave in this or that country; and occasionally there are songs in praise of beloved wives and husbands. Bitter commentaries like those of Swinburne:

> . . . love is more cruel than lust,
> Time turns the old days to derision,
> Our loves into corpses or wives;
> And marriage and death and division
> Make barren our lives. (Dolores)

may be balanced by deeply moving tributes to a mate, like that of John Stuart Mill in the dedication of his great book, *On Liberty*:

To the beloved and deplored memory of her who was the inspirer, and in part the author, of all that is best in my writings—the friend and wife whose exalted sense of truth and right was my strongest incitement, and whose approbation was my chief reward—I dedicate this volume. . . . Were I but capable of interpreting to the world one half the great thoughts and noble

195

feelings which are buried in her grave, I should be the medium of a greater benefit to it, than is ever likely to arise from anything that I can write, unprompted and unassisted by her all but unrivaled wisdom.

The discussion that follows is by no means intended to summarize the literature on marriage, but merely to elaborate a little upon some of the curious dynamics of marriage which illustrate why the marital state is often so untenable. Today, even more than in the past, it is a bold if not foolhardy person, indeed, who will presume to suggest how to make marriage "work" happily; for in recent years, as we have noted, the "institution" has lost much of its former meaning and has yet to formalize new meanings, and men and women are in the position of having to "make do" as best they can in an ambiguous relationship. No wonder people are exploring alternative possibilities.

When Admiral Byrd went to Antarctica for a winter he refused to take a companion with him, reportedly because he felt that murder would result from two people living so closely together under the conditions.

In 1957 a man, who as a Boy Scout had accompanied Byrd on an expedition, headed an expedition near the South Pole. He said that his men got along well because they were taught to be *always* agreeable and pleasant in their dealings with one another in spite of all hardships, and to keep busy. Otherwise the circumstances of such intimate living together would quickly become intolerable and dangerous. One of us has an old friend who was on the 1908 Amundsen expedition to the North Pole, and he is very much in agreement with the foregoing views.

It is our feeling that marriage amounts to a kind of "polar icecap of human relations" and that it too requires a very special kind of social adjustment. Not only does it constitute, perhaps, the most intimate and complex of interpersonal relationships (Ambrose Bierce defined marriage as "The state or condition of a community consisting of a master, a mistress and two slaves, making in all, two"), but also it is usually saturated with mundane threats related to money and social status. Moreover, it is pre-structured and pre-jeopardized by our traditional notions of what our sexual attitudes and practices are supposed to be and what our role as male or female is supposed to be. This, generally, is a fantastically complex, loaded, and difficult situation.

But into marriage wander or leap inexperienced, immature, uninformed, and actually deluded young people. They have been led to believe that a certain age and some kind of ceremony have qualified them to live happily ever after in an essentially delightful state of loving bliss. Little has been said to them about the endless obligations of marriage, or the fact that its chief activities are hard work and head-to-head conversation with, in important ways, a stranger. (Wendell Johnson has pointed out that everyone gets some training in public speaking—which most people almost never do— *but no one gets training in private speaking—which everyone does all of the time.*) It is fancied that somehow, over the years before marriage, young people have learned all about how to behave in the marital state, how to talk together, how to make love, who does what, how and when, who "wears the pants," and so on. If we bother to stop and think for a moment, we recall that when we got married we were profoundly ignorant of the realities of married life. But we assume or hope that by some magic, some stroke of fortune, these young people will have learned what we did not (and perhaps still do not) know. We are very likely to forget that we ourselves, their parents and others of an older generation, are the only models that these young people have for their marriages. This we find to be a disturbing thought, for most can recall so much immaturity, bickering, littleness, and perhaps even deliberate cruelty, as well as impatience, nagging and other forms of unkindness, even inhumanity, in their own marriages—that we must shudder to contemplate the only model that our newlyweds have to follow.

The extent to which actual experience of marriage differs from young people's prefabricated notions of it is usually fantastic. (Listen to what young people contemplating marriage have to say with regard to what is important in marriage. Then listen to what couples who have been married for some time have to say on the same topic, and compare the ideas. This exercise can be worked into an excellent educational activity for persons of junior high school age on up.) In the first place, it tends presently to dawn upon each that he or she has married a stranger, that the excited and total love that may at first have existed was more of a projection of an ideal dream mate—a Prince Charming, our ideal mate out of Hollywood—than the actual person one is now living so closely with. Moreover, among other things, each partner is inclined to feel that he or she has a right to expect his or her mate to know how to operate skillfully in the married state. This is quite an expectation considering the lack of realistic preparation each receives for marriage. It is always amusing to get high school and college males talking about what they expect of their future wives: good cook, meals on time, "can iron my shirts" and other capabilities for "Mom-like" behavior, well educated. But will you want her to work on the side to help out with the income? Well, okay, some. But I still want my meals on time and good. What if she stops off on the way home to bowl or have a beer—as you probably will want to do . . .? All sorts of things come up at this point.

Before marriage, men tend to have certain ideas about

women, but not many that will prepare them to live intimately, day in and out, with the particular women they do marry. They come into marriage feeling obligated, by virtue of their maleness, to know all about sex and making love; but they tend to be jolted by many unexpected developments. Incidentally, one of the reasons Kinsey was so unpopular in some quarters is that his studies of thousands of men and women led him to believe that sexual experience prior to marriage increases the likelihood of good adjustment in marriage because it amounts to a kind of pre-training. He said that sexual experimenting before marriage provides a training period for learning sexual techniques and discovering the kind of partner with whom one can hope to live happily. "We have seen a few marriages get into difficulties because they were based on sexual interests alone; but we have seen many hundreds of marriages ruined by the failure of partners to learn before marriage that they could not adjust emotionally or sexually to each other" (1953, p. 266).

What are some of marriage's unexpected, jolting developments to which we refer? To mention only a few of many possible examples, most men take a long time to realize that their wives' moods and behavior are likely to fluctuate considerably with the phases of the menstrual cycle (Bardwick, 1972). Many men are astounded and alarmed at quite a few things of a sexual kind, such as finding that their wives may not only initiate but enter into the sexual act as enthusiastically as they themselves do and, perhaps, apparently find climax an even more intense experience than their own. Some men have wondered whether their wives were quite normal to behave in this way and, of course, their feeling was communicated in one manner or another to their wives. And again, we have heard men say that they never felt the same about women, especially their own wives, after seeing their new wives in the act of "relieving" themselves or after hearing them emit wind. (This kind of thing is also likely to bother women, too, but they are prone to think that men are fundamentally rather crude animals anyway—after all, there was dear old dad—so they rather expect it.) One must wonder what in heaven's name they thought they were marrying—some nonbiological symbol of "womanhood"? More than likely.

And of course, many men are shocked if their wives seem to have even an experimental interest in any but the most customary means of coitus. Of course, too, the reciprocal of this often applies to women as well. Such reactions are without regard for the fact that different people find different ways of making love more satisfactory than others, and playful experimentation is considered most enjoyable by many.

Women generally do not seem able to express verbally and directly a desire for coitus—this being something of a linguistic problem for most people, considering the vocabulary we have to work with—and if they do, at a certain point, their husbands are likely to respond by thinking that they are perhaps "over-sexed" or lacking in a proper degree of modesty. In one instance, a man became impotent as far as his wife was concerned because she exhibited what she considered to be merely a good, healthy, frank interest in sex. Her behavior raised his grave doubts as to her normalcy and his own competency.

There are women who, if they are treated as intellectual equals, have contempt for their hubands because they feel deeply the alleged inferiority of femininity which has been taught to them via psychological osmosis by a long tradition. Such women are prone to feel too that a husband who offers them equal status is not really masculine, is weak—and is therefore a source of insecure feelings in that he is not playing his proper pants-wearing role. A woman of this kind is not unlikely to be grateful for a beating by her husband, for this reaffirms her faith in the dominant male who, like father, can provide her protection and security while keeping her in line. Many a husband in a dark cloud of guilt feelings and apprehension as to consequences for having blackened his wife's eye has been amazed the following day to find himself receiving unusually considerate treatment and respect from his victim. There seems no end to the perverse, self-defeating ingenuity of *Homo sapiens.* (Certainly we do not intend this to be construed as a recommended self-help technique for husbands. Actually a man who has the sort of relationship with his wife described above is usually in a double bind; damned if he does and damned if he doesn't. That is, if he doesn't "stand up like a man" he will be "dumped on" for being considered a "slob." But if he tries to avert this by playing a "John Wayne role" he will be dumped on anyway—for being a "brute.")

Well-structured situations tend to give people a feeling of security. For example, games are never enjoyable or even workable until the rules are set and side lines marked—that is, until the players know what they can and cannot do, who is on whose side, and what the objectives are. In marriage, males and females do not always see eye to eye the matter of just what rules are to be observed and why, what the objective is, and so on. At any rate, the rise of feminism notwithstanding, generally women are more anxious than men that certain things be done in some customary manner—*i.e.,* "the right way"; and thus the perennial popularity of Emily Post's and various newspaper columnists' dictums and decisions, which come from heaven only knows what divine source. Some women, and men too, remind you of a football or basketball official, running around confidently calling the play—as though they knew what the game is that people are supposed to play. This predominantly, but by no means exclusively, feminine notion of propriety tends to give wives the idea that they have a certain superiority over their husbands, who seem fantastically ignorant of the rules of the game. In fact, there is sometimes no question that they are playing a quite different game or at least using a considerably different set of rules. More often than not women have some pretty firm ideas about how couples should walk down the street together, how introductions should be made, what position toilet seats should be in, who should open the door for whom, when kissing should and should not occur, how often sexual intercourse should be engaged in, and how it should be done.

A man who may be a figure of some importance in his work, and who may be accorded an appreciable amount of respect when on the job, may permit himself to be treated like a wayward child by his wife because he, too, tends to feel that she, like mother, "really knows best" how things should be done. Thus, one of the most painful experiences of the senior author's life was seeing his wonderful old classics professor bullied about by his wife. Perhaps the most tragic aspect of this sort of situation is that usually the wife suffers even more than the husband. She repels most other people by her "bad" behavior. And, having been raised in the same general traditions as those who find her unattractive, she feels unhappy about her own behavior, which is to say about herself.

At any rate, when a man starts to leave the house, if his wife says, "Well, where do you think *you're* going?" he is likely to fumble for some explanation, in effect accepting the relationship implied by such a question. It is likely that the woman feels that she has a right to ask such a question in that particular way because she knows that she has a better understanding of what married people are *supposed* to do. Anyway this was, as likely as not, the kind of thing her mother did to keep her dad in line. She is likely to have some quite definite opinions about how Saturday and Sunday mornings should be spent, and how man and wife really *should* spend their evenings—and these probably do not include his wandering off to some bar.

To repeat, when we decide to participate in a game, the first thing we want to know is, How is the game played? What is it all about? It is disconcerting to think you are playing basketball and have some person think the game is football and go around tackling you. But this is the kind of thing that happens all the time in marriage, into which game two people enter, each with some preconceived though perhaps vague notions as to its goals and rules and who is on whose side. Because of both nature and nurture, these two people perceive and react to the world in profoundly different ways. Under the circumstances, it is surprising that so many marriages make out as well as they do. The situation would be very amusing were it not for the fact that from this strange game of marriage—this cold war in which the opponents eat together, sleep together, and share each other's destinies—issue the children who, we hope, will be understanding and skilled in matters of interpersonal relationships, even those of the polar icecap of human relations.

All the talk about equality of the sexes has created its own problems. These days most people are willing to admit that men and women are equally human and should have equality of opportunity to achieve their life's objectives—to fulfill themselves. They should be equal before the law. But being equal in such matters does not mean they are not different from each other in some very fundamental ways. Anthropometrically, anatomically, and physiologically, they are obviously different in some respects. We have concluded that the world looks somewhat different "on the average" to men than it does to women. We are among the many who believe that women, generally, use language somewhat differently. As indicated earlier, men emit stronger odors than women, but women have a keener sense of smell than men. Any elementary school teacher can tell you whether the little girls, as a group, behave the same as the little boys.

It may be noted that we have made no effort to account for real or imagined differences. Of course, the little girl is taught from infancy to begin acting to a male audience, all manner of traditional sex role expectancies are set, and so on. However, it seems that there is much to be said for that old state of mind which permitted a woman to dismiss and forget a husband's behavior with the statement, "That's a man for you"; and conversely for the husband, "That's a woman for you"— without insisting that both sexes should behave the same or feel that the other is inferior or that they can really understand each other. This was a healthy recognition that women are not men and men are not women—even though they may both be human and equal.

The perplexities of modern marriage have led various observers to propose a familiarization and training period in the form of a socially sanctioned "trial marriage," which would precede permanent marriage and which could be terminated relatively easily. The intent of these proposals has been to give "permanent" marriages a better chance to last and to provide a tested, secure, and stable relationship within which to have children. After all, it is argued, adoption agencies tend to require that couples be married at least two years before adoption can occur, and many other criteria must be met by the would-be parents; even animal shelters usually make stiff demands of would-be animal adopters. In contrast, all married persons are deemed competent for parenthood. However, trial marriage plans are frequently dismissed as immoral and probably communist-inspired, except, that is, by people like college students who tend to see considerable merit in the idea. Many unmarried couples we've known describe themselves as not being ready for marriage and certainly not ready for parenthood. They are eager for a close relationship with a particular person of the other sex for an indefinite period of time. Their friends and, in some cases, families know of their involvements and they report almost no social pressure against what they are doing.

Often these couples have analyzed the situation in something like the following manner: "In previous generations when there was no dependable way to separate social approval to cohabit from social approval to procreate, in exercising its legitimate interest in regulating at least to a minimal degree the circumstances under which children were born, society needed to exercise influence over cohabitation. However, now that couples may reliably choose to live together without procreation, the state should get out of the business of selling marriage licenses and into the socially urgent matters of regulating child-bearing and/or rearing."

At any rate, in our present scheme of things, we cannot go at this home-making, procreating, and child-rearing business alone, as Byrd tackled the polar winter. But perhaps we can apply something of the policies of Byrd's recent followers to the pole. They insisted upon having all possible knowledge of the polar situation to which they committed themselves. They developed skill in advance in solving its problems and were trained in how to deal with the unexpected. They were a *doing* group, partly because they knew that idleness is hazardous when people are living with one foot in the other man's boot, so to speak; still, in so far as possible, they respected each other's privacy. They were by conviction, training, and necessity spontaneously and unfailingly friendly, considerate, and cheerful to each other, no matter what happened—just as many married people behave in just the opposite way to each other purely out of habit, and because one's mate may be the handiest verbal punching bag on which to vent one's bad feelings.

To these requirements for a successful expedition in the polar or marital situation, we might venture to add that husband and wife would do well to learn to play together, sexually and otherwise; to give some thought to what they *say* about sexual and other personal matters; to give at least as much thought to what they can contribute to the value of life of their mate as to what they think their mate owes them; to identify and explore their own life meanings and thereby grow in humanness and understanding; and to respect each other's right to adulthood, right to solitude, and right to be a unique individual with what may be the unique perceptions of his or her own sex.

But then, with our traditional attitudes and under present circumstances, is the giving of such love and the granting of such freedom possible in marriage as traditionally constituted?

REFERENCES

Bardwick, J. M.: Her body, the battleground: the psychology of female anatomy. Psychology Today, 5:50-54, 76, and 82, February, 1972.

Kinsey, A., et al.: Sexual Behavior in the Human Female. Philadelphia, W. B. Saunders Co., 1953.

9

What is "Natural" Sexual Behavior?

WHEN people think about some of the more peculiar circumstances of modern life—how people goose-step to the tick of the clock, joust angrily in murderous traffic, push various kinds of buttons for a living, feed their dogs scientifically and themselves whimsically, watch gland-tickling television into the late hours as their large muscles atrophy from disuse, follow the hourly news breathlessly as it bounds from tragedy to emergency, work diligently to make their habitat uninhabitable, dwell in giant ant hills, puff lethal smoke, produce large numbers of children who shortly become strangers to them, and make an ideal of sexlessness in a sex-centric society—they are prone to conclude that this is not an entirely "natural" way of life. As a more healthy opposite, they are likely to think of animal life in the wilds or to conjure up a picture of humans in the natural state, the "noble savage." We must confess that terms like "noble savage" tend to make us visualize a red-skinned fellow with feathers in his hair, lurking alone in a fairly dense forest. He seems to be hunting nuts or mice or possibly a female noble savage and to be suspicious that someone is hunting him.

In this chapter, we will be concerned with the meaning of "natural." For perspective regarding evolutionary implications of human sexual behavior, we shall consider certain aspects of animal sexual behavior, and for perspective concerning the varieties of human behavior in different circumstances, we shall consider sexual practices in some other societies. We may then be in a position to consider what behavior—if any— might be called "natural" to us. In the next chapter, we shall survey some modern societies for interesting contrasts and for ideas as to how societies may make deliberate attempts to mold patterns of sexual attitudes and behaviors.

It seems that the farther down the evolutionary scale one goes, the more subject is the animal in his sexual behavior to hormonal control. As opposed to humans, whose sexual behavior is highly subject to learning and to social conditioning as well as to perceptual and glandular influence, animals below the primate level tend to respond mainly to periodic reproductive excitation. In other words, you don't expect a pack of dogs to be following a bitch around unless she is in heat—which is to say, actually prepared to reproduce. The rest of the time the dogs are relatively free to go about their business, out of the absurd trance imposed on them by their glands which play a lively tune under the directorship of the female's glands. Remove the female animal's ovaries and she loses interest in sex and males lose interest in her. Humans, on the other hand, may accomplish what appears to be a perpetually "in heat" state which has little reliance on periodic glandular initiation (eunuchs sometimes remain sexually active) and have no relationship with reproduction (the sex life of a hysterectomized woman need not be altered). This is to say that if you are the parent of a shapely young female, you should expect to be plagued continually rather than just occasionally by a pack of young males.

Before returning to animals, let us make it clear that we do not mean to appear dogmatic about what animals do and do not do, because in individual cases some are capable of surprising versatility. For example, one of us once saw a large water snake chewing wolfishly away on the neck of an eel. It was literally cutting the big fish's head off. Now everybody knows that snakes swallow their victims whole, usually head first, and that they cannot chew them up into smaller pieces. However, this snake did not seem to know this, and considering the limitations of his teeth for this kind of work, it was doing quite a credible job of dissection.

Once the male animal is aroused, by the female in estrus or by heightened sex hormone levels due to other causes, his copulatory efforts may be directed toward objects other than fertile females of his own species, particularly if females of his own species are not available. Thus interspecies and like-sex copulatory behavior and self-stimulation, if physically possible, may be observed in animals all along the evolutionary scale. Evolutionarily speaking, apes are at an intermediate level between humans and lower animals. Their sexual behavior is less dominated by glandular cycles than that of other animals. The female may be receptive while not in estrus; she may be selective as to which males to encourage and which to discourage; and she may for unknown reasons be unreceptive to any male even when at the peak of estrus (Ford and Beach, 1951, pp. 204-06). Otherwise nonreceptive females will sometimes, as an emergency measure, offer themselves to males even though not in heat if they wish to use sexual appeal as a device to avoid attack or obtain food. Male apes seem to retain interest in sex even when not excited by estrous females, and they may seek a variety of outlets ranging from disinterested females and other males to self-stimulation. In a word, they are almost human. These are all evidences of considerable liberation from purely glandular control of sexual behavior and are sug-

8

gestive of a greater flexibility than is found in lower animals.

In brief, and generally speaking, subprimate reproductory behavior is tied as intimately to cyclical glandular action as is the menstrual cycle of the human female. Sexual receptivity tends to occur only when the female is prepared to conceive. (On the other hand, if the female dog discovers clitoral gratification, she may find ways of masturbating to climax with considerable frequency, whether or not in heat.) At such times she is as likely to initiate mating as the male, and if necessary will utilize various stratagems to bring his thinking into harmony with her own. (This is true also of human females in societies which do not require sexually passive behavior of the female—which is to say that without anti-sexual brain washing, the receptive or ardent female tends to play a 50-50 part in sex.) Evidences of most sexual behavior observed in human beings may also be observed in a variety of animals, thus suggesting an evolutionary continuity behind much human behavior including sex play among the young, self-stimulation, homosexual contacts, and efforts at inter-species matings ("bestiality") (see Ford and Beach, 1951, Chapt. 13).

It is a shame, by the way, that Professor Yerkes' female ape's famous efforts to seduce him are not preserved on film. At any rate, if we are to find a guide to what is "natural" by studying animal behavior, it appears that we have to include all of these kinds of things as "natural."

Now for sexual behavior in some exotic societies. An informant who was in Korea toward the close of World War II tells us that when he would enter a village, the children, all of whom were naked, fled to their huts in embarrassment. However, presently they would return "properly" dressed to receive a stranger—"properly" dressed meaning that they wore clothes from the shoulders to the waist only. He also reports that in the Philippines he saw mothers quiet their upset children by gently stroking their genitals.

Our informant was able to take this practice in stride as a foreign curiosity. But another traveler to the Philippines was not able to take in stride the discovery that his native maid was employing this technique to quiet his son. This was a little too close to home to be considered a quaint native custom. He seemed to be particularly incensed because his son responded so well.

Lord Avebury's 1902 review of some sexual customs provides a series of interesting snapshots (Avebury, 1902, pp. 541-42). Note especially his concluding remark.

It seems to the Veddahs the most natural thing in the world that a man should marry his younger sister, but marriage with an elder one is as repugnant to them as to us. Among the Friendly Islanders the chief priest was considered too holy to be married, but he had the right to take as many concubines as he pleased, and even the chiefs dared not refuse their daughters to him. In Western Africa the women of the reigning families might have as many lovers as they wished, but were forbidden to degrade themselves by marriage. Among the natives of New South Wales, though the women wore no clothes, it was thought indecent for young girls to go naked. . . . In endeavoring to estimate the moral character of savages, we must remember not only that their standard of right and wrong was, and is, in many cases different . . . and it would open up too large a question to inquire whether, in all cases, our standard is the correct one.

This broad-minded Victorian would also probably be prepared to question whether all games need to be modelled after English cricket.

It is pretty clear that one of the fundamental problems in the understanding of one person by another is this matter of extraordinary variability of human be-

havior. Let us point up a contrast. Suppose that someone asks you how a wolf (the four-legged type) be-
haves. The chances are that you can say some things
about wolfish behavior that have pretty accurate application to wolves in Alaska, Siberia, or any other place
where wolves still happen to live. But if someone asks
you to describe how humans behave, unless you have
been completely shut up in your own tribe you must
ask, "Humans—where and when?" before you can hope
to answer the question. If the only human beings you
know are those with whom you grew up, you will of
course suppose that theirs is typical human behavior
and not just local. If, suddenly, you find yourself confronted with people from somewhere else, the chances
are that when you watch them do things, you will decide
that they are quite odd or even abnormal. You may even
begin to doubt that these new people are really people
in the same sense that you are—after all, a wolf that
does not behave like the other wolves you've known
probably has something wrong with him.

Perhaps another example would be worthwhile.
Anthropologists report that the name of each tribe
of American Indians means, actually, "the people."
Whether the name is Zuni, Apache, Navajo, or what
have you it means "the people." Clearly, if you are not
one of "the people," you are something else—which,
very possibly, does not need to be treated as a person;
and this, presumably, is why a Ute, Comanche, or
Apache could carve up a nonperson, *i.e.*, neighboring
tribesman or non-Indian, as coolly as he would a coyote.
This is also the kind of mentality which led white men
to amuse themselves by shooting and thereby virtually
exterminating the African Bushmen and actually committing genocide against the Indians of Newfoundland,
and which generally leads us to feel less distress over
the slaughter or starving of Chinese or Nigerians than

of Americans or Canadians. But let us continue with the Indians.

Of course each tribe had its own ways which, to each, was the right way; and these ways included some interesting sexual practices. Permissiveness was quite common; however, some tribes, in striking similarity to our own a few years ago, did not permit their women to associate pleasure with sex. In some, the young girls' thighs were tied tightly together at night for protection against visiting temptations, and at least one tribe carried its stoicism to an extreme by having husband and wife hold intercourse through a small hole in a rough wool blanket. We don't suppose that people have these kinds of things in mind when they talk about returning to a more "natural" way of life.

Masturbation has been found in virtually all societies that have been studied. In some it is condoned or even encouraged among children, although it is usually either ridiculed or condemned among adults. Universally, as among primates, it is presumably more commonly practiced among males than females. A few societies take an extremely dim view of masturbation. Among the Kwoma of New Guinea, if a woman sees a boy with an erect penis, she will beat it with a stick, with the result that boys even learn to urinate without touching their genitals.

In many societies, homosexual activity is viewed very much as it is in America, that is, very negatively. In some societies, it is tolerated in childhood but not in adulthood, and there are still other societies in which homosexual activity is required of all males. For example, all the Keraki bachelors of New Guinea practice homosexual anal intercourse, which is an obligatory part of the puberty rites of those people (Ford and Beach, 1951, pp. 184-85). Similar requirements, we may note, have been made for admittance to membership in some boys and girls "gangs"—or tribes—in North America. Homosexual behaviors are also widespread among women in the various societies studied, and as in the case of the men, the social attitude varies from approval to indifference to strong disapproval.

Among some American plains Indians, a man who did not wish to play the role of a man in his tribe could become a transvestite (*i.e.*, one who may or may not be a homosexual, but who desires to wear the clothing of and perhaps be accepted as a member of the opposite sex). As such "he" could have a respected status, wearing the clothing of a woman, doing women's work and perhaps being one of the wives of a man.

Universally it seems, homosexuality occurs more frequently among men than women. It is never the dominant mode of sexual expression of a society. Although other forms of sexual expression tend to give way to heterosexual matings, there are individuals in many societies who function successfully both homosexually and heterosexually at the same time, and there are some who have none but homosexual interests. Social conditioning determines the way in which the homosexual is evaluated.

Extramarital and premarital sexual relationships are also regarded in a quite different light by different societies. In many societies, both of these types of behavior are forbidden, although, as in North America, there is always a considerable discrepancy between theory and practice. On the other hand, people like the Toda of India permit women to have several husbands and several lovers, and there is not even a word in the language for adultery. Attitudes toward premarital relationships also vary tremendously, ranging all of the way from complete permissiveness, to permissiveness only after the girl has begun to menstruate, to most severe penalties if premarital intercourse is discovered. In any event, the young put their minds to finding a way. The

Hopi Indians make every effort to keep girls and boys of ages ten to twenty apart and an older woman accompanies the girls wherever they go. However, it should surprise no one that meetings are sometimes agreed to by the girls in spite of the fact that they alone shoulder full responsibility if they are caught or become pregnant. It is no mean trick for the boys to sneak into the small, often crowded dwellings at night. But even if dire punishments might await those discovered in premarital relations, no system seems to be entirely successful in preventing this behavior—except that of the Wapisianna who "define cohabitation as marriage, and thus rule out the possibility of intercourse between two unmarried people. At the same time, of course, they eliminate the problem of the unmarried mother" (Ford and Beach, 1951, p. 190).

Evidently because menstrual blood is almost universally considered "unclean" (and in some societies dangerous to a man's physical or mental health), most societies taboo intercourse during menstruation. In some societies the menstruating woman is considered a source of contamination and is forced into virtual isolation during her period. Sexual interest of human females, which generally tends to increase before and/or after menstruation, seems to be low during this period. Interestingly, other primates that menstruate do not tend to be receptive at this time either (Ford and Beach, 1951, pp. 211-12).

One sexual taboo that is virtually universal is primary (*i.e.*, parent-offspring) incest. Murdock's explanation of this taboo is perhaps most satisfactory, *i.e.*, by avoiding intra-family sexual rivalry it might very well have been a major factor historically in preserving the family (Durkheim and Ellis, 1963; Murdock, 1949). In other words, this strongest and most widespread of taboos seems to be a product of social conditioning and is not found in lower animals. However, in humans it is so firmly established that most people are not aware of a wish to violate it, although psychoanalysts report finding ample evidence of the wish and dream at unconscious levels of mental functioning.

There is a popular notion that women in industrialized countries make an unnecessary fuss about the business of childbearing. Childbirth is a "natural" function, people—especially men—argue, and should not be any more painful or traumatic than any other natural function. This point of view seems theoretically sound enough. Experience with various forms of psychoprophylaxis of pain in childbirth lends considerable support, as does the usual performance of animals when giving birth. But we cannot be sure that something as small as a cervical os or a vaginal tract can be depended upon to be entirely at peace when an object as large as a baby's head is squeezed through it. At any rate, there is evidence that childbirth in the "natural" state is not always an easy matter. Some primitive people suspended a woman by her armpits and then had individuals hang by her waist in order to force the reluctant child out. Others favored the sit and bounce on the abdomen approach. Still others expedited labor by bouncing the woman in a blanket, fireman rescue net fashion (Ford, 1945).

At this point it seems fair to say that: (1) human sexual behavior has much in common with primate and subprimate behavior; (2) human sexual behavior in a given society seems to be profoundly influenced by social conditioning and individual learning, and is characterized by marked liberation from glandular control;[*]

[*] Frank A. Beach has expressed this thought in the following way: "Considering mammals only, it has been suggested that evolutionary changes in the direction of increasing corticalization of sexual functions seem to be associated with increasing complexity and modifiability of the individual's sexual patterns and also with a decreasing reliance upon gonadal hormones for sexual activation and performance" (Beach, 1958, p. 97).

and (3) returning to a more "natural" sex life is not necessarily an attractive prospect—if by natural one means behavior found among animals and "primitive" people generally.

Let us now survey three contrasting societies in somewhat closer detail. In each of these it appears that there is considerable permissiveness with regard to the sexual activity of children, and we gather that equality is accorded females in sex matters.* Beyond these similarities, the differences are rather striking.

The Mundugumor of New Guinea (Mead, 1950, pp. 139, 152-54) have (or at least did have at the time of Mead's famous study in the early thirties) a social organization which might have been developed by delinquent baboons. Mothers are so bored with feeding their infants that it is a wonder that they bother. The moment infants stop suckling at the breast they are popped back into their basket cages. Thus they develop a fighting attitude, struggle for the nipple, choke from swallowing too fast—which angers the mothers and infuriates the children—and learn to associate the entire relationship with anger and struggle rather than affection and reassurance.

This situation is a kind of prototype for future love making. Pre- and even postmarital sexual relationships tend to be quick and violent and involve much scratch-

---

* It is generally supposed that the human male is naturally the sexual aggressor and the Kinsey material lent support to this belief. However, anthropological data reveal that where active repression of female sexuality is not practiced, the female is just as likely to initiate sexual activity and engage equally in whatever sex play, experimenting or roughness that is practiced by the males. Moreover, if an orgasm is expected of the female in a particular society, she routinely experiences one (Ford and Beach, 1951, p. 271). Similarly, if a society expects the man to maintain an erection and withhold ejaculation as long as the woman wishes, he learns early to do this (Ford and Beach, p. 270).

ing, biting, tearing of clothing, and smashing of ornaments, all of which are intended to produce maximum
excitement in minimum time. Neighbors' fields are
sometimes pretty well torn up in such encounters. But
for greater credibility we will quote Mead at this point.
"Sometimes the bush meetings are varied by an accepted
lover's slipping into the girl's sleeping-basket at night . . .
If she receives a lover in her sleeping-basket she risks
not only discovery but actual injury, for an angry father
who discovers the intruder may fasten up the opening
of the sleeping-bag and roll the couple down the house-
ladder, which is almost perpendicular and some six or
seven feet in height. The bag may receive a good kick-
ing and even a prodding with a spear or an arrow before
it is opened . . . Whereas a bush encounter between
lovers is violent and athletic, a tryst in a basket must be
in absolute silence and comparative immobility . . ."

The Mundugumor are such a savage people that one
wonders at the courage of investigators to work among
them. They call to mind the wonderful cartoon showing
two visiting anthropologists fleeing before spear-waving
natives; and the caption reads something like: "I guess
we'll have to report that next to nothing is known of
their sex lives and let it go at that." But let us move on
in our study of sex in the "natural state."

In Polynesia (Danielsson, 1956), where there are no
words for sexually "obscene," "indecent," or "impure,"
and sex is never a source of shame or embarrassment,
love is the Life Force, the "essence of existence." It is
worshipped as something both divine and delightful
to be carried on as gaily as fishing from the time when
children are old enough to learn to dance. It is a game
to be played in joy. Instead of fighting and battling like
the love-bent Mundugumor, the Polynesians commonly
establish a love-making mood by dancing, in which the
girl is courted with graceful play-acting and pleading

gestures as friends clap and cheer in the group emotional intoxication which becomes, by our standards, downright immoral. Delightfully so.

Such words as illegitimate, faithlessness, adultery, bigamy, and divorce (which are our words for game violations and are of the same order as "out of bounds," "icing," "off side," "double dribble," and "unnecessary roughness") are unknown in Polynesia, but a family becomes concerned if a girl does not bear children early because her function is to be as fertile as the generous soil of the islands. Childbearing is surprisingly easy for the mother and everyone is delighted when a child is born. It is loved endlessly, and no one is seriously concerned about who the father may be.

The light-hearted liaisons of boy and girl can be broken easily by one or the other simply saying, "I am tired of it"; and this is true also of marriage. The incomparable Lichty has summarized the Western attitude toward Polynesia and what it stands for in our Puritanical-escapist tradition in his cartoon depicting a couple of ministers watching South Sea natives at play; one "man of the cloth" is saying something like: "Come, come, Dr. Truffle. Even if we've failed to lick the gay and carefree indolence of these people, let's have no talk of joining them!"

Modern technology has in recent years been sneaking up on the Eskimos as well as most other primitive societies. Their traditional way of life has been generally altered, if not basically destroyed. However, we have some eye-witness information about Eskimos of the past which adds an interesting dimension to our picture of varieties of human sexual behavior.

The late Peter Freuchen, a Danish explorer and writer, lived with the Eskimos in Greenland and was happily married to an Eskimo woman for a dozen years. (Students are always relieved to learn that she died.

Peter did not desert her.) According to Freuchen (1956), the Eskimos had an easy-going attitude concerning sex which struck him as being both healthy and realistic. Their marriages were exceptionally harmonious and husbands and wives very faithful. They were entirely permissive regarding the sexual behavior of the young and, by our standards at least, of adults as well. For example, Eskimo parents never worried about the whereabouts of the teenagers, taking it for granted that they would be enjoying themselves in vacant igloos in the area in couples or in small parties. The jolly sport of wife trading was also common. That is, if your wife is pregnant but you need a woman along to help with the distant bear hunting, you leave your wife behind with a friend who needs some sewing done and take his along. Or it might be purely a matter of fun. A pair of hunters decide to show up at each other's homes for the night. Or under certain circumstances you might even call partner-trading a matter of psychological necessity. An igloo full of naked Eskimos (the stiff, cold clothing was always left in the entrance way and body heat was a major factor in keeping the igloo comfortable) are feeling the devastating effect of the long, cold, and threatening Arctic night; so someone puts out the light and everyone runs around in the dark and ends up with a partner. After a while the light is lit again and everyone is in fine and gay spirits once more "and a psychological explosion has been averted."

Freuchen and others who knew them well considered the Eskimos a decent and happy people, and he was profoundly saddened that "bad white men" took such advantage of their customs—and "good white men" taught them to be ashamed of what had always been right to them.

But perhaps the isolated Marquesans of Polynesia have carried to unique heights the role of sanctioned sex in a primitive society. Chastity is viewed as the extreme sexual aberration, and virginity is anything but prized. "Romantic" love, sexual prohibitions, and jealousy are unheard of. According to anthropologist Menard (1972), Marquesan mothers instruct their very young daughters in coition and contraception, and long before puberty, girls are expected to enlarge the clitoris by stimulation and to cultivate a highly responsive vagina capable of "milking action" by means of using smooth, carved phalli (dildoes) of graduated sizes. Medical examinations have indicated that adult Marquesan females do indeed have highly developed and sensitized genitalia, both internal and external, which make orgasmic response possible merely by pressing the thighs together and when dancing, and which make possible a common form of partying: one girl willingly spending the night on the beach with several males.

Such socially acceptable "gangbanging" (heterosexual intercourse between several boys and one consenting girl) behavior provides a dramatic example not only of societal differences, but also of the effects of societal attitudes upon psychological health. The female Marquesan gangbanger is accepted and even admired, especially for exceptional performance, as when one girl successfully "took on" the entire Tahitian rugby team of thirty boys one night (Menard, 1972, p. 55). In contrast, our gangbanging females tend to be "very ill psychologically" (Kinsey, 1972). Here, unless done as a prank, for a lot of money, or other non-neurotic reasons, acting out this common female fantasy is identified with psychiatric disorder. The behavior is evidently within the range of "normal" for males in both societies, although it is illegal here.

For their part, the males have their genitals massaged for growth and responsiveness almost from infancy, and in time the boys are gradually and gently introduced to coitus by older, experienced girls selected by their fathers. In brief, deliberate efforts are made to encourage maximum sexual interest and responsiveness in both males and females—sex, fun, and enjoyment being considered of the essence in life.

Diseases introduced especially by the whalers of the past century nearly destroyed the Marquesans, but when they were again isolated from outside traffic, they resorted to their ancient sex cultures and managed to rebuild their population. Children are idolized and belong to everyone. The oldest able persons are involved in sexual ceremonies, such as marriages. Menard found Marquesan "freedom from inhibition and sexual hang-ups entirely refreshing." Missionaries have never made progress with these people. What an incredible contrast between sex life styles: our traditional sex squelching versus Marquesan cultivation of sexuality—as we do intelligence and artistic ability.

We may note in passing that white people have not always had smooth sledding when it came to persuading these or other peoples to abandon their own beliefs for theirs. For example, Malinowski was unable to convince the Trobriand Islanders that there is such a thing as paternity. This they considered a silly story invented by the missionaries. Their attitude made teaching them about Christianity impossible because Christianity is a patriarchal religion and can only be intelligible to people who comprehend fatherhood. " 'God the Father' would have to become 'God the Maternal Uncle' to make sense to the islanders—but this does not give quite the right shade of meaning, since fatherhood implies both power and love, whereas in Melanesia the maternal uncle has the power and the father has the love." These people cannot grasp the idea of people being God's children because they don't believe that males have anything to do with the creating of children (Russell, 1929, pp. 21-22).

A study of the sexual behavior of exotic societies is much more than a stroll through a museum of human curios. Indeed, its implications for education are profound because it shows convincingly that people are not tied to a single stereotyped pattern of behavior, but are sufficiently flexible to shape themselves to a pattern or patterns which, we may hope, will be conducive to human happiness under modern circumstances. But as Mead has pointed out, this potentiality for flexibility is "a two-edged sword that can be used to hew a more flexible, more varied society than the human race has ever built, or merely to cut a narrow path down which one sex or both sexes will be forced to march, regimented, looking neither to the right nor to the left" (1950, p. 209).

In the next chapter we will attempt to discover what some modern societies have attempted and are attempting to do along these lines of deliberate self-molding.

REFERENCES

Avebury, Rt. Hon. Lord: Pre-Historic Times. New York, Appleton, 1902.

Beach, F. A.: Evolutionary aspects of psychoendocrinology. *In* Behavior and Evolution. Edited by A. Roe and G. G. Simpson. New Haven, Yale, 1958.

Durkheim, E., and Ellis, A.: Incest: The Nature and Origin of the Taboo, and The Origins of the Development of the Incest Taboo. New York, Lyle Stuart, 1963.

Danielsson, B.: Love in the South Seas. New York, Reynal, 1956.

Ford, C. S., and Beach, F. A.: Patterns of Sexual Behavior. New York, Harper and Row, 1951.

Ford, C. S.: A Comparative Study of Human Reproduction. New Haven, Yale University Publications in Anthropology, No. 32, 1945.

Freuchen, P.: Love among the Eskimos. American Weekly, September 16, 1956.

Mead, M.: Sex and Temperament. New York, Mentor, 1950.

Menard, W.: Love Marquesan style. Sexual Behavior, 2:52-56, September, 1972.

Murdock, G. P.: Social Structure. New York, Macmillan, 1949.

Russell, B.: Marriage and Morals. London, Liveright, 1929.

10

Sexual Behavior and Sex Education in Some Modern Societies

In the previous chapter we were chiefly concerned with surveying sexual behavior in some "primitive" societies in an effort to discover whether there is a "natural" kind of human sexual behavior. We may not have reached a very conclusive answer to this question other than that wherever you find people you find sex and that human beings are capable of adopting any of a variety of patterns of sexual behavior as "natural." You also find some forms of sexual behavior that are considered acceptable and some that are deplored, even though what one society accepts, another may deplore. Thus, just as one person's lovemaking is likely to appear ridiculous to any other person, people in one society are likely to find the sexual behavior of any other curious or absurd, if not downright wicked.

People in different primitive societies have tended to have superhuman explanations of why they do things as they do; and in these explanations an assortment of deities has been involved in the sculpturing of the many ethnological pathways through time. However, in more recent years, people have been prone to blame some god less and evolution more for what has befallen them. Thus, if a brainless interplay of forces may be said to evolve an animal species, similar forces might produce a society.

Indeed, it could be argued that most, if not all, societies have "just growed" under the pressures of circumstances surrounding them and within them—to a great extent quite "brainlessly." But from time to time people have dreamed of systematically structuring all aspects of human existence, and a few societies have attempted to shape themselves by plan in order to achieve more or less clearly defined objectives. Thus, Plato's idea for the Republic included controlling and directing sexual behavior—in part in a curiously underhanded manner for one so concerned with the idea of Justice. That is, in the mass marriages people drew each other by lot, supposedly, but the rulers manipulated chance enough to bring certain couples together. Nazi Germany undertook to concentrate Nordic virtues by selective breeding and the inculcation of traditionally defined gender roles. Today, the "hard as Krupp steel" male image and lack of realistic sex education are blamed for widespread male impotency and female discontent. Similar problems are reported in South Africa—and, by George, in Canada and the USA!

There has unquestionably been a growing tendency for modern societies to attempt self-molding in sexual behavior as well as in other ways. Although this chapter is in part intended merely to suggest the varieties of modern sexual behavior in different countries, it is also concerned with exploring some more or less systematic and large-scale efforts to control sexual behavior.

Just as we observed that primitive societies have failed to conform themselves to any single pattern of sexual behavior—even though all that survived evidently managed somehow to produce babies—we shall see that "modern" societies have by no means produced a pattern of sexual behavior that is likely to be adopted soon by any considerable number of other countries. Let us consider an especially selected sampling of modern societies. First, here are some observations made some years ago after one of us (Johnson) spent some time in Trujillo's Dominican Republic, which was dominated by traditional Spanish values.

"I gathered that there were three classes of people: the well-to-do and leisured who enjoyed polo, excellent local rum and, in some cases, American movie actresses; the soldiers who made the place a kind of armed camp and who guarded El Presidente with machine guns; and the poor who, of course, did the work. The rich were plump if not fat; the poor were as lean as their burros.

"I was told that people of the upper class took it for granted that if a young man and woman were alone together, they would very likely copulate as soon as possible. Since the parents did not wish to deal with the several possible consequences of such behavior, in the Spanish manner they invariably provided a chaperone whenever their daughter was to be in the presence of a man. While visiting there I was interested to note that the social conditioning was highly successful. The girls tended to act as though they felt rather naked if by chance a chaperone was slow in putting in an appearance, but they greatly enjoyed kissing games and drinking parties when Aunt Julieta was standing by.

"Indeed lively flirtations were common, but well supervised. This seems to make for a very neat and moral situation. But the men rescued themselves from it by maintaining something approaching complete control of the women, and by associating freely with attractive women of the lower class for whom chaperonage was contraindicated. I was told by a Dominican of relatively high position that wives and upperclass women know all about this really, but they are carefully trained to pretend that they don't and so avoid inconveniencing the men in their adventures. Even though I was married, I was told I'd be a fool not to marry a wealthy Dominican girl because their religion forbids divorce under any condition, and the whole tradition requires lifelong, docile, and skillful service on the part of the women. My wife was not amused by this recommendation.

"At any rate many of these ladies made a practice of letting the hair on their legs grow very long in order to publicize the fact that their hair is straight and that therefore they are truly of Spanish—probably Castilian— rather than Negro ancestry. To our American eyes their hirsute legs extending below very handsome dresses made for a somewhat peculiar sight to say the least.

"But we discovered that they considered our ways rather queer too. For one thing the lady professors with us were viewed as being unduly forward, masculine, bold, and lacking in lady-like decorum. For another, whereas the Dominican women were capable of looking placidly on while a visiting male dog mounted their handsome silver female beside the dinner table, we visitors were not nearly so placid. At a certain point one of us, the senior member of our group, felt compelled to spring up, redfaced and desperate, to interfere with this mating behavior. The Dominicans thought this frantic response inappropriate and rather odd, but out of courtesy they ignored it."

Switzerland is another of those countries that have utilized strong past traditions as a way of controlling the modern situation. The Swiss have, we understand, a highly patriarchal society in which the father is truly the boss. The mother is expected to play a submissive role and the children are said to be extremely well disciplined. What little delinquency there is, is very severely dealt with (Brown, C., 1958). Moralists are prone sometimes to point to Switzerland as a country that knows how to rear its children, and the men are much admired in some quarters for continuing to "wear the pants."

This scheme of things sounds almost too successful, and it is something of a relief to be able to say that perhaps all is not entirely as it appears to be from here. For example, an old Swiss gentleman who enjoyed telling about life in Switzerland when he was a boy made a convincing case for the argument that there is a good deal of spirit in the young people of Switzerland that neither their elders nor writers on this subject seem to know much about. His very serious descriptions of contests involving carrying for distance a bucket of water on an erect penis were little classics in their own right, and tended to expand one's awareness of athletic event possibilities. We also understand that Switzerland, like most other countries, has its episodic scandals involving raids on houses of prostitution, including male houses, which are occasionally given wide and red-faced publicity. Such episodes must be embarrassing, to say the least, for a country that has won the reputation for knowing how to deal with this business of sex, "delinquency," and the "controlling of women."

But such episodes are not nearly the setback for Swiss traditionalists as was the February, 1971 federal election in which the Swiss voters (all male) finally decided to give women the right to vote in federal elections and to hold federal office. As their sisters around the world could tell them, Swiss women face a long, uphill struggle if they are to divest Switzerland of its reputation for "controlling its women." In contemporary Switzerland, upon marriage a husband claims all his wife's money; a married woman can neither buy property nor contract debts unless her husband is co-signer; no woman in Switzerland holds a top position in business, industry, or banking; and a Swiss woman receives about 25% less pay than does a man for the same sort of work (Swiss Women Tackle Inequalities . . . 1971). Do similar anomalies exist where *you* live?

Now for the Soviet Union. Churchill once said: "Russia is a puzzle wrapped in a mystery inside of an enigma"—or something like that, and the discussion that follows will doubtless do little to straighten out that situation. However, some available sources do seem to give us the basis for sketching in a hint of what has been taking place there with regard to sexual behavior and sex education.

There seems to be no question that the U.S.S.R. is one of the countries of the world in which systematic planning has been and is being attempted in the interests of structuring society and molding the behavior of its citizens. When the Czarist state was overthrown, the spirit of revolution against things past inevitably lashed out at such religion-linked institutions as marriage, and "free love" seemed to symbolize at once a debunking of the bourgeois ideas of marriage and the emancipation of women. Needless to say, whether earned or not, this reputation for accepting "free love" won the Communists few friends in those parts of the world that refer to themselves as Christian. But, we gather, when large numbers of war-orphaned children were added to the normal burden of illegitimate children, the Soviet leaders faced a vexing problem that they set about solving by educational means. The general idea seemed to have become: value chastity, deemphasize sex and associate its gratification with marriage exclusively. The following passage was quoted from the official U.S.S.R. publication, *Soviet Education* by *U.S. News and World Report*:

The October (1917) Socialist revolution wiped out the political, legal, and economic inequality of women, but some people have incorrectly understood this freedom and have decided that human sex life can be carried on with a disorderly succession of husbands and wives.

In a tightly organized society, a socialistic society, such practices necessarily lead to a laxity and vulgarization of relationships unworthy of man, cause difficult personality problems, unhappiness, and disruption of the family, making orphans of the children . . .

Every parent must work toward training the future citizens to be happy only in family love and to seek the joys of sex life only in marriage. If parents do not set such a goal for themselves and do not reach it, their children will lead a promiscuous sex life full of dramas, unhappiness, misery, and injury to society . . .

Questions of sex must be simply treated, not made a treasured secret . . . The fact that the child often asks where children come from does not mean that one must explain it through and through when he is too young . . . There is much he does not know about other life problems, and we need not burden him prematurely with knowledge beyond his understanding . . . The proper time will come for such knowledge, and there is no danger in answering him: "You're still a little tyke; when you grow up you'll find out."

Discussions of sex should preferably be held with a doctor or organized in school. A wholesome atmosphere of confidence and delicacy always desirable between parents and children is sometimes disrupted by too outspoken conversations on such difficult subjects.

Sex education is and should be education for love. That is, great and profound unity of life, yearnings, and hopes. But such sex education must be conducted without too open and downright cynical selection of physiological problems.

We advise parents to be extremely careful with regard to the child's feelings towards people and towards society. It is necessary to see that the child has friends (parents, brothers, comrades) and that his relationship with them is not casual and egotistical, but that his friends' interests should be his (Russia Takes a New Line . . ., 1949)

We understand, too, that the Soviet slant on sex education includes a recommendation that systematic planning should fill the time of the young. That is, instead of being left to themselves to follow their whims and impulses, they should be fully involved in a program of exacting school work and physical training.

One cannot help wondering how successful these official statements of policy are in altering the behavior of the Soviet people. Many visitors to the Soviet Union sing the praises of the young people, their diligence, sense of purpose, and their behavior generally. Still, they have their "hooligans" too, we are told. At any rate, as an example of what is required in the way of adjustment to shifts in official policy, we may consider what has happened with regard to induced abortion since the revolution (Gebhard et al., 1958, p. 215). Shortly after the revolution, abortion was legalized as a measure in the emancipation of women—and presumably because smaller families would provide women more time for factory and other work. However, a decade or so later abortion was outlawed unless for strictly medical reasons. Considerable publicity was given to dangers of induced abortion—dangers to the women's health, enjoyment of sex, and future fruitfulness. Whether induced abortion was outlawed for reasons of health or a need to increase the labor and military manpower, we cannot say, but in 1955 abortion suddenly again became safe and legal.

For a striking contrast with the allegedly puritanical trend in the U.S.S.R., we may turn now to a consideration of the Swedes who, if anything, have caused even more grief to moralists than have the Russians.

As one would expect, there is a history behind "the state of affairs" existing in Sweden. A permissive attitude toward premarital sexual intercourse which results in approximately 98% of married Swedish couples having such experiences does not just happen overnight (Barnard, 1971). (Barnard reports that whereas 94% of the 16-year-olds in a recent study *didn't* want the schools to advocate sexual abstinence for teenagers, 70% of the Swedes between ages 20 and 63 believed that the schools *should* advocate premarital abstinence. Even Sweden has the perennial generation gap!) At any rate, the background seems to be something like this. In the past a great premium was placed upon making marriages fruitful. There is no way of guaranteeing fruitfulness in marriage quite like accomplishing pregnancy before marriage. If a couple is dating for a while and the girl fails to become "with child,"* each had better seek another partner with whom he or she might be more successful in starting a family. Such a tradition could hardly avoid making premarital sexual activity more or less socially acceptable, as it apparently is today. Young people are not encouraged to marry early, and long engagements are therefore very common. In spite of systematic instruction regarding contraception, premarital pregnancies are apparently very common. Induced abortions are frequently resorted to, but illegitimate birth reportedly account for about 10% of the total births. Neither the illegitimate child nor the unmarried mother is ostracized in a Puritan manner. Indeed, such terms as "illegitimate child" are not used. Matters pertinent to children born out of wedlock are dealt with under the rubric of "one parent families," an expression now in wide use in North America, too.

Factors other than historical traditions undoubtedly influence modern Swedish attitudes and practices with regard to sex. Sweden is a small country which has succeeded in establishing for itself what is very possibly the highest standard of living for "the average" person that the world has ever known. From a materialistic point of view, at least, they may be said to have "arrived" if one compares them with other countries, most of which are still waging battles against poverty, unemployment, insecurity, and disease. The Swedes evidently have an efficient educational system. They are socially secure "from womb to tomb," as the old saying goes,

---

* An expression reminiscent of the lady penguin who was "with Byrd" at the South Pole.

and apparently everyone enjoys unprecedented amounts of leisure time.

In brief, Sweden's tradition and modern circumstances have evidently contrived a unique situation in which sexual intercourse is frankly accepted as important and decent for the unmarried as well as for the married. The subject of sex is considered worthy of study in school, and since sex among the young is not for reproductory purposes, contraception is encouraged and induced abortion accepted. All in all, the Swedish point of view is so outlandishly different from our own that many think that they should be pitched into the middle of the Pacific Ocean along with the incomprehensible Samoans. However, others are attracted by the idea that a society is fond enough of its children to want them to experience the good things in life—including sex for those who desire it—and they believe that we have much to learn from the Swedish approach.

Americans have commented upon the sexual behavior of the Swedes in articles with such titles as *Sin and Sweden* (Brown, 1955). In that commentary Brown reported widespread "promiscuity," great numbers of unmarried mothers, a low birth rate for the country and large numbers of legally induced abortions performed upon both married and unmarried women. He asserted that unwed mothers are considered heroines in Sweden.

Most of all, he seemed incensed at the sex education imposed upon the young of that country. The leading sex educator of Sweden is quoted as having said, "The important thing is that they must be in love. I tell the girls it is alright to sleep with a boy but first they must be in love . . ." A psychiatrist is quoted as having said, "The only differences between our behavior here and behavior in other countries is that we face the facts. Young people sleep together. We don't frown and tell them that it is sinful and expect that it will prevent it.

Since they're going to do it anyway, we try to give them training and teach them to be honest." The American newspaperman wrapped up his story with his heel by quoting a Swedish boy: "I have no real morals . . . I would never marry a girl because I had made her pregnant. Why should I give up my liberty for the sake of a child?"

For their part, of course, the Swedes are prone to take a dim view of such foreign critiques. They consider them inaccurate and unfair. They do not consider that they have reached the end of social evolution of sex roles, and of education relative to human sexuality. Sex education was introduced into Sweden's schools in 1940, and became compulsory in 1956 for children from age 7 on up. A recent Royal Commission on Sex Education took a fresh look at the compulsory sex education program. In their report to the Minister of Education in 1971, the Commission presented two main objectives for the Swedish program. "First, it should give insight about human anatomy, physiology, and sex life, so that any shortcomings arising from ignorance could be successfully counteracted and harmonious relationships between two people promoted.

"Secondly, it should teach that sex life is closely linked with personality, social relationships, and the society as a whole. Full awareness of this bond would restrain worst intentions of human beings and encourage greater responsibility, consideration, and concern (Vaigo, 1971)." The Commission's guidelines to schools also advised that the schools inculcate such values as: no person is entitled to force his or her sexual attentions on others; notions that women occupy different social positions from men should be eradicated once and for all; there should be tolerance toward people belonging to "sexual minority groups"; contraceptives should be used unless both parties consciously desire to produce a baby.

The section in the previous edition of this book which dealt with the Australian scene stated that former Australians living in the United States reported "as the standard of living is rising in Australia, the country is becoming more like America every year"; and they predicted that "in time the Australian youth will be able to have more unsupervised leisure and automobiles and become indistinguishable from American youth." How prophetic!

We have had the good fortune to be able to talk at length with a number of highly educated Australians in the United States and Canada. Our queries about sex education and sex practices in Australia leave little doubt that there is considerable, rapid change occurring in some areas. There appears to be a generation gap of major proportions developing.

Basically, the *traditional* Australian approach seems to appeal more to North Americans than do the other plans outlined here. In the first place, it does not offend us "morally." Quite the contrary. In the second place it suggests an enviable restoration of control of things to adults. That is, we have tended to feel toward the Australians as one might toward a neighbor who is able to control his dog or the weeds in his rose garden. Or his wife. And—oh yes—there has been a certain appeal to us in the fact that the kids of Australia have apparently been quite happy with their lot. What an achievement—to control people without angering them or making oneself feel the persecutor deserving in his turn of punishment! But, alas for those who look to Australia for a model, their Paradise (has been) Lost. For Australian youth have been looking northward for *their* model.

In essence, the traditional Australian idea seems to

be that the best way to solve sexual problems of the young is to avoid them. Thus, in practice every effort was made to de-emphasize sex, "sexiness," and sex play, and to fill the time of the young with studies and sports. It would appear that the plan worked, if one may judge by such things as: the traditional very low juvenile delinquency rate, few marriages among high school pupils, and an almost total absence of pregnancies among school-age girls.

Following are some of the techniques that were reportedly used to avoid sex problems (Teenagers and Sex in Australia, 1958):

1. Sex was not publicized. It seems to have occurred to someone "down under" that certain human drives do not require "selling" and that if you prefer not to make an issue of something, you do not harp on it constantly. Of course, they had their scandal type tabloid newspapers which relied heavily upon sex, often associated with violence, for their sales appeal. However, we understand that such publications are now virtually nonexistent, their stock in trade having been pre-empted by the "straight" newspapers which are taken by the majority of the population. One tongue-in-cheek informant has told us that during a recent two-year stay in his native Australia he shared the impression with many others that "gang rape is the national sport of Australia." This impression was attributable to the frequency of banners affixed to news shops advertising the contents of that day's newspaper, and to newspaper headlines themselves, which so often read something like "Man Eats Nude Picture," and "Thirteen Bikers Rape Girl (Picture Inside)." You may be either relieved or disappointed to learn that the "picture inside" was likely to reveal only the gum tree beneath which the alleged assault took place. On the other hand, the traditionalists still hold power, and strong efforts are made toward

mass social censorship under the aegis of the Minister for Customs and his staff, who censor all books and films coming into Australia. Certainly none of the "gay literature" which is so readily available in any large North American city gets past the Minister, and perhaps only five of the twelve annual issues of *Playboy* are admitted.

2. In urban areas, all Australian boys and girls used to attend separate high schools. Currently, however, sexual segregation in the schools is being phased out, even in private schools. No new public schools are sexually segregated.

3. Girls were and are forbidden to "doll up" in the Hollywood sense, and the wearing of cosmetics to school is discouraged if not forbidden. Students still wear uniforms to school. But after school hours, the garb of young people quickly changes. One Australian claims that his country "leads the world in brief swimsuits and short dresses." Surprisingly, he reports that the older generations do not seem scandalized by this. This same Australian has told us that Australian-produced T.V. shows have included nudes. (Of course, the Minister for Customs does not deal with domestic T.V. shows.)

4. Heavy home study requirements did and still do leave little time for much in the way of socializing. Boys and girls still tend to be discouraged from spending unstructured time together, and displays of affection in public are still considered "outside the mainstream."

5. Australia has an ongoing tradition of compulsory sports participation for youth. All elementary and secondary private and public schools shut down other activities for at least one half day each week so that the students can participate in at least one team sport and also in aquatic activities. Nothwithstanding the recent influence of the North American "hippy" models, much

youthful Australian energy is channeled into such activities as mountain climbing, adventuring in the wilds, and striving for championship level performance in a variety of sports.

6. Young people were and still are discouraged from marrying until they have reached the level of social maturity symbolized by home ownership. If they do marry before they have their own house, they are wont to postpone having children until this social benchmark has been achieved.

7. In most of Australia the attitude of the schools continues to be that sex education is up to the home. Here again, however, the winds of change are blowing. "Hardly had Queensland's Education Ministry declared that sex education was taboo, when it was announced that a liberalized policy of sex education, in which parents would be asked to play an important role, was projected for New South Wales schools next year" (Smith, 1972).

Well, here we have a hint—but of course only a hint— of what the world looks like today, sexually speaking. Again, as in the case of our survey of "primitive" societies, we find considerable diversity in outlook and practice from country to country, and again the lesson is clear that humanity's self-molding capabilities are growing and can be expected to produce varied and perhaps unexpected patterns of behavior. Our impression is that there is a widespread tendency among the world's peoples to make deliberate efforts to plan the lives of their youth in such a way as to avoid sex-related problems among them. Avoidance of sex-related problems can be approached from opposite directions: (1) the traditional, unsuccessful method of stomping out the sexual behavior, and (2) the more imaginative and now feasibile method of *altering the consequence* of the behavior. That is, sexual gratification need not result in unwanted pregnancy, disease, humiliation, or guilt. Many people in the United States and Canada believe that their societies may soon be forced to make renewed efforts along sex education lines but there is certainly no unanimity of thought as to the most desirable direction to take.

More typical of the times than the way things are around the world is the way things are changing. We may conclude this chapter by making brief note of some interesting examples of sexual behavior in transition in a few parts of the world.

England—our immediate source of the Jewish-Christian tradition—has responded to widely publicized studies of homosexual behavior by altering its stand on the subject. Our impression is that homosexuality is now deplorable rather than criminal or sacrilegious, as it used to be. The theater may deal with the subject—artistically, we presume—without threat of censorship. For another example from England, the kinds of serious writing that are now reaching the public in volume and are sharply at odds with traditional notions of morality seem well worth citing. Alexander Neill, Headmaster of "that dreadful school" Summerhill in England has been acclaimed and denounced for his educational ideas, which include permissive views on sexual behavior (Neill, 1960). In some respects, his ideas seem more or less in harmony with those of the American psychologist, Ellis (1958). When Neill and Ellis speak of freedom in masturbation and remain placid in the face of swearing, lying and sex play of children, and sex before marriage, they run counter to a stream which must be losing force or it would long since have drowned them. Their underlying gospel, though, is love and human happiness—a dangerous enough gospel in any age.

One of the strongest currents of change in the sex and sex education realms is that associated with population, its explosion and its control. Such countries as Sweden and Japan have brought their numbers under control by means of contraception and induced abortion. The Swedes and Japanese are literate people capable of responding to mass persuasion programs, but the peoples of the poverty-stricken, starving, exploding countries are not readily reached by the mass media. And they tend to cling to their old ways as though they were lifelines. For example, in a certain typical rural region in India, efforts were made to persuade men to limit the number of their sons to two, on the grounds that this is all that the land would support. These men would have no part of the idea, declaring that a man's sons are and always have been his wealth. The more the better. This traditional belief withstood even the argument that in the past, if a man had six sons, all but one or two surely died very young, whereas now because of modern medicine, all six live and have to be supported by the same small piece of land. Not even this implied threat of raising sons to starve them moved these people.

In those countries where birth control is feasible, it is not always practiced. A prominent view in both Canada and the United States, for example, is that each new pregnancy is a harbinger of a new outlet for products in years to come—a new consumer on the way. The more babies the better—the better for business—in the short run. In Japan, on the other hand, where there was apparently no alternative to population control except national disaster, there is resistance to another "writing on the wall." There, the liberated female and feminist uprisings do not seem to be making the men especially happy. There are reports that some of the men have retaliated by making use of a rubber substitute for female

9

sexual partners. However, a Japanese health educator, who was doing post-doctoral studies in Canada as this third edition was being prepared, acknowledged that this is the case, but certainly did not think it could be considered a peculiarity of his people. His response to a question about this matter was, in effect, "Yes, but there are individuals with unusual sexual practices everywhere." At any rate, in the grand tradition of Heroditus and Marco Polo, we are merely reporting what we hear from travelers as well as what we see and read!

More cheerfully, then, we may return our thoughts to the impact of one people's way upon others. An English doctor visited friends in Finland. He was soon taken to a Finnish bath, where he was shocked to find men being soaped and massaged and dried by very business-like women in white aprons. When asked by his friend to take off his clothing he said, "But what about her?" indicating the middle-aged woman at the cash desk. "Well, what about her?" his friend responded as he took off his own trousers. The good doctor then resolved the problem very gracefully. "Like any non-nudist Englishman I have heavy inhibitions about appearing undressed in front of a woman, but I couldn't be impolite to my host, so I compromised by keeping my pipe in my mouth" (Gordon, 1958).

REFERENCES

Barnard, D.: Most Swedes want sex in curriculum. The Times (London) Educational Supplement, July 30, 1971, p. 8.

Brown, C.: No juvenile delinquency there. The Evening Star, Washington, D.C., November 17, 1958.

Brown, J. D.: Sin in Sweden. Time Magazine, April 25, 1955.

Ellis, A.: Sex Without Guilt. New York, Lyle Stuart, 1958.

Gebhard, T. H., et al.: Pregnancy, Birth and Abortion. New York, Harper, 1958.

Gordon, R.: A bath to the Finnish. *Holiday,* August, 1958.

Neill, A. S.: Summerhill: A Radical Approach to Child Rearing. New York, Hart Publishing Co., 1960.

Russia takes a new line on sex. U.S. News and World Report, 26:25-26, July 22, 1949.

Smith, R.: Meta-clinical sex education. The Times (London) Educational Supplement, February 11, 1972, p. 14.

Swiss women tackle inequalities but see long fight. New York Times, February 9, 1971, p. 3:3.

Teen agers and sex in Australia. Ladies' Home Journal, January 1958.

Vaigo, A. C.: "Be frank about sex," say Commission. The Times (London) Educational Supplement, September 17, 1971, p. 19.

11

Theories of Sex Education

THERE are about six and one-half different points of view which we shall call "theories" of sex education. (At least two of the seven that are listed are too similar to really add up to two; therefore the total seems more properly between six and seven.)

Theory 1. This theory holds that the best sex education is no sex education of any kind at all. *We will call this "The No Sex Education Theory."* After all, any sexuality in the young shouldn't be there anyway; so why bother teaching about it—and perhaps create problems? If, by mistake, it should appear, ignoring or punishing it may make it go away. In marriage, suddenly, "you'll know what to do!"

Until very recently, few people would admit to approving of this theory. For one thing, it is considered rather obvious that people need some kind of preparation and guidance for difficult and complex situations, such as those involved in the business world, warfare, and marriage. However, in actual practice most North American parents, teachers, and perhaps especially school administrators still behave as though they believe in this particular theory and carefully sidestep opportunities to provide the young with instruction on sex. This avoidance behavior is due, usually, to feelings of personal inadequacy to handle the job, to lingering and still very potent traditional attitudes, and to the language barrier.

Of course, too, teachers and school administrators are doubly motivated to avoid the whole business, because our schools are so subject to pressure from individuals and groups in the community. Unhappy citizens often drive school principals wild for reasons far less sensitive than sex education, and teachers still lose their jobs or at least are disciplined for attempting to deal even cautiously with the subject of sex in the classroom. Clearly, circumstances encourage a dedication to don't-rock-the-boatism.

To appreciate the treacherous ground the public school administrator finds himself/herself treading to fulfill the role of homeostatic balance keeper, consider the following anecdote. In one of our sex education classes for teachers, a junior high school English teacher commented with some irritation that those in the class were exaggerating the sex-related problems in our schools. "I have never seen any of these things," she declared.

"You don't see them!" snarled a junior high school principal, looking like something just about to leave a launching pad. He then described what he had been dealing with during the last two weeks.

It seems that the eighth and ninth graders had spread the word that such-and-such Thursday was famous "All Queers' Day"—to be celebrated by the wearing of green shirts. As planned, the seventh graders endeavored to comply, insisting that their parents buy them green shirts, whereupon the principal was swamped with irate calls: "What's this All Queers' Day business?"

But that is not the whole story. The principal continued, still sputtering on his launching pad, that he finally got this episode quieted down only to discover that he was right in the middle of another public relations fiasco, this time brought on by the fun-loving little girls. The eighth and ninth grade girls had spread the word that to celebrate Thursday properly, a red skirt should be worn. Dutifully, the seventh graders showed up in skirts containing red—for "All Whores' Day."

To a degree, this avoiding of sex education is doubtless a good thing, considering the qualifications of many teachers for such teaching. Are other groups prepared to step in and handle the job? Not that we know of. Although in recent years North American medical schools have begun to "tool up" to help prepare physicians to deal with the myriad sex-related problems with which their patients are apt to be beset, they certainly do not pretend to be preparing "sex educators" for the schools. And conversations with various clergymen lead us to doubt that many of them feel qualified along these lines either. How could they?

It is our understanding that some countries make it a matter of policy to conform as nearly as possible to this theory in their dealings with children. For example, as we have seen earlier, the Soviets generally de-emphasize the subject of sex in school, and endeavor to so fill the time of the young with school work and physical activity that leisure time problems such as those commonly associated with boy-girl relationships are to a considerable degree avoided—as is also, presumably, the need for any but the most scanty of sex education.

Many Americans and Canadians tend to be attracted to this approach; but we make it unworkable here by granting youth extraordinary freedom and wealth in an environment saturated with sexual stimulation. Inevitably, formal sex education is proposed as a desperate measure to deal with the resulting problems.

Sweden, as we have noted, has a quite different view of the entire matter.

Theory 2. There is now a widespread notion, perhaps

the most widely accepted in both Canada and the United States among educators, theologians, and physicians, to the effect that there should be sex education and that it should be quite frank. But, too, it must be on a highly moral and/or religious plane. We will not discuss this theory at any great length because its major features are known and accepted by, perhaps, most people today.

This theory might best be designated "The Sex Sublimated Theory; and it fits very well into the four mythological stages of sexual behavior in the course of life that were outlined in the chapter, "Growing Up and Sex." Thus, sex exists only in marriage and is necessarily and invariably associated with love, beauty, in a non-phallic kind of way with God, and preferably with procreation. Sexual intercourse is seen ultimately as purposive behavior, aimed if not always at reproduction at least at a spiritual kind of union between kindred souls. Conception is sometimes conceptualized as "God creating a soul."

It may be a little hard to believe that so respectable-looking a theory could generate an opposition, but it has. Ellis, as we shall see, considers it quite unrealistic; and Neill—again, as we shall see—considers all this a gilding of the lily. They claim that such verbal white-washing or sugar coating is done by people intent upon making a generally "bad" thing occasionally "good"— the perennial alchemist at work, trying to transform the baser metal into gold.

On the other hand, lacking these elements of marriage, love, and certain moralistic and religious overtones, sex in any form is likely to be regarded as deplorable if not degrading, filthy, immoral, crude, animal, and very possibly against God and the law. The need to transcend elemental biology is reflected in many ways, including the frequent bitter complaint of wives:

"Sex means nothing to you but a physical act. A prostitute could take care of your needs just as well." (And
many a husband has taken this kind of complaint as a
suggestion.) It is undoubtedly of great psychological
importance, as well as interest, that sex can be viewed
in such opposite ways, so positively and so negatively,
by the same society as acceptance of this theory requires.

As we have noted, the Soviet approach to sex education is not entirely devoid of the point of view of this
theory: religion, and Judeo-Christian sex morality being replaced by Marxist-Leninist morality and overriding service to the state.

*Theory 3. There is the theory that the best place to
learn about sex is in the gutter—"The Gutter Theory."*
A distinguished physiologist has seriously advocated
this point of view, his idea being that in the gutter kids
laugh at sex, and anything that you can laugh at won't
make you sick.

Now of course it is a very easy matter to criticize this
theory, both on the grounds of its apparent lack of a
base in some kind of morality and on the grounds that
the gutter approach may easily give rise to the spreading of misinformation, some of which is potentially
harmful.

On the other hand, however, some writers maintain
that the gutter approach, with all its obvious flaws, is
to be preferred to the common "sugar coating" of sex
(*e.g.,* by many proponents of Theory 2) which is sometimes done to remove it from the subhuman level to the
superhuman. To illustrate, in a chapter called "When
Are We Going to Quit Stalling About Sex Education?"
in his book, *Sex Without Guilt,* Ellis argues against a
spiritualized approach to sex education which in effect,
he says, instills irrelevant guilt-producing notions and
fears. He has written:

No one, for example, would begin to teach a child homemaking skills and responsibilities by beginning: "The home is a sacred place and cooking and cleaning are beautiful God-given occupations which must always be carried out in a serious and sober manner so that the fundamental purposes of life may be gloriously fulfilled." Yet this is the kind of hokum with which our books and talks on sex education are commonly filled. Naturally when handed this type of "enlightenment" the bright child quickly begins to wonder what it is about sex that is so intrinsically filthy that mealy mouthed words by the dozens are needed to help clean it up (1958, p. 139).

As a psychotherapist he is afraid of this kind of sex education and contends that we might well return to more meager, but in some ways more true to life, alleyway sex education of several decades ago.

At any rate, it is possible to argue that most of what most people know about sex today they did acquire "in the gutter," even though gutters tend to be fancier and better scrubbed places than they used to be. However, exceedingly few people would admit to being adherents to this theory.

Theory 4. There is also the theory that sex information should be presented with unrestrained frankness and bluntness; and we may therefor term it "The Blunt-Blitz" Theory of sex education—the shock treatment. Needless to say, proponents of this theory do not tend to be popular, especially not among educators and theologians. Its shock effect tends to drive off many who would otherwise find the position reasonable. This theory is usually not taken very seriously by most of its opponents because it is "so far out" that its spokesmen are readily dismissed as being mad, communist, or anti-Christ. Only very recently has it begun to assume proportions as a popular point of view which might be considered threatening to the traditional morality.

Proponents for this theory are prone to argue that the shrouding of sex in secrecy and sacredness is, in effect, pitting social regulation against instinct to a dangerous degree. They argue that this practice gives rise to repressions and other mental gymnastics which are likely to be damaging to mental health and social adjustment. The contention of some psychologists, including Ellis, who are in private practice and therefore can't be fired by an outraged board of trustees, is that the only way out of the present dilemma, which is constantly reinfecting people with psychosocially damaging sex conflicts, is a frontal attack which will smash certain traditional attitudes. They sometimes wax violent because only thus, they claim, can we hope to see the sexual component of the human personality liberated in our time—freed from second or tenth class citizenship among the structures, functions, and behaviors of the person. Freed to become the healthful, important, joyful—even, some maintain, the "sacred life force" which has brought us to this present point in time and, with luck, will propel us into the future. Most people see no such urgency. There is plenty of time.

But Ellis' behavior borders on the fantastic—to anyone, that is, who has so much as half a root in our sexual tradition. He is a Western version of the hot-coals walker; also a human fly. In fact, defying the laws of traditional gravitation has become his stock in trade. He goes around the country in person and in print recommending to young people that they engage happily and freely in premarital sexual relations to their heart's content—for the pure joy of it and perhaps to discover a person with whom a more or less permanent relationship would be desirable. In a matter of fact manner, he says that heavy petting is bad only when *not* followed by intercourse or climax achieved by other means. Considererate parents, he suggests, will not only instruct their daughters on contraception, but also will take them, if they wish, to a physician for prescription of diaphragm or pill. Masturbation is a boon to humanity and is often the only available way of gaining relief from sexual tension before and during marriage. On special occasions, really mature husbands may encourage their wives' going to bed with old flames—and grow in stature as human beings by facilitating the reunion (Ellis, 1960 and 1962).

Former Governor Faubus of Arkansas probably never felt more in the right—and this is going some—or more sure of public support than when he began hurling his thunderbolts at the faculty of the University of Arkansas for someone's having invited Ellis to lecture there, of all places. Ellis may be something of a hero among avant garde college students, but he is doubtless realist enough to know that any widespread official acceptance of his views is likely to be posthumous—if then. But who knows? His more enthusiastic enemies wish him posthumous already.

In addition to some psychotherapists, certain novelists have been believers in this point of view. D. H. Lawrence was one of these, and in spite of the fact that his book, *Lady Chatterley's Lover,* was perhaps the most censored of modern literary works, he considered it *his major effort at sex education,* molded in literary terms.

In Lawrence's Paris edition of this book he says in the introduction:

The great necessity is that we should act according to our thoughts, and think according to our acts. And this is the real point of this book. I want men and women to be able to think sex, fully, completely, honestly, and cleanly. Even if we can't act sexually to our complete satisfaction, let us at least think sexually, complete and clean (Ginzburg, 1958, p. 84).

So far so good. But why was *Lady Chatterley* censored so much when books exploiting sex in almost every imaginable way and in the most blatant manner, and having no deliberate implications for sex education whatever, have been distributed freely before and since Lawrence's book without much if any opposition from the censors? We don't pretend to know all of the reasons, but certainly one of them was that Lawrence's abrupt-shock treatment of the subject led him to use the old four-letter words—of all places—right in the middle of his tenderest love scenes. He thus profaned love. Love-making, sexual intercourse, and sex play have, as it were, been on tenuous enough grounds in Christendom without having someone come calmly along introducing the language of the bad boy, the gutter, the backhouse, into the hopefully sacred situation.

Of course, Lawrence's intent in doing all this was to pull our language about important personal things out of the long-dead Latin language and/or the infantile and put it into the English language of day-to-day usage. In using these and other "bad" words—that is, the words that we are taught from infancy are unspeakable and painful and insulting to the ears of nice people—Lawrence outraged almost everyone. Romantic love and this kind of language clash in most people's minds as few things can. (For information on the earlier respectability of "the four letter" words, see Partridge's *Dictionary of Slang and Unconventional English*.)

When Lawrence rolled little hand grenades like these onto the laps of his readers and the censors, he was by no means naive concerning the current attitude toward such language in such places, but he insisted that he was trying desperately to break down barriers between men and women, between people and their bodies and their bodily functions, including language barriers. Unfortunately for his motives, he walked directly into what the general semanticists term a "signal reaction"—which is now known to be extremely difficult to extinguish or alter. For as Hayakawa has pointed out, "In every language there is a long list of such carefully avoided words whose affective connotations are so un-pleasant or so undesirable that people cannot say them, even when they are needed. Words having to do with physiology and sex . . . have, especially in American culture, remarkable affective connotations" (Hayakawa, 1949, p. 86).

Counterattack against Lawrence's attack upon what he considered to be the unnaturalness and dishonesty of modern society's dealings with sex was as inevitable as it was violent. Perhaps he should have assailed the scatological and the sexual in separate volumes, but I'm afraid that, to his mind, this would have been missing part of the main point. It would have taken no great genius to predict that if he would ever achieve any widespread acceptance of the philosophy behind *Lady Chatterley*, it would be posthumous. (Posthumous is as posthumous does.)

The point of view represented by the frank-blunt theory has even succeeded in infiltrating the field of education slightly. A. S. Neill, who has run a private boarding school in England since 1921, would prob-ably resent being accused of trying to shock anyone, but to most people his views are shocking enough. He has spoken calmly of freedom of masturbation for chil-dren—as something of a natural right and as one means of avoiding the usually devastating guilt and shame re-actions commonly associated with this virtually univer-sal behavior of the healthy. Although sex knowledge is not forced on the children at Neill's school, whatever interest or curiosity they may have is responded to fully and frankly. Neill contends that:

If the child is to have a healthy attitude toward sex and a subse-quently healthy love life, sex must remain on the earth. It has in itself everything, and all attempts to enhance it by raising it to a higher power are futile attempts to paint the lily (1960, p. 223).

Neill does not permit boys and girls to room together at his school because he is sure that the government or somebody would close the place down. We all must make our little concessions.

Theory 5. The traditional and currently mainstream Australian approach to the education of the young seems to represent a theoretical orientation which is somewhat different from the others. As we said earlier, the Australians have tended to strive for a no sex education type of sex education. But since it is not at present possible to shut off sex in the young completely, *we might more accurately identify a "Theory of Minimal Sex Education" in a situation contrived to avoid sexual problems,* and thus to minimize the need for sex education. North Americans, especially those who are the parents of girls, commonly view this approach sympathetically, in part at least, because it purports to save the young from sex and themselves from sex-related problems that tend to ambush the young. At the same time it keeps children and youth busy and reportedly happy with healthful and educational pursuits.

As was pointed out earlier, young people in Australia are subjected to a heavy regimen of school work at home as well as at school, but as a sports-minded people, they keep the young happy by placing a great emphasis upon play, games, outdoor sports, and athletic competitions. The systematic efforts made to minimize the sexual stimulation of the young, so effective for generations, are breaking down. Who knows when it began to do so significantly? Perhaps it was when . . . such people as American marines and sailors with their completely different sets of conditioned responses visited the fair shores of Australia in large numbers during World War II. There is no end to the accounts of how a great many women behaved as though they were "sex starved"—a highly commendable condition in the opinion of the visitors, but one having important implications for this theory.

Could it be that the young adult males respond better to the desexualized atmosphere of athletic Australia than the females, just as males seemed able to adjust to *coitus reservatus* at Oneida Creek, New York, where many men were apparently content for about thirty years to surrender the orgasm almost all of the time to the communal wives (Gardner, 1957, p. 246)? In this connection, it is quite possibly significant that when American undergraduate classes were asked whether they would prefer to grow up in America or Australia, many men hesitated because the sports and outdoor life of Australia has its appeals. However, the women almost never hesitated. They turned thumbs down on the Australian way immediately.

During World War II a fighter pilot, who had just returned to the combat zone from a week's "rest" visit to Australia, asked one of us (Johnson) to go with him to confession in the improvised church. What could the boys have found to do in such a place that would require confessing? However, it seemed that a group of priests had been flown in to handle things for the Catholic marines on the island. The confessor seated his friend where he could not help seeing the priest's face, and this individual's expression soon indicated clearly that he was not by any means listening to a commonplace confession. Later explanation revealed that he had confessed to having "shacked up" with twelve women during those seven days in Australia, and that the priest, a youngish man himself, had had some difficulty taking all this in stride.

Theory 6. This theory tends to make the accepting, and even a blending, of sex and love essential to human happiness. It proclaims that sex is a foremost rather than a rearmost aspect of the human personality. Most blunt-blitz proponents agree with the objectives of this theory, but differ mainly as to methods of reaching the objectives (*e.g.*, compare writings by Neill, Maslow, and Guttmacher with those of Albert Ellis and D. H. Lawrence). Whereas people like Ellis seem to be saying, "Come on, jump in *now*, the water's fine," proponents of Theory 6 agree that the water is fine but that many things need to be taken into account before a jump is made—and then, perhaps, it might be better for lots of people to "ease in" or even stay out. Recall that Neill does not permit the boys and girls in his school to room together for the very practical reason that this would probably cause his school to be closed by the authorities. Proponents of Theory 6 tend to realize that the consequences of violating the taboos and restrictions of a Judeo-Christian society are very real things to be reckoned with in sex education, regardless of how objectionable they may seem.

Disconcertingly, the language of Christianity and of proponents of this theory are frequently confronted nose to nose, despite the usual insistence that the meanings are categorically different. For example, how might holders of different points of view interpret the following: "With my body I thee worship" of the marriage ceremony; "He walks with me and He talks with me and He tells me I am His own" (some Sunday School teachers skip over this one); "joy in thee"; "ecstasy"; "heavenly bliss"; "mystical experience"; Love.

How might different schools of thought interpret William Blake's famous lines:

> Children of the future age
> Reading this indignant page
> Know that in a former time
> Love! sweet Love! was thought a crime.

After all, Blake was a "mystic."

Both views profess a fundamental concern for the welfare, happiness, morality, goodness, and decency of humanity, but still they are fundamentally and adamantly at odds. Views on sex and sin appear to be among the major points of difference which make the Judeo-Christian sex tradition unacceptable to "believers" in this theory. On the other hand, critics of this theory accuse them of promoting an immoral, pagan, anti-religion, even animal kind of behavior. To the proponents of the traditional Christian view, Theory 6 is especially vulnerable because of its tendency to recognize and accept the possible and even moral existence of sex outside of monogamous marriage.

Supporters of this theory contend that humanity cannot hope to be happy or healthy—or free from the powerful tendency toward crime, war, compulsive preoccupation with sex and sexual quirks ("perversions")—until such time as sex is accepted as a good rather than as a bad part of the self. After all, they argue, the human species has survived thus far *because of* sex, and moreover, it is an incomparably wonderful and joyful thing—if not spoiled by ignorance, ineptitude, or the anti-sex education of the sexually ill. Perhaps the gift to humanity which, in a way and to a degree, compensates for the inevitable suffering and death?

Perhaps as good a label as any for this theory is "The Naturalistic-Humanistic-Love Theory." Its advocates tend to feel that if children are dealt with honestly and lovingly, there is little need for formal sex education.

One can only guess at the proportion of the North American population that would declare itself against the spirit of this theory. Recent personal experience has impressed us with the large numbers of individuals of all ages who are for it—but most see little hope for putting it into practice on a large scale. Certainly, something approaching 100 per cent of people acting in some official capacity would have to at least *say* they oppose it utterly, regardless of their private opinion. Almost everyone has been trained from infancy to be stoutly against it. Still, out of curiosity and in the interests of laying all of the theories open for inspection, it seems sporting to see what some of the gentle heretics have to say.

To begin with, there is frank-blunt-gentle Neill who has written: "Sex affords the highest pleasure in life. Sex with love is the supreme form of ecstasy because it is the supreme form of both giving and receiving" (1960, p. 213). He is too old and famous to be trying to get attention; and we gather that he is too philosophical to expect a few left jabs to floor the giant traditional attitudes toward sex. Moreover, any critic could point out that there are grounds for suspicion concerning him. That is, in the past it has been older men who have set the standard concerning the *restricting* of sexual behavior of the young. Neill is something of an inside-out version of St. Augustine. After a wild sex life as a young man, St. Augustine imposed an anti-sex morality upon the youth of Christendom for centuries to follow. Neill had by no means such a jolly youth and wound up in his seventies writing a book in which naturalness, play, fun, happiness, and sex are presented as being of the essence of life among the young as well as the wealthy. Neill has written:

For a parent there is no sitting on the fence, no neutrality. The choice is between guilty-secret sex or open-healthy-happy sex. If parents choose the common standard of morality, they must not complain of the misery of sex-perverted society, for it is the result of this moral code . . .

All of our leering attitude toward sex, our guffaws in music halls, our scribbling of obscenities on urinal walls spring from the guilty feeling arising from suppression of masturbation in infancy and from driving mutual sex play into holes and corners. There is secret sex play in every family.

The fact that nearly every motion picture deals with love proves that sex is the most important factor in life. The interest in these films is, in the main, neurotic. It is the interest of sex-guilty, sex-frustrated people. Unable to love naturally because of sex guilt, they flock to film stories that make love romantic, even beautiful. The sex-repressed live out their interest in sex by proxy.

Hate sex and you hate life. Hate sex and you cannot love your neighbor. If you hate sex, your sexual life will be, at the worst, impotent or frigid; at best, incomplete.

I do not forget that many parents have religious or other negative views on the sinfulness of sex. Nothing can be done about them. . . . On the other hand, we must fight them when they infringe on our own children's right to freedom, genital or otherwise . . .

When the sex relationship is a failure, everything else in the marriage is a failure. The unhappy couple, reared to hate sex, hate each other . . . The worst problem children come from such parents . . .

If the child's questions are answered truthfully and without inhibition on the part of the parents, sex instruction becomes part of natural childhood . . . Sex instruction [of the formal kind] should not be necessary . . . for the term instruction implies previous neglect of the subject (Neill, 1960, pp. 212ff).

By implication, Maslow had some important things to say with respect to this theory. Maslow, a psychologist, became tired of the practice of building personality theories on the basis of what is learned from the study of neurotic and psychotic persons. He decided to reverse the usual procedure and, with considerable difficulty, identified a group of people who, by all the criteria available, were found to be symptom-free, mentally healthy people. He then proceeded to study them, their ways of thinking, acting, and feeling, minutely. Their loving behavior and sexual behavior were of special interest.

Maslow used the term "self-actualizing" to describe the behavior of such healthy people whose basic needs for security, food, esteem, love, and so on, are sufficiently

well met for them to be able to live freely and spontaneously. They sound like adult versions of Neill's "self-
regulating" children. But let us flavor Maslow a little.

> It is amazing how little the empirical sciences have to offer
> on the subject of love . . . I must confess that I understand this
> better now that I have undertaken the task myself. It is an
> extraordinarily difficult subject to handle . . . And yet . . . we
> *must* understand love; we must be able to teach it, to create it,
> to predict it, or else the world is lost to hostility and suspicion
> (1954, pp. 235, 236).

Here, then, is a suggestion that love is of sufficient
importance to be made the subject of research and
teaching.

There are important educational implications in Maslow's statement that people want to love and be loved,
but that they just don't know how to go about it.
Healthy people "can and do so freely and easily and
naturally without getting wound up in conflicts or
threats or inhibitions."

> My subjects were loved and were loving, and are loved and
> are loving. . . . this tended to point to the conclusion that . . .
> psychological health comes from being loved rather than from
> being deprived of love. . . . We can learn a very great deal from
> the peculiar and complex nature of sex in the love-life of self-
> actualizing people. . . . For one thing it can be reported that
> sex and love can be and most often are very perfectly fused
> with each other in healthy people.
>
> Another finding . . . is the very strong impression that the
> sexual pleasures are found in their most intense and ecstatic
> perfection in self-actualizing people. . . . Experiences described
> in reports . . . have been at so great a level of intensity that I
> felt it justifiable to record them as mystic experiences.
>
> Another characteristic I found of love in healthy people is
> that they made no really sharp differentiation between the roles
> and personalities of the two sexes.
>
> That is, they did not assume that the female was passive and
> the male active, whether in sex or love or anything else (Maslow,
> Chapter 13).

Proponents of such views of human sexual behavior tend to feel that if children are reared properly, little in the way of formal sex education is needed, but they have exceedingly little to say on the subject of the re-education of those who are improperly reared in regard to sex—which is to say, the vast majority of the population. For example, Freud, in his famous little essay on sexual morality (1931), wrote:

> We may well ask . . . Is our "civilized" sexual morality worth the sacrifice it imposes upon us . . .?

And he went on:

> It is not a physician's province to come forward with reform schemes . . . however, I could confirm the imperative necessity of reform in this direction by showing the damage caused by our "civilized" sexual morality and pointing out the part it plays in the spreading of nervous disorders in modern times (1931, p. 48).

Whose province is it then—this matter of re-education and reform? The educator's? Which educators!? This problem seems no more approachable at the present time than is that of the geometric increase in the world's population.

Theory 7. This theory might be called the "Do-It-Yourself Theory" of sex education. Just a few years ago it could not have been included in this list at all because the vast majority of people had no place to go for information but to their parents, ministers, teachers, and physicians—where almost no one in his or her right mind was willing to go unless, of course, a problem, likely a growing problem, forced him to.

Things have been changing very rapidly. You can now walk down to your corner drug store and get paperback books by leading authorities. Books by Wardell Pomeroy, Albert Ellis, Mary Calderone, Masters and Johnson, and Allan Guttmacher are to be found easily in book stores and public libraries. Popular magazines publish articles by outstanding people every month, and *Sexology, Journal of Sex Research* and the *SIECUS Report* can be counted upon to keep one current with new developments and in touch with some of the franker thinking on the subject of sex.

It is noteworthy that many, if not most, serious contemporary writers express some degree of resentment about the barriers that continue to exist between what is known and those who wish to know it. One of the more eloquent protests is that of Guttmacher, a top-ranking physician associated with both Mt. Sinai Hospital and Columbia University Medical School, who felt compelled to begin his book, *Babies by Choice or by Chance*, as follows:

THIS IS AN INDIGNANT BOOK!

I am indignant that the liberal side of the sociomedical issues we discuss is rarely, if ever, portrayed to the American reader by a physician. I am indignant that organized American medicine is more interested in its own economic security than in the social health of those it serves. I am indignant that the Church wields such stultifying power in certain areas of medical care.

It is high time that men of good will burst the medical, political and religious shackles which bind them, to analyze and solve health problems by frank, free, and unbigoted discussion. Perhaps my book will advance that day. If so, it serves its purpose (1961, Introduction).

Dr. Guttmacher's feelings are not quite the same today as they were when he wrote the above in 1961, and he has since expressed gratification at the progress being made by physicians and clergymen in trying to qualify themselves for teaching and counseling in this field. But the causes of his indignation are far from vanished.

A number of years ago a legal battle took place in the United States over the question whether *Lady Chatterley's Lover* is too obscene to be mailable. *Lady Chatterley* finally won out over the Postmaster General. This was all very interesting, but even more interesting to us was the fact that at about this same time such serious studies as Lewinsohn's *History of Sexual Customs* and Henriques' *Love In Action* were being delivered to our desks and to university libraries through the mail from entirely respectable publishers. The pictures alone in these books (expurgated in the paperback editions) would, we suspect, have been more than enough to get them banned had they come to the attention of postal officials. We were also somewhat surprised to receive by mail, at about the same time, such delightful, though plateless, books as Ginsburg's *Unhurried View of Erotica*, which provides insights into some of the preoccupations of various important people, including Ben Franklin, and into the problems that the serious student of sex encounters when trying to obtain books on sex from the world's libraries that possess them. Incidentally, the U.S. Post Office has, *ex officio*, one of the world's foremost collections of erotica—as does, too, the Vatican, also *ex officio*. Apparently, only high ranking officials and their friends can view such collections without danger of damage to their moral fiber.

To our minds the development which has made possible what we are calling Theory 7 is perhaps the major breakthrough in the sex education of modern times. People are now able to obtain literature that helps to make possible realistic and rational thinking and informed choice-making. As indicated, people who can read can now bypass or leap-frog some of the major obstructions that stand between sex information and those who need and want it. In fact, SIECUS* and SIECCAN† were organized to help people do just that.

---

* Sex Information and Education Council of the United States; 1855 Broadway, New York, N.Y. 10023

† Sex Information and Education Council of Canada (Toronto); 293 Burnhamthorpe Rd., Islington, Ontario.

Unless one wishes to argue that ignorance is a more solid foundation than knowledge upon which to base decisions and build attitudes and practices, it will have to be admitted that this is a good, rather than a bad development. Of course, many still do choose to argue for ignorance.

REFERENCES

Caprio, F. S., and Brenner, D. R.: Sexual Behavior: Psycho-Legal Aspects. New York, Citadel Press, 1961.

Ellis, A.: If this be heresy. The Realist, *31*, Feb., 1962.

Ellis, A.: Sex Without Guilt. New York, Lyle Stuart, 1958.

Ellis, A.: The American Sexual Tragedy. New York, Lyle Stuart, 1959.

Ellis, A.: The Art and Science of Love. New York, Lyle Stuart, 1960.

Ellis, A.: The Folklore of Sex. New York, Grove Press, 1960.

Freud, S.: Modern Sexual Morality and Modern Nervousness. New York, Eugenics Publishing Co., 1931.

Gardner, M.: Fads and Fallacies in the Name of Science. New York, Dover Publications, 1957.

Ginzburg, R.: An Unhurried View of Erotica. New York, The Helmsman Press, 1958.

Guttmacher, A. F.: Babies By Choice or By Chance. New York, Avon Books, 1961.

Hayakawa, S. I.: A note on verbal taboo. *In* Language in Thought and Action. New York, Harcourt, Brace, 1949.

Lawrence, R. H.: Lady Chatterley's Lover. New York, Grove Press, 1959 (from the 1928 Italian edition).

Lief, H. I.: Physicians declared ignorant about sex. The Washington [D.C.] Post, May 11, 1962.

Maslow, A. H.: Motivation and Personality. New York, Harper and Row, 1954.

Neill, A. S.: Summerhill: A Radical Approach to Child Rearing. New York, Hart Co., 1960.

Pomeroy, W.: Boys and Sex. New York, Dell Publishing Company, 1971.

Pomeroy, W.: Girls and Sex. New York, Delacorte Press, 1969.

Russell, B.: Marriage and Morals. New York, Bantam Books, 1959; also, New York, Liveright, 1929.

12

And in Conclusion

The foregoing discussions suggest something of the range of perspectives and gravity of problems associated with human sexual behavior and sex education. We have considered the nature and scope of the challenge to education. The challenge was then seen to have important biological, psycho-developmental, historical, linguistic, legal, moral, and cultural aspects. Contrasting society-wide experiments in sex education were considered, as were also the possible theoretical orientations which determine what form sex education will take.

In brief, the coverage of this volume makes apparent a magnitude and depth of subject matter which is sometimes not fully appreciated in sex education circles and which is awesome to say the least. For its implications would seem to suggest to humanistically inclined persons a need to reexamine and, perhaps, in fundamental ways alter a whole way of life ranging from child rearing practices to moral codes, education, language, and laws relating to sex. In the past, social changes of such enormity have tended to have many years, even centuries, to work themselves out more or less gradually. But the transitional period that is upon us provides little time for leisurely contemplation or acclimatization. It is like the research of Freud or Kinsey or Masters and Johnson: suddenly, seemingly out of nowhere, it is

10

there, a fact of life; and it does the shocked objector no good to deplore, denounce or try to wish it away.

The situation today continues to be characterized by widespread enthusiasm for initiating sex education programs, mainly in the hope of doing something about VD, out-of-marriage pregnancy, and teenage marriage —although self-discovery, self-understanding, and other-sex-understanding have resulted. It is also characterized by what at present seems a declining, but in some places deeply entrenched, anti-sex education movement, as, for example, in California. There is still a lack of teachers who are qualified to teach either the teachers or the pupils, uncertainty as to qualifications of persons to do the teaching, what should (and should not) be taught, what literature and other teaching aids should be used, and what to do about possible parental and other community reaction. On the brighter side, far more teachers have had at least a course or workshop on sex education. And when reasonably capable and honest teachers do start a program of some sort, they tend to be amazed at the willingness, even eagerness of the young to communicate openly, questingly, seriously, and thoughtfully, not only among themselves but with the teacher, supposedly the representative of the out group. Those of us who have undertaken sex education for parents have tended to be encouraged by this group's willingness to learn facts, consider them objectively, and try to apply them rationally. Indeed, some of us have concluded that parents, and perhaps the general public, are more ready for factual, objective sex education than they are usually given credit for.

In brief, a good many educators are trying to help the young to think through real concerns and problems honestly and knowledgeably. This kind of thing is a step forward in almost anyone's book. There tends to be a lot of self-perpetuating re-enforcement in a situation like this—if the educators will but be honest and not merely try to move the old hypocrisy to another level.

Some very definite and specific progress has been made to date with regard to both knowledge and education about sex. True, as Wardell Pomeroy has emphasized repeatedly (1972, p. 2), there are still fewer than a hundred high quality, replicable scientific studies of human sexual behavior. Still, by drawing from those that do exist and from data from related fields, e.g., history, sociology, psychology, linguistics and law, it has been possible to synthesize and put to practical use a body of knowledge. By way of illustration: masturbation upsets far fewer people about themselves or their children than it used to; homosexuals are more commonly viewed as human beings and fellow citizens; morals are more commonly considered rational guidelines in the service of humanity than as rules in the service of deity; sex laws are being questioned and even changed as they are judged by the usual criteria of laws in the United States and Canada; communication about sex has become much more easy and open, even with regard to personal problems—with the result that such problems are now more often soluble, to the benefit of the individual and perhaps his or her family; and it is now more respectable to teach and do research in this field. Sex is becoming more like other important matters that can be considered objectively in terms of their human meaning.

The Sex Information and Education Councils of the United States and of Canada and the American Association of Sex Educators and Counselors have been especially important developments, perhaps not so much because of their activities and meetings, but because they represent established and respected rallying points of common interest and common cause. An official organization of dedicated people is not easily put off or put down. Moreover, undertakings and statements of such groups tend to carry special weight. For example, the SIECUS Study Guides on Homosexuality and Masturbation were evidently more influential than articles on those subjects published elsewhere by the same authors. Similarly, AASEC's *Professional Training and Preparation of Sex Educators* will doubtless carry more weight in university training than guidelines proposed by any individual—as will also its forthcoming pronouncements on the certification of sex educators.

With regard to the future of sex education, say during the coming decade, leading professionals tend to feel that it will continue to be concerned mainly with reproduction ("the birds and bees jazz") and VD, and with remedial efforts aimed at common misconceptions. It will, they believe, continue to shy away from contraception education for some time yet, for of course, this subject implies to the young something that they presumably do not know, namely that sex is not just for making babies. It will refuse entirely to consider coital techniques, even coitus at all, and will be dedicated to the morality that middle class mother, father, and teacher were brought up on. A gradual improvement in the quality of sex education is foreseen but with occasional, temporary setbacks.

Paradoxically, setbacks will likely occur at points which some consider to represent greatest progress. For example, relaxation of puritanic restrictions on language often give rise to backlash, as does also frankness in sexual portrayal (pornography). Many consider it real progress that people with sex problems can now seek professional help which may include learning to respond sexually with another person even though not a legal mate. Grounds for serious backlash? Yes, because: (1) the idea of moving intellectual sex education to a primarily feeling-doing level is abhorrent to many; and

(2) the utilizing of paid partners (prostitution?) when other partners are not available is also abhorrent to many and raises legal questions. Incidentally, the publicity given the sex clinics, which are primarily for the well-to-do, has given rise to comparable efforts by college students to set up their own grassroots "clinics" for fellow students with sexual hangups. After all, directors of professional clinics tend to describe their work as basic sex education aimed at teaching people what should come naturally: bodily pleasure and sexual fulfillment. But student clinics with no charge? What backlash such undertakings invite! The idea could spread.

At any rate, there seems no turning back, and in spite of turbulence, political campaigning on platforms of "morality," legal barriers, and what not, the obvious foment will give rise to a brave new world, sexually. Both the American and Canadian education systems place the control of education in the hands of the individual states or provinces, and communities have a great deal of leeway with regard to policies and offerings. In other words, at least it can be said that innumerable opportunities exist for testing out different approaches to the subject and, hopefully, for evaluating experimental programs. Then, for some time to come, as we have pointed out, education in this area will, to a considerable extent, need to be *remedial* in nature, concerned in considerable part with clearing up misconceptions. One can only wonder about the degree to which sex education will attempt to deal with the deeper issues associated with the subject. Most enthusiasts who wander into this field tend to be myopic or naive in their perception of its depth and expanse. Their reactionary adversaries do not ordinarily intellectualize their hostility very well, but to their credit, they sense the profoundly revolutionary meaning of the undertaking as the surface-scratching sex educator often does not. We are reminded of an ardent Catholic acquaintance's response a few years ago, when he went to Rome and was shaken, no almost shattered, upon finding priests eating meat on Fridays in anticipation of the lifting of the ban. If this truism is no longer true, what about all of the other truisms?

Then there is the matter of the mind's response to facing itself from opposite corners of the ring; for sex is one of our fundamental psychological conflicts. Generally speaking, new learnings at an intellectual level, which are contrary to a pattern of long-held, deeply ingrained beliefs and attitudes, are not likely to dominate thought and action overnight. In fact, we have sometimes been astonished at the discrepancy between what we have known educators to learn about human sexual behavior and sex education, and what they actually did and said about them at home and school. For example, some high ranking school administrators would give every indication of having gained important insights, would make specific plans for translating these into usable educational terms—and shortly thereafter be hounding teachers mercilessly for trying to do what they themselves had contemplated doing. True, their new-found adventuresomeness may have been repressed because it became too unmanageable or threatening to linger in consciousness. Or, behavioristically, a different set of contingencies "on the firing line," as compared with those found in the sanctuary of a university class, may have doomed any but the most conservative thinking. Only some clear-cut evidence of concomitant or instrumental value could be likely to override the cultural set regarding how educators *should* feel about sexuality of the young. (A principal was driving himself and everyone else wild in his efforts to supervise lights out in a camp-out for coed, young adult "retardates." "If you hear a zipper, get your flashlights on them!" he ordered. All this in spite of the fact that he was aware that all of the girls were on the pill and, with parents' consent, some were spending weekends with their boy friends. Absence of negative consequences did not quiet him. However, had he been assured of possible positive consequences of some happy coed sleeping, such as re- duced day time discipline problems, he would probably have relaxed and gone to sleep himself.)

Let us speculate further as to what lies ahead with regard to our sexual customs, our laws, morals, practices, and education. Taking an unreservedly optimistic view that there *will be* a future of any considerable duration seems impossible these days; and our views of the future of our patterns of sexual attitudes and behaviors are not naively optimistic, nor are they selectively blind to ugly possibilities. However, in consideration of the various scientific, technological, economic, and social develop- ments of modern times, and the fundamental adapta- bility of the human organism, it seems reasonable to consider the possibility of the approaching of a better way of life generally—in which sexuality will be more fully understood, freely felt, and reckoned with as a major factor in the totality of healthy personality func- tioning.

John Steinbeck made the following remarks about his belief in "the perfectibility" of people in his acceptance speech on the occasion of his receiving the Nobel Prize for literature:

The universal fear is the result of a forward surge in our knowl- edge and manipulation of the physical world.

It is true that other phases of understanding have not yet caught up with this great step, *but there is no reason to presume that they cannot or will not draw abreast. (italics ours)*

With our long proud history of standing firm through the millennia in the face of almost certain defeat, we would be not only cowardly, but stupid to leave the field on the eve of victory.

So it is with our knowledge of and dealing with human sexuality. There are grave dangers and many problems ahead; but there is a chance worth working and fighting for that—being a boy or a girl, or being a woman or a man—all can in the future have a new and better and happier and fuller meaning. Such is our hopeful belief, and the remarks that follow are in the spirit of that belief. If this book has any value, it is in terms of contributing a little to the coming of that time.

The sex laws do not seem likely to change very much, very soon, although some old laws are being interpreted differently now. For example, homosexual behavior may not be construed to violate sodomy or indecent behavior statutes. Many sex laws are being studied intensively and modified, to a degree, in terms of what legislators consider to be greater harmony with modern circumstances. Witness for example changes in abortion laws during the last few years. Unfortunately, despite these revisions there continues to exist in North America widespread *de facto* discrimination on such bases as sex (men are never required by law to keep unwanted growths inside themselves) and socioeconomic status (well-to-do women can always get abortions) and to reflect metaphysical dabbling (e.g., how could anyone possibly know when a "soul" enters a conceptus?).

Another hot issue that looms ahead is whether or not prostitution should be legalized. As usual, whether prostitution should exist will be confused with whether it should be legalized; and the naive will go on supposing that illegalizing it will dispose of it. The majority of those wishing to see it legalized will argue that this is the only way to bring it and much VD under control of the public health authorities. They will be accused of favoring vice. Women's Lib will, with justification we think, insist that equal opportunity, as pertains to regulation, apply to both male and female prostitution. Our question is: should education at some or any level concern itself with such subjects as prostitution? We think that young people need to be prepared as well as possible to make objective decisions concerning all important matters, "nice" or otherwise. However, education and prostitution would make unlikely bedfellows. This is true also of pornography, another issue disqualified from school consideration.

In this connection it is interesting to note that many problems, legal and otherwise, are often solved not on the basis of arguing out the apparent issues, but on the basis of developments that may not have figured in the controversy at all. For example, quite some years ago, in spite of major Catholic opposition, officials of the state of Illinois decided to begin giving contraceptive information and equipment to certain mothers, married and unmarried. The decision was evidently not prompted so much by a stand on principle concerning the "morality" of contraception, but by a financial crisis. Illinois no longer felt that it could afford *the luxury* of innumerable unwanted, impoverished, unprovided-for children or the associated maintenance, delinquency, school, and employment problems. Since that time the federal government has become very much involved in encouraging birth control because the child, family, and economic problems do not mark time for high-level moral-religious controversies to be resolved. This situation is similar to the conflicts between capitalist and communist countries which will never be resolved because communists decide to like capitalists or *vice versa,* but because overriding circumstances may draw the two systems together. The Nobel Pize-winning scientist, Albert Szent-Gyorgi, has commented on this tendency for major problems to "work themselves out" in unexpected ways, assuming of course, that there is sufficient time:

Our history knows of various problems which man was unable to solve; eventually, they solved themselves. A few hundred years ago, western history was dominated by religious differences. In those days it must have seemed most logical for a Catholic to kill a Protestant, or vice versa. There could have been no way to explain why they should not do so. Today, we hardly understand what it was all about, can only smile about it, forgetting the endless suffering these ideas caused, depopulating Europe to a great extent. We only can bless fate that atomic bombs were not known then, or else we could not be here. These problems exist no more; they solved themselves. We have grown out of them. . . . We look back on dueling today as a children's disease of our history. [In the old West] there could have been no possible way to explain that everybody would be safer without a gun. Dropping it must have been paramount to accepting one's death sentence . . . Today nobody wears a gun . . . Total disarmament has been achieved—again not by logic. We have grown out of it (1962, p. 32).

Szent-Gyorgi then goes on to point out that humanity may in like manner outgrow some of its major problems of the present day. This very likely will be the case with aspects of the evolution of our sex attitudes, practices, morality, and laws. If there is but time.

Everyone knows that dating and courtship practices have changed considerably in recent years. One need not be a scientist to determine that there is much greater permissiveness concerning intimate physical contact than there used to be. It seems reasonable to believe that the Kinsey data, which showed a continued increase in premarital sexual intercourse of both males and females since the turn of the century can be extrapolated to reflect a continuing increase in this behavior. Most sociological studies conducted to date indicate no significant increase in the incidence of premarital coitus on the part of college students since World War II. However, most of us who have been teaching at the university level for many years are quite sure that there is something very fishy about these findings. In the course of a discussion of the concept of socially approved, childless "trial marriage," an undergraduate student commented: "It's happening already and people are taking it for granted without any official decisions. Most of us here in this class are or have been involved in some such relationship and we don't see it as a moral issue and society apparently isn't trying to stop us." No one in the class of about a hundred chose to take issue with him.

Women who, in the past, usually had the most to lose by an unwanted pregnancy, but were at the mercy of the male's possession of and willingness to use a condom, can now make provisions for their own safety, and apparently they are doing so. Druggists report that totally unlike the situation in the past, women are now accounting for an appreciable percentage (some claim the larger percentage) of the sales of contraceptives. Contraceptive foams and condoms are now being displayed openly on counters of many respectable drug stores, whereas in the past all such things were "under-the-counter" items. What has happened to bring about such changes?

We had not until fairly recently fully appreciated the extent to which the pill has spelled liberation from the unspeakable dread of pregnancy that has haunted countless married women. Women seem to be all for having access to their own protection. For another thing, the traditional sexual morality, a major condition of which has been the dependent, vulnerable status of the female, has never before been confronted to such a degree by big, really big money. To some, this may well be a gross, commercial, and unpleasant consideration, but it is a very real one and it must be taken into account if the dynamics of the situation are to be appreciated. Whereas the average female might be counted upon to menstruate perhaps five days out of the month—and thereby she has created a huge industry devoted to the disposal of menstrual flow—she might, between the ages of perhaps fifteen and fifty-five, use a contraceptive many times per month. The potential market, disregarding the possibilities for sales in desperate, overpopulated countries, is almost beyond belief. Sales knowhow, which in the last forty years has made it respectable for women to smoke, drink beer, and even perhaps to menstruate, should not be underestimated. The contraceptive industry is well aware that it is not catering to a fad that is likely to vanish with the new season, but rather to one of humanity's major drives and preoccupations. In consideration of the widespread need and desire for contraceptives and the profits to be made from them, it is hard to imagine any development short of world catastrophe that will reverse the sales trend.

Even Roman Catholicism, which a few years ago backed away from blanket condemnation of masturbation, has become more lenient concerning contraception. Rather typically, priest R.H. Springer, S.J., has argued: "Should contraception information be given at all? . . . Mindful of the harm and human suffering occasioned by sexual ignorance in the past, I cannot cast my vote for omission. If knowledge is not a virtue, far less so is ignorance." (1972, p. 19). Nearly coinciding with this development will likely be the appearance of the first effective, safe abortifacient, the prostaglandins. (Already approved for use in England.) This will be a "morning after" kind of pill and will therefore probably renew the controversy, for Catholicism has not softened its position on abortion at all. Before long now, perhaps, you may take the pink pill but not the white.

In a special kind of way, dating and courting couples are in a more difficult position these days than they used to be, if they have been at all steeped in the prevalent Judeo-Christian-Puritanic tradition concerning sex. As was pointed out earlier in past years, no matter what their actual sexual behavior was, they *knew* what was "right" and what was "wrong." No matter what they actually did, they knew how they stood on a right-wrong basis. Today, however, the actual wrongness of "wrong" behavior is being questioned—not only by impassioned lovers but by scientists, therapists, and even, as we have noted, by various theologians, some of whom claim that traditionally "wrong" behavior, sexually speaking, may sometimes be better for individual and social health than "right" behavior. The belief that sex outside of monogamous marriage is, by definition, bad is being challenged before the eyes of the young and others who must make the decision and attach some kind of personal meaning to what they choose to do. (It may be noted that, these days, a great many young people no longer have the least concern over this controversy, viewing it as incongruous as the continuing religious wars of the Irish. They are more likely to be worrying about specific sexual matters and hang-ups such as what is expected of them as males or females, how to respond well, why they can't climax as they've been led to believe they should, how to communicate more adequately with a mate, how to disengage gracefully from a tiring relationship, whether to marry or have children.)

Thus, we have such spokesmen of the extremes as Billy Graham and Albert Ellis. "Give your sex to God," admonishes Graham. And he goes on to argue that sex is not so important after all, and that there are quite adequate substitutes prior to, and otherwise outside of, marriage. On the other hand, Ellis says: Your sex is a wonderful, incomparable part of you. Be informed, take the necessary precautions; and then enjoy it freely and guiltlessly before, during and even after marriage. This, he maintains, is the healthy way. But again, on the other hand, "Give your sex to God." Authority pulling from both ends at once.

The sexual morality tradition is now in the ring with a formidable opponent—a composite of basic biology, a cultivated skepticism toward the dogmatic, the chronic stimulation of sexually knowledgeable entertainment and advertising, increasingly available and respectable birth control techniques, potentially controllable and curable venereal diseases, leisure, affluence, and the feeling of urgency to *live* today because of the chronic threat of global war and other disasters. The Judeo-Christian-Puritan sex tradition is in for a tough fight.

But it is pointless, it seems to us, to get involved in shadow boxing over whether some formalized view, traditional or otherwise, is the Right one. On the contrary, we have found it more useful in our discussions of sexual behavior with students, parents, and professional persons to evaluate behavior in terms of three interrelated considerations which are reducible to the key words: (1) *knowledge,* (2) *meaning,* and (3) *tolerance.*

1. *Knowledge.* When we are confronted with a sex-related problem in personal or professional life, it is well to bear in mind that we are not the first person in history to have run up against this kind of thing. There is information; the amount of information is increasing, and it is becoming much more available. Few things are less productive or more repetitious of treacherous stereotypes than discussions of various sex-related behaviors which have not been preceded or accompanied by study of current, objective literature. For example, if one assumes that masturbation causes insanity, that exhibitionism usually is followed by violent attack, or that pornography produces antisocial behavior, then of course "problems" in these areas will be dealt with quite

differently than if more valid knowledge were the starting point.

2. *Meaning.* People tend to react to episodes involving sex without making an effort to determine their
meaning context. In contrast, for example, the informed
adult may know that the masturbating of mentally retarded children is neither the cause nor the effect of
their being mentally retarded; and upon looking for the
meaning of frequent masturbation may discover that
the children are bored from lack of interesting things
available to do, are being put to bed too early to sleep
and are diverting themselves as best they can—or are not
really masturbating at all but responding to the irritation
of too tight-fitting clothing or a skin problem. Similarly,
as in a specific case, a young man's exploding with an
"obscenity" in a junior college class took on new meaning when the teacher came to realize that she had humili-
ated him needlessly before his classmates at a crucial
point in his desperate effort to overcome drug addiction,
support his family, succeed in college, and perhaps most
of all, win the respect of his peers. More typically, a
clergyman-counselor did not think to look for meaning
in a man's "masturbating on his wife in bed" and simply
attributed subsequent divorce to masturbation; and
again similarly, a father came upon his son and another
boy engaged in sex play, and his outbreak—not the sex
play—has resulted in over forty years of more or less
severe anxiety on the son's part over the question of his
normalcy.

Looking objectively and knowledgeably for meaning
in observed sexual behavior has extremely important
implications for sex education.

3. *Tolerance*—of human differences. This has to do
with becoming aware of the enormous differences
among people—differences in sex attitudes, preferences,
strength of sex drive, maturation rate, etc.—and learning

to get over using oneself and one's own background as the standard for others, including one's mate and children. Ellis refers to learning tolerance as not being a sexual fascist. Intolerance commonly takes the form of considering people "abnormal" or even "perverted" who are not like oneself or who live by other codes. We tend to be trained systematically to be intolerant from an early age, but tolerance also can be taught and learned. Sometimes we are least tolerant of ourselves, and fail to grant ourselves the same right to be different that we may grant others.

Homosexuality makes a good model of the application of our threesome: knowledge, meaning, and tolerance, and of the need for us to stop trusting our conditioned responses in dealing with sex "problems."

1. There is a body of knowledge about homosexuality which, among other things, informs us that even though we do not really know what "causes" it (and this is true of heterosexuality also), we do know that so far there is no convincing evidence of genetic or constitutional causation. Few consider it a sin any more, the prevalent medical opinion being that it is a sickness brought on by early environmental factors; but a growing view is that it may often be simply an unexplained but potentially healthy sexual preference.

2. Homosexual activity may mean different things to different individuals who participate in it, which is true also of heterosexual activity. It may be a compensation for being deprived of heterosexual outlets, it may be associated with disliking or fearing the other sex—which is to say about one-half of the world's population. It may be encouraged by fear of failure with a heterosexual partner; it may be purely for profit via prostitution; and we have known individuals who had some preference for heterosexual relations, but usually engaged in homosexual ones so as not to have to bother with the time,

money, and energy usually required to achieve heterosexual seduction. Sometimes, however, none of these
negative motivations seems to apply. The individual
merely finds his or her greatest amative and sexual enjoyment with his or her own sex. And the meaning of
homosexuality to society? Since its practice has never
constituted a serious threat to human survival, unless
homosexuals attempt to force sexual attentions on others
(they evidently do this considerably less often than
heterosexuals do) or attempt to exploit minors or defec-
tives, opinion is growing that homosexuality practiced
between willing adults in private has no negative meaning for society.

3. Tolerance enters the picture when we can view the
person who is homosexual, for whatever reason, as being
basically a fellow human being and who, as such, is not
to be judged by us, disdained, despised, or discriminated
against—but helped, if possible, if he or she needs and
wants help. We may think the person wrong or unwise
for not seeking to change if he or she does not do so,
but that is really none of our business.

We recommend the triumvirate—knowledge, meaning, and tolerance—as being most helpful guidelines in
the evaluating of human sexual behavior and problems.

It is sometimes asked or implied: is the intent of sex
education to place still greater emphasis upon sex? Many
of us think not, in the sense usually conveyed by the
question. Perhaps, curiously, we feel that in a certain
way, a major objective of sex education is to *de-emphasize* sex. The following may make our meaning clear.

Some teachers were up in arms because pupils were mutilat-
ing valuable volumes by cutting pictures of nude art work from
them. All kinds of traps were planned to catch the culprits; but
the principal handled the matter in another way. He purchased
a large statue of a Venus figure, a nude woman sitting on a flat
surface, knees wide apart, ankles crossed, holding an infant to her

full breast. This large figure was placed in the most attractive hall-way in the school. Of course throngs gathered and eyes were riveted on ~~breasts and~~ labia. Then in less than a week an interesting thing happened. Instead of seeing the statue as almost nothing but a set of exposed sex organs, the pupils began to see it as the statue of a handsome woman feeding her child. Sex had been de-emphasized in the sense that it was restored to reasonable perspective as a part, but only as a part, of the whole. Of course the damaging of art books stopped, but more importantly, many teachers and pupils learned a profound lesson in sex education.

It may be noted that in the foregoing discussion, we have made reference to a number of "forbidden sexual behaviors," discussion of which is taboo in most classrooms and households as well. What can the teacher do who cannot or will not deal with such subject matter, perhaps even with the subject of sex at all?

Whatever educators feel they can or cannot do in the way of direct sex education, they are furthering the improvement of human relations generally, including the various aspects of sexual adjustment, whenever they predispose young people to feel more involved in humanity than in their feelings against people; to be more respectful of themselves and of their fellow human beings than respectable; to be more loving than lovely; to be capable of friendship and not just of friendliness; to be more accepting of themselves, physically and mentally, than rejecting; to use language with proper awareness of its potency, especially perhaps for evil; and to be free of a feeling of obligation to prescribe how other people, including future mates and children, should live. All this kind of thing is, in a way, basic sex education, and it is excellent preparation for any close personal relationships including those of marriage and parenthood.

One of the major problems associated with modern "marriage" is that people tend to think they know what the word means. Whereas in the past, it meant some quite specific functions and relationships—and children grew up, in effect learning what their future role as husband and wife would be—today the word is the same but the "institution" is often quite different. Married people frequently have the eerie feeling that one might have if, while expecting to play a nice, neat game of European football (soccer), were instead suddenly to find himself or herself in the middle of an American sandlot football game of uncertain boundaries, debatable rules, and fortuitous responsibilities. In like vein, people "have children" in the spirit of the past, but without the past's need for children.

Observers of the dating-marriage-child scene are inclined to feel that the rug has been pulled out from under society. Typically, the moral fiber of the nation is called into question, and dismal comparisons are made with fallen nations of the past. It is possible, though, to take a somewhat different view of the meaning of what we see about us these days.

If change is bad, *per se*, then of course the irreversible changes that are occurring are bad, but as we have seen, there is much in our traditional attitudes, practices, "morality," and laws that is absurd, unfair, inappropriate, unrealistic, and very likely in need of change if human values are deemed important. For example, the "second sex" business. The position of women has not, historically, been an enviable one to most men. Nor, we gather, has it tended to be so to most women. This situation may be changing in fundamental ways, and the implications are enormous for both women and men. Increasingly now, women are in a position to choose their way of life, whether it should be as home makers and child rearers, as scientists, educators, physicians, or workers in the business world, or as a combination of these various alternatives during different parts of their lives. Increasingly, women may marry or not *as they choose* without the feeling that not to marry is in some important way to fail. Moreover, if they do choose to marry, they may have children or not, *as they* wish. In an article entitled "A Vote Against Motherhood," Gael Greene champions this growing freedom to choose, stating:

I don't want to have any children. Motherhood is only a part of marriage, and I am unwilling to sacrifice the other equally important feminine roles upon the overexalted altar of parenthood. Instead of condemning myself to the common syndrome of the unhappy creature who is mother first, wife second, woman third and human being last, I champion the wondrously satisfying love of a woman and her husband, two adults enjoying the knowledge and mystery of each other, tasting dependence, accepting responsibility, yet individual and free (1963, p. 10).

In recognition of the fact that large numbers of people do not choose to or cannot marry, and large numbers of married people do not choose to or cannot have children, it is certainly unrealistic for the sex educator to aim his or her entire approach toward preparation for family life.

An increasingly safe and potentially wholesome sex life is said to be becoming available to the married and the unmarried who desire one; and there seems to be a growing feeling—by no means a universal feeling, of course—that this is a decision to be made by individual women and is not the business of society at all. For example, such religious groups as the Quakers and Unitarian-Universalists have recently questioned the validity of the traditional morality in such matters. At any rate, those who talk about these developments are divided in their evaluations of them, but they are facts of modern times, however they may fit into one's value system.

Many people view the new era for women with alarm. We have known many men and even a few women who believed that women should be kept in the status some-

what like that assigned to them by the early Christian
fathers. Such a way of life is available to those women
who want it, but the dominant female view is not likely
to be in these terms, and it is the women who will decide. Part of a letter from a young woman reflects what
we suspect will be a growing feeling among women in
regard to the sex education of young people:

> In short, sex education for teenagers has got to be more
> human, deep, and spontaneously affirmative—as wonderfully
> positive as possible—to help the young person realize he/she *is
> not* alone; his experiences, feelings, and needs are common, fine,
> and simply human; to air out and bring light and freshness and
> enjoyment into those darkest, most disturbing, lurid, guilt-ridden
> realms of sex memories and current activities and desires. Other-
> wise one's sexuality cannot be dealt with rationaly, realistically—
> and the whole of one's self cannot be healthy and integrated.
>
> I feel very strongly that parents, teachers, and authors should
> be honest and realistic in their approach to youth, and give
> them the reassurance and relief, the ability to accept themselves
> and to enjoy life wholly and intelligently, that they deserve. No
> more uneasiness, hedging, antiseptic "rationality," or brief,
> matter-of-fact neutrality (which is taken as negativism) please!

So much for what *is not* wanted. But what *is* wanted?
This is a more difficult question. Is something wanted
that is so positive that it would resemble the child rearing practices of the Marquesan Islanders described
earlier (Chapter 9)? Not only an entirely accepting attitude toward childhood sexuality, but systematic, deliberate cultivating of it from infancy onward, just as we
are accustomed to try to cultivate intelligence and creativity? This is at the opposite end of the spectrum from
the traditional way. It is hard to imagine significant
numbers of American or Canadian parents or teachers
carrying "positiveness" this far. Trying as we do to keep
sex education off the affective level and on the cognitive
level, would we soon be able to make such a readjust-
ment in approach? At the moment, we think that moth-

ers are doing rather well if they confide to their daughters that they themselves are on the pill, or some such —thereby communicating to them that they engage in sex guiltlessly and for fun. The new era for women will certainly include more honesty, self-acceptance, and joy in living being communicated to and encouraged in the young.

Our personal view is that the new era for women, with its opportunities for independence and choice, is one of the most important and encouraging developments of history for men as well as women. At any rate, modern circumstances make change in the meaning and status of womanhood as inevitable as the transition in popular transportation from horse-drawn carriage to automobile. To our minds, this is a good rather than a bad thing. We are appalled by the duration of modern wars and of the Thirty Years' War and the 100 Years' War. We should be, too, by the "eternal battle between the sexes," which may at last be drawing to a close because of, not in spite of, the spirit of People's Lib, not just Women's.

To elaborate, it is hard to think of a very strong argument against the increasing ability of both men and women to marry or not as they please, rather than from economic or other necessity, or dependency or weakness or social pressure or the desire to exploit someone whom custom and the law render exploitable. It seems much better to marry simply because of a wish by two people to become more or less deeply involved in each other and perhaps to share the rearing of children.

It tends to be upsetting to many when they are confronted with the fact that children have lost much of their historical function. (We have sometimes had to emphasize that we are merely reporting the facts of a situation, not creating it.) But here again, the new era *can* mean a better rather than a worse state of affairs with respect to children. There is an attraction in the idea that offspring are intrinsically valuable and do not have to have an immediate economic or political value to a family or to a tribe-minded people to justify their existence.

The loss of a social function, other than as consumers, of childhood and youth has given rise to innumerable problems. But a realization seems slowly to be growing that children are too important to have their conception left to chance, mistakes, ignorance, indifference, or any sexual arousal that is not related to intent or qualification for parenthood.

Of course, this realization has not grown to any great proportions as yet, and many thoughtful people are sick to death of the arguments about the right of married couples, any married couples, to have children at their whim or slip-up. It is still commonplace for men to impregnate women who will have one, two or more children, be divorced, and adventure about while a relative or public welfare agency or someone, anyone, tends the children. Parenthood may still be entered with no license other than that required for a marriage, and perhaps the absence of a venereal disease. Increasingly we will demand: What about the rights of the children? What about the rights of society, which badly needs understood, respected, well-loved, well-reared, well-educated children?

At another level, the inquirer must ask: How long does our society wish to afford, or think it can afford, the luxury of the whimsically conceived children who become the solid base of our delinquency problem and an aspect of our chronic education problem, and so on, and soon become the creators of a new and bigger crop of unwanted, unprepared-for babies? These are not merely rhetorical questions to be played with verbally, but questions that are urgent and can now be framed in scientific terms and approached by methods that the new era is making increasingly available.

The new era, which is aborning, can give rise to a new appreciation of children, both individually and collectively. For several decades now, children have not had to be viewed as necessities or even as assets to families in any "practical" way. They neither work in the fields nor "bring in wages." They have been made to feel this lack of function, to feel purposeless and resentful because of it, but we wish to emphasize that the new situation need not be viewed in an entirely gloomy light, by any means.

As things are going, the new era can leave the matter of childbearing and child rearing to those who identify these functions with their own life objectives—people who by temperament and training have some basic qualifications for the job—and a job it is—and want it. As we have pointed out, other married people can be relieved of the feeling of obligation to have children and, like the unmarried, can have little or no difficulty avoiding having them.

It will become widely realized that having and rearing children is like other demanding and complex occupations. That is, it is too hard and exacting to be carried out well by the untrained, unwilling, and irresponsible, or those who take little or no joy in the company of children. We should surely be tired of a situation in which relatively simple functions, such as driving a car or directing traffic, require evidence of qualification, whereas the enormously complex business of parenthood in present circumstances requires nothing but a marriage license, and perhaps the absence of a venereal disease.

The new era can make possible a new and better attitude toward parenthood as a supremely valuable social function. And it can bring to childhood the dignity and maximum consideration that its social value deserves.

REFERENCES

American Association of Sex Educators and Counselors: The Professional Training and Preparation of Sex Educators. Washington, D.C., AASEC, 1972.

American Association of Sex Educators and Counselors: Certification Conference in New York City, December 17, 1972. Washington, D.C., AASEC.

Greene, G.: A vote against motherhood. Saturday Evening Post, 236:10, January 26, 1963.

Szent-Gyorgi, A.: Solving the unsolvable. Bulletin of the Atomic Scientists, 18:32-33, October, 1962.

Pomeroy, W.: The now of the Kinsey findings. SIECUS Report, 1:1-2, September 1972.

Springer, R. H.: Quoted in Georgetown Today, Georgetown University, Washington, D.C., November, 1972.

Index

Please remember that this is a library book, and that it belongs only temporarily to each person who uses it. Be considerate. Do not write in this, or any, library book.